For Kaori + Neil, with all Best's

Roman Mittau
1999

Sonny's Story

Sonny's Story

A Journalist's Memoir

by Rollan Melton

**University of Nevada
Oral History Program
1999**

UNOHP

Mail Stop 324
University of Nevada
Reno, NV 89557-0099
775/784-6932
ohp@scs.unr.edu

Editor and Publisher:
R. T. King

General Manager and Associate Publisher:
Mary Larson

Production Manager:
Kathleen Coles

Production Associates:
Linda Sommer
Kathryn Wright-Ross

Production Assistants:
Kevin Kolkoski
Beth Opperman

Contributors:
Ken Adams
Victoria Ford
Mark Gandolfo
Michael Green
Susan Imswiler
Dwayne Kling
Nina Koch
Brad Lucas
JoAnne Peden
Meredith Rucks
Bill Stobb

Consulting Designer:
Robert E. Blesse

A department of the
College of Arts and Science
University of Nevada, Reno

Publication of *Sonny's Story* was made possible in part by gifts from:
Carl and Bette Dodge
Link Piazzo
Dean C. Smith
The Gannett Foundation
The John Ben Snow Trust

Copyright 1999
University of Nevada Oral History Program
Reno, Nevada 89557

All rights reserved. Published 1999
Printed in the United States of America

Library of Congress Cataloging-in-Publication Data

Melton, Rollan, 1931-
Sonny's story : a journalist's memoir / by Rollan Melton.
p. cm.
Includes index.
ISBN 1-56475-376-x
1. Melton, Rollan, 1931- 2. Journalists—United States—Biography. I. Title.

PN4874.M486 A3 1999
070'.92—dc21
[B]
99-054890

DEDICATED TO

MARILYN
and

JUD ALLEN	Bless him for not hiring me.
CHARLES J. ARMSTRONG	A rejection slip from him, too.
ANNE GIBBS BERLIN	The best teacher I ever had.
JOHN BRACKETT	I got the editor's job he turned down.
HATTIE BROWN	Her "F" grade got my attention.
TY COBB	His days and nights belonged to his readers.
MARK CURTIS SR.	A friend who had to say "no."
DON DONDERO	Great pal; exemplary photographer.
RON EINSTOSS	Noble enemy of dime store journalism.
WES GOODNER	"To be the best, practice more."
JAY POWELL HAMMOND	The first to urge me to write my memoirs.
A.L. HIGGINBOTHAM	Hero or villain? Both, actually.
KENNETH A. INGRAM	"That's not writing, it's typing."
JOSEPH R. JACKSON	In the background, doing the work.
KEISTE JANULIS	"Tell the people what's going on."
DAISY LENZ	"Warlord" who rescued Sonny, the dropout.
PAUL A. LEONARD	The epitome of civic virtue.
WARREN LERUDE	Top editor, publisher, teacher, friend.
E.J. (JACK) LIECHTY	Paragon of clear thinking.
RUSTY MARRS	An absent mother, with due cause.
CHARLES G. MURRAY	Star-bright newspaper icon.
ALLEN H. NEUHARTH	Twentieth-century newspaper giant.
KENNETH ROBBINS	Good! He got the job I wanted!
MIKE SCHON	Suggested a pivotal element in my life.
EDWIN SEMENZA	"All must understand your lyrics."
CLAUDE H. SMITH	"Improve, or we'll let you go."
DEAN C. SMITH	Youngest, feistiest, best.
ETHEL SMITH	First Lady of the *Fallon Standard*.
RAYMOND I. "PAPPY" SMITH	Master of ballyhoo and good sense.
CHARLES H. STOUT	He came bearing opportunity.

Contents

The Hobo Kid	1
Choosing Journalism, Sticking With It	43
Striking Opportunities	95
Going Public, Getting Hitched	151
Gannett VP, G-J Columnist	187
Sonny's Five "W"'s	205
Index	215

The Hobo Kid

Rusty Marrs, 74

Reno, NV Aunt Neta seldom phoned. When she did, it would always be about something important, but she would ease up to her news as though working to create an O. Henry ending. One night in the fall of 1959 Aunt Neta called. She opened the conversation by saying that she hadn't heard from me for a while, and she hoped that my family and I were well.

"Couldn't be better, Auntie." I told her the latest on the Meltons. "And how are you and Jimmy doing?" I asked.

"Well, Jimmy took a bad turn. The brain tumor just had too much of a head start." Her voice fell to a whisper. "I'm sorry to tell you, Sonny, that Uncle Jimmy slipped away from us last night."

Neta was my mother's sister. The two of them lived in Stockton, California, but even after Jimmy's death they did not live together—Mother lived alone in a rental home. Mother's health and general physical condition were not good, and she depended on Neta to do her grocery shopping, run other errands, and pay bills.

Aunt Neta called with news of another death in the family in 1962. Following our preliminary exchange of pleasantries, she said, without emotion, "Your grandma Daisy has passed on. It's better this way, because she had suffered so long with arthritis. It crippled her hands so that she could no longer write to your mother and Wilbur and me, and you remember how she loved to write those letters."

The years passed, and as our family ranks thinned, calls from Neta increased in frequency. The news was never good: "Cousin Tomlin has passed; Uncle Cecil is gone; Aunt Lillian is lost; your Uncle Wilbur's condition won't be getting any better."

My sister Bronna lived east of Reno in Fallon, where she and I had gone to high school. She had contracted emphysema, caused by a lifetime of smoking cigarettes, and when she died in 1985 at age fifty-two, it was my turn to call Aunt Neta with bad news.

When I told my mother about Bronna's death, her reaction was stoic—she had been prepared for the news by my many calls over the previous months chronicling Bronna's declining health. I urged Mother to come to Fallon for the funeral, but she felt that she just wasn't physically or emotionally up to it.

With Bronna's death, gone was my closest childhood pal, my sibling soul mate, cheated out of the long and healthful life that she deserved by tobacco dependency. Her death was a great loss to me.

In December of the following year, Auntie phoned with more bad news, and this time she skipped the preliminaries: "Your mother fell off a small footstool at home and banged her head hard. I got her to the hospital. She wants to see you, Sonny, and I think you'd better come fast."

My mother had been a robust young woman when I was growing up, with flaming red hair worn in a pageboy cut, and her personality had had two sides—one that enjoyed laughter, humor, and song, and another that was brooding and anxious. "It's the Irish in me," she would state, referring to both her frequent melancholia and her red hair. She had always been Mother to Bronna and me; everyone else called her by her nickname, "Rusty." Arriving at Stockton's Saint Joseph's Hospital, my wife, Marilyn, and I quickly found my mother's room. Although her health had declined as she aged, I was shocked by how diminished she now was. Mother had become a frail and pale woman, much thinner than I had ever seen her. If she was pleased that we had come, she concealed it well: "I knew Neta would call you about my fall. I'm not feeling too good, Sonny."

"Mom, you'll be OK. Just stay here as long as they tell you to."

"Well, do I look in any shape to leave here?"

Marilyn took her on a wheelchair tour of the hallways. In her young womanhood, Mother had loved needlework. When Marilyn steered her past a hospital craft exhibit, she made her only upbeat comment of the day. "Good god," she said, "what lovely crocheting!"

My mother died not long afterwards. I wrote her obituary for publication in the *Reno Gazette-Journal*, focusing on the years she had lived in Fallon. The item was just four inches long, not enough to tell her full story. My opening sentence read, "Rusty Marrs, 74, died of complications from injuries suffered in a fall." Aunt Neta read the obituary and offered a suggestion: "Wouldn't it have sounded better to have written 'passed on'?"

"Possibly, Auntie. But that's not our newspaper's style."

"Well, it ought to be."

Mother had been a well-known restaurant waitress when she was raising Bronna and me in Fallon, but in Stockton, where she had lived for thirty years, she was as far from being a public figure as anyone could be. Mother's reclusiveness was by choice. She associated with only a few, and they had to be people she trusted deeply. There were just seven of us at her grave-side service, including a minister whom the mortuary had rounded up and a former *Stockton Record* newspaper colleague of mine who had read the obituary and seen that I was Rusty's son.

Daisy Claims Husband Deserted Family

Danville, IA Standing next to my mother's grave that gray winter's day, saying goodbye, I thought back on her life and its turbulent start. She had not grown up in a stable family.

Mother's mother, Daisy Edgington Williamson, had been raised in a small town in Iowa, one of nine children born to a farming couple of Scotch-English-Irish descent. To the end of her life, Daisy remained hazy about how far in school she had gotten. She would say, "There was much to do on our farm, and my brothers, sisters, and I had to help with chores. We worked in the fields and looked after our family's livestock. It seemed I went directly from being a little girl to being a woman, skipping childhood." Daisy's paternal grandfather had served with the Union forces in the Civil War.

Mother's father, Hugh Osborn Williamson, a Missouri native, was a young barber when Daisy met him in Iowa. Of Irish descent, he had eleven brothers and sisters and was unschooled. It was said that some of his forebears had fought with the Confederacy. Photographs of young Hugh standing alongside Daisy show that he was short and, like her, had wavy red hair.

Daisy and Hugh got married in 1911 in Danville, Iowa. Their first child, Beulah, my mother, was born six months later at New London, a tiny farm village near Cedar Rapids. Their second child, Wilbur, was born in 1916. Wauneta (whom I always knew as Aunt Neta), arrived in 1920. Each had red hair. "It's the Irish in them," Grandmother Daisy would say, over and over, virtually to the end of her life.

Daisy's marriage to Hugh was rocky from the start, and it would end in divorce. She told her parents, and later her children, that Hugh was cruel and inhuman, and that she felt in danger living with him. There was more. Daisy asserted that her husband was a confessed adulterer, and she branded him a marital deserter. Two of her children, her grandchildren, and her great-grandchildren knew that Hugh Williamson had been a rascal, because Daisy so declared.

Hugh filed for divorce and custody of their children in New Mexico in May, 1925; Daisy filed for divorce and custody in Iowa in July. Neither responded to the other's petition. After fourteen stormy years of marriage, they were granted a divorce by the New Mexico court; but on jurisdictional grounds, that court refused to address the issue of custody of the children, who had remained in Iowa with Daisy. Hugh left New Mexico and moved to Denver immediately after the divorce decree was entered.

As a child, and then as an adult, I believed my maternal grandfather to have deserted his family. Grandmother Daisy said that this was so, and I believed that it must be true. "He just up and vanished," she explained, "and by now, he probably is dead."

"For damned certain," my Uncle Wilbur vowed repeatedly, "if the son of a bitch does live, and he ever comes around us, I'll shoot him."

My mother, who was thirteen when her father was said to have deserted her, shared her mother's animus for him. When I was a boy, only Aunt Neta questioned Grandmother's story. "Our father has apparently passed away," she would say, carefully avoiding the "dead" word. "And those who have passed cannot speak for themselves."

Meltons Go West

Boise, ID My father's side of our family can be traced to Scotland and the birth in 1773 of Elijah Melton. As a young man Elijah emigrated to the American South. From family records kept in the Melton Bible, we know that he eventually married Ann Green, who was eleven years his junior. The couple had six children, setting a precedent for sizable families on the Melton side; and Elijah married more than once, establishing another Melton tradition, one that was to be repeated among his descendants, often with regrettable results.

Ann Green was Elijah's third and last wife. Her father, Captain Benjamin Green, owned two merchant ships and had an interest in a large dry goods establishment in Savannah, Georgia. The captain's commercial enterprises did not enjoy good fortune. On one voyage, returning fully laden from a foreign port, his vessels were overtaken by pirates who made off with the ships and their cargoes. Back in Georgia, Captain Green learned that in his absence his partner in the dry goods business had sold all their merchandise and property, and had vanished from the country with the proceeds.

Generations of Meltons carried Christian names common to the times, with not a "Rollan" among them. Inexplicably, there was one Tiny Melton. I doubt that any Melton since has been accused of being tiny. Melton occupations varied widely and included farmer, clergyman, handyman, barge worker, mailman, feedlot worker, country printer, and storekeeper. There was not to be a journalist Melton until well into the twentieth century.

My paternal great-grandparents, Sarah and William Melton, lived in Burksville, Kentucky. They had seven children, of whom my grandfather, John Allen Melton, was the eldest. He was born in 1868, and as a young man he served with the U.S. Army in the Spanish-American war. (His father had been in the Confederate army in the Civil War.)

My grandmother Isabelle married John in Burksville in 1900. Isabelle's parents, Mary and James E. Miller, carried a grudge against John for marrying their daughter, who was thirteen years younger than he. "It was robbing the Miller cradle," they always maintained.

My grandparents were neither better nor worse educated than most Americans of the time. They often boasted that they had gotten as far as the sixth grade, but that might have been stretching it. "I was busy working; there was no time for schooling. It seemed that all children went to work early back then," my grandfather often said.

Isabelle and John had six children, five of whom were born in Kentucky. The oldest two, Bufford and James, died in infancy. In 1904 my grandparents packed their belongings and their surviving children (Margaret, John, and Jack), and left Kentucky on a river boat. Their parents never saw them again.

A few of Grandmother Isabelle's seven siblings had earlier moved west, settling at Idaho's capital city, Boise. My grandparents followed them to Boise, where my grandfather found work with fuel companies and feedlots, and ultimately with railroads that had operations in Boise. His last job was shoveling coal onto steam locomotives, an occupation that he followed until he was into his eighties.

Like a number of other new Boise residents near the turn of the century, Isabelle and John Melton brought with them the slow, Southern manner of speaking. Being from the South was a source of pride: "Too bad the United States got Abraham Lincoln instead of Jefferson Davis for president," my grandfather once told me. He was serious.

Isabelle and John's youngest child, Rollan (my father), was born in Boise on March 23, 1909. He was the only one of the couple's children who was not a Kentucky native. Later my grandmother would tell people how the curious spelling of her youngest child's name came about: "I was pregnant with my son when I came across the name Roland. I liked it, and after his birth, I told a nurse that that was the name we wanted for our son." She should have been more specific. On the birth certificate, the name came out "Rollan." My grandfather was not fond of his youngest child's given name, so from the time Rollan was a baby, John Melton would say, "You're the bunk. Just a little bunk." Thus, in the family and among friends and fellow workers, Rollan Melton was "Bunk."

Tragedy struck the family midway through World War I. Dad's brother Johnny was stricken with a severe pain on his right side. Isabelle was certain that the discomfort would pass, but she was wrong. Johnny's appendix burst, gangrene set in, and the infection got too much of a head start. Johnny died on April 2, 1917, at the age of fifteen. My grandmother felt heavy guilt, and she grieved for the rest of her life. There was an unwritten, yet widely understood, rule in our family: neither the name of her lost Johnny nor the circumstances of his death were ever to be spoken around her.

There were two additional unmentionable subjects. My grandparents' marriage unraveled in 1918, six children and eighteen years after it had begun. The precise cause was uncertain, but it was said a few times, well out of the earshot of my grandmother, that John liked his liquor more than he liked Isabelle. After their divorce, Grandmother did not permit John Melton's name to be mentioned in her presence.

The other not-to-be-discussed-in-Isabelle's-presence topic was her second marriage. The family always tippy-toed around that, as though it were an evil fiction. Yet, it was real. She did marry a William Shoemaker of Boise. Mr. Shoemaker's occupation loosely fit his surname—he was a shoe salesman.

Grandmother Isabelle and Shoemaker were married in 1919. Later, family members always were vague about how long the marriage lasted, as though they had been struck with amnesia, but one sensed that Isabelle and William were husband and wife for no more than a few months.

Beulah Williamson and Rollan Melton Wed
Union Doomed From The Start

Boise, ID Beulah Erma Williamson moved to Boise from Iowa as a teenager. She was eighteen when she met my father, Rollan Melton, at a party early in 1930. He was twenty-one. "I loved to dance, and Rollan didn't know his left foot from his right, so I set out to teach him," she would later say. "At least on the dance floor, he was somewhat coachable."

They were married on December 8, 1930, in Boise, in the presence of Daisy Williamson, the mother of the bride. Later, I would be told time and again that my maternal grandmother had "glared a hole right through your father" at the wedding ceremony. Daisy was concerned about her daughter's choice of husband, for she had sensed during the courtship that this union was doomed.

In the beginning, the marriage was loving and serene. I was born on July 24, 1931, slightly more than eight months after the wedding. Father insisted that I also be named Rollan, thus ensuring that I would have to cope with a lifetime of others misspelling my name. My baby sister, Bronna Lu (known as "Brownie"), was born on September 26, 1932, the same day our Uncle Jack turned twenty-nine.

Despite the heavy laying-off of workers because of the Great Depression, my father had steady employment as a baker, having followed the work line of his older brother, Jack. (Father had begun his apprenticeship when he was thirteen.) My mother looked after Brownie and me. Still, Mother had a difficult time paying the bills,

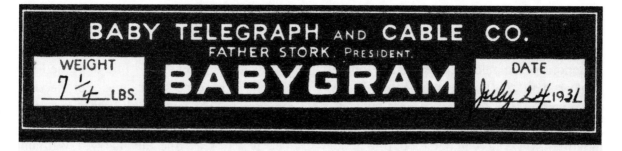

"I was born on July 24, 1931.... Father insisted that I also be named Rollan, thus ensuring that I would have to cope with a lifetime of others misspelling my name."

---

for although Father's work was steady, his income was small. (And, as it later turned out, he was not bringing home to Mother all the money that he was earning.)

Soon after his marriage, Father began writing flowery letters to his mother-in-law, who by the end of 1931 had returned to her native Iowa. "Sure do miss you, Mother," he wrote. Still later, his Western Union telegram to her lamented that "Money wired us not yet here." He also wrote often to Aunt Neta, addressing her as "Sis." The affectionate letters described how well "our little Sonny and Brownie are doing."

By then my parents and everyone else were calling me by my nickname. One R-o-l-l-a-n spelling per household could be a big-league challenge; two would have been no hits, no runs, and an avalanche of errors. They also let my hair grow long. It flowed in ringlets, and things got to the point that passersby would look at me and exclaim, "Oh, what a lovely little girl!" Brownie's hair grew long too, and some persons believed that we were twins. Then, one day when I was two years old, Father told Mother, "I'm taking Sonny over to my mother's house for awhile." Instead, he took me for my first visit to a barber. Shorn of my locks, which my father saved from the barber's floor, I was returned home, where my mother is said to have nearly collapsed from shock: "You've robbed our little Sonny of his boyhood," she cried.

My mother and father were so different from one another. As a baker, he had to be up hours before the sun rose; she read late into the night and would sleep late in the morning. She could swear like a sailor on shore leave, but I rarely heard my father use profanity. He would one day tell me he was an alcoholic before he turned twenty, but into the mid-1930s, I don't remember ever seeing my mother take a drink. She was just a shade over five feet tall, and he was five-feet-nine. She liked to socialize, and he was a little shy—he was ready to leave the minute they arrived somewhere, but she loved to visit family and friends for hours at a time.

Mother and Father did have at least two things in common: they loved Brownie and me unreservedly, and each loathed the other's mother. Father blamed Daisy for much of their marital trouble and called her "the warlord," while my mother alleged that Isabelle had much in common with a viper and was a woman to avoid at any cost.

By the time I was four, my father was convinced that I might well be left-handed. "We can't let him grow up as a southpaw. Why, no one in the family has ever been left-handed," he shuddered, as if it were some kind of crime.

Father's solution, which my mother approved without protest, was to permit me to use only my right hand. He rigged a crude, confining sling to my waist, and I spent that summer with my left arm strapped behind me, trying to will my right hand and arm to do my bidding. Meal-times were difficult, but in general I enjoyed the experience, because people who saw my restricted arm believed I had been injured. They sympathized, and I basked in the attention and pity I received.

When autumn arrived, I was doing most things right-handed. My father, as though reassuring himself that he had done the proper thing, would tell me, "Thank God I stepped in and did something so that you wouldn't be so different."

My conversion to the "right way of doing things" went satisfactorily, but the opposite was true of my parents' marriage. Just past my fourth birthday, I began to sense that something was seriously wrong. Sometimes night would fall and Father wouldn't be home—that seemed odd, in that as a baker, he would have to be up and off to work by 4:00 in the morning.

I became concerned about the constant loud arguing between my parents, something I hadn't been aware of earlier. I would see black and blue welts on Mother's arms and ask how she had hurt herself. She would answer, "I took a fall, Sonny." I would hear her crying, and she would explain that she didn't feel well. Once when I asked my mother why her eye was swollen shut, she said she had bumped into a door.

Late in 1935, a few months after my fourth birthday, Father was no longer coming home at all, and when I questioned his absence, Mother brought Brownie and me together. She told us, "Your daddy don't live here anymore. He is still your daddy, but I have to divorce him." She went no further in explaining the reasons for the breakup, but she did tell us that divorce meant that their time together was at an end. I began to cry, but she soothed me and said, "There now, you'll still get to see him at times, perhaps as much as you're seeing him now."

Father was the first to take legal action. On April 10, 1936, he filed a complaint. He alleged that mother had inflicted upon him "extreme and repeated cruelty, causing mental suffering." He said that she drank and stayed out all night, and that she nagged and scolded him and used abusive language. He asked for custody of me, and further asked the court to "permit daughter, Bronna Lu, age three, to remain with the defendant, Beulah Williamson Melton."

Our mother filed a counter complaint, denying all allegations. She asked that a divorce decree be granted her and that she be awarded custody of Brownie and me. She declared that Father was earning twenty-six dollars a week, and she asked that the court order him to pay to her child support of twenty dollars per month for each child.

While the court deliberated, our parents' separation continued, and Brownie and I remained with our mother. But in October, Father moved back in with us after promising Mother, "I will quit my excessive drinking and will not again strike you or do anything to cause you mental or physical suffering."

Father honored his pledge until the night of January 16, 1937. Sister Brownie and I saw and heard what happened. He came home late, accompanied by a fellow baker, Jess Hug, and talked Mother into letting him in. She trusted that she would be safe, but she badly misjudged. Sister and I saw Father lunge at her, and Mr. Hug was applauding and cheering him on, as a spectator would cheer a boxer at a fight. We took cover, cowering first behind the stove and then in back of a bed.

Father's fists hammered Mother's body and face. She was knocked against the sewing machine, bruised, bloodied, and pleading with him to stop the beating. Our wounded mother finally collapsed, and Father and his friend left laughing, Mr. Hug congratulating my father on a job well done. When the men had gone, Sister and I rushed to Mother's side and did the only thing two small children could do—we told her how much we loved her, and that we were sorry for what had happened.

The court granted Mother her divorce on March 26, 1937. She was given custody of my sister and me, and our father was ordered to pay child support totaling forty dollars per month. He ignored the support order, so on October 23, 1939, the court ordered him to pay support or go to jail. The monthly payments arrived for a time; then they stopped altogether.

My father's abuse of my mother has remained always in my memory. As a boy, there was little I could do to help, except to try and understand. As time passed, I came to know that alcoholism was the root cause of my father's behavior. A lovable man when he did not drink, he was a savage drunk.

One day I would use my influence and my public writing to fight against the mental and physical abuse of girls and women. And one day my father would forever give up alcohol and become the wonderful parent and friend Brownie and I had always hoped he could be.

Nomadic Family Roams Boise
Chicken-Coop Tenants

Boise, ID   After the divorce Mother was on her own, with Brownie and me to look after. Our gypsy lives began. We wedged our way into the small Boise home of Grandmother Daisy and her second husband, Clair Lenz. (Clair was a truck mechanic; Daisy was a waitress.) A block away lived Mary and Wilbur Williamson, my mother's brother and his wife. Mary and Wilbur were only fifteen years old, but they were already the parents of a two-year-old daughter, Sherma. The Great Depression was in full force, and even though Uncle Wilbur's work skill was auto body repair and painting, he would take any job he could find; in fact, he even rode the rails around southern Idaho in search of jobs.

Mother's sixth-grade education had prepared her for nothing but domestic work. Along Warm Springs Avenue in Boise there were homes of wealthy families, and she was able to get jobs in some of them as a domestic. Returning home each day, she spoke disparagingly of what she termed the filthy rich: "If they had a lick of fairness and sense, they'd be paying me twenty-five cents an hour rather than fifteen cents," she asserted.

In the late summer of 1937, Mother announced that we were moving away from her parents' rental home. She said she had found a little house in South Boise. "It's close to Garfield School, son, and that's where you will enter the first grade in September." The house was owned by a family named Dykus.

To a child's eye, small things often appear huge, and our new one-room house seemed palatial to me. In reality, it was a converted chicken coop. There was just enough room for a stove, a bed for Brownie and Mother, and a cot for me. A water pump, activated by hand, was outside our front door. Alongside the house was a one-holer outhouse—I had to stand on my toes to reach its wooden door latch. Mother felt she could afford the rent, which was five dollars a month.

On the first day of school, Mother walked me to Garfield School, enrolled me, coached me on how to find my way home, and went on to her job up on Warm Springs Avenue. After that I timidly showed up for school each day on my own, wearing floppy pants that were held up by suspenders.

The people from whom we rented our converted chicken coop claimed that they had fumigated it before we moved in, but we discovered that it was infested with tiny, reddish-brown mites. They were in the walls and the ceiling, and soon they were in our bedding. Mother called them bedbugs. Brownie and I would wake up every morning with red welts all over our bodies from their bites.

Our house was also invaded every day by flies from the adjacent cow pasture. In an attempt to keep their numbers down, we hung lots of flypaper strips from the ceiling—curiously animated streamers, swaying gently as captured flies buzzed on their sticky surfaces.

Our first winter in South Boise was a challenge. Mother attempted to ward off the cold blasts by plugging spaces between the coop's poorly-fitted boards with rags and newspapers. She sent Brownie and me out into the neighborhood to fetch pieces of wood, and she hammered these slats in place in the gaps until the walls of our little home resembled a wooden checkerboard. They were still far from air tight. When summer arrived, Mother boasted, "Nothing beats our air conditioning, and it isn't costing us a plugged nickel."

My father would occasionally visit us. He almost always brought a quart of milk and a couple of loaves of day-old bread from Holsum Bakery, where he worked. Brownie and I loved seeing our dad, and he would invariably bring each of us a candy bar or an all-day sucker. Best of all, he usually gave us a brief ride in what he called his fancy new car. It was a beat-up Ford Model-T sedan that he had to crank to start. On one of his visits, Mother snapped a picture of Father, Brownie, and me in front of the one-holer outhouse.

Our South Boise adventure ended abruptly, just after I completed the first grade. Late one summer night I awoke to voices outside. One belonged to Mother, and

"On one of his visits, Mother snapped a picture of Father, Brownie, and me in front of the one-holer outhouse." 1937.

there were two men talking aggressively to her. I peeked out our door and saw a police car, its headlights illuminating a pasture adjacent to our shack of a home. The policemen were loudly warning Mother, "Do not do this again!"

When the police left, Mother stepped back inside, gently scolded me for being up so late, and then explained what had occurred: "I had climbed through the barbed-wire fence and was milking the neighbor's goat. I have done this before," she said, "and nobody has seen me. This time somebody called the cops and squealed on me. It's a hell of a note, son, when they deny us milk for breakfast." The Dykus family evicted us the following day.

Mother found a new home for us, closer to town and to the homeowners for whom she did housework. Uncle Wilbur came over in his car, loaded up all we owned plus the three of us, and drove us to our next stop, a two-story apartment building owned by a family named Gagnon. Our one-room apartment was on the second floor.

The location of Gagnon Apartments was convenient. It was close to a mom-and-pop grocery that specialized in candy, and it was near the Holsum Bakery, where we could visit our father while he worked. Just three long city blocks distant was Park School, where I was to spend the second grade in 1938-1939. Our father was proud that he had also gone to school there. One weekend he walked me to the school and said, "Sonny, look at that huge crack that runs down the front steps." He went on proudly, proclaiming, "Me and some other boys swiped a big freight wagon one Halloween night, hauled it up those steps, shoved it down, and the runaway wagon left that big crack. It was our special mark on the school, and it was fun; and the best part was that they never caught us."

Sister Brownie began first grade as I entered third grade at Park School, and we would walk hand in hand, to and from school. One afternoon that autumn, Brownie and I arrived home from school and found Mother out front of Gagnon Apartments perched atop our large family trunk. She was crying, and she broke the news to us: "Kids, these bastards are shoving us into the street. In another few days, I'd have had enough to pay them some rent. But no, they haven't a merciful bone in their bodies."

I asked mother, "How much do we owe them?"

She answered, "Well, it's probably for three months, maybe a little more."

"Sister Brownie began first grade as I entered third grade at Park School, and we would walk hand in hand, to and from school." Brownie and Rollan c. 1939.

Sonny Keeps Moving

Idaho Our little gypsy band was on the move again. Mother had always declared that no matter what, Brownie would remain with her, but after the eviction, she told me, "You may have to keep moving, Sonny, until I can get my feet on the ground and bring you back."

Uncle Wilbur took in Mother and Brownie. I was sent to live with Grandmother Daisy and Clair, and I transferred to a Boise Bench District school. Shortly thereafter, Clair was hired as a diesel mechanic at a tiny Idaho mountain town called Banks, about fifty miles north of Boise. We moved to Banks, and I transferred to my third school that year, a one-room schoolhouse with eight grades taught by a single teacher.

My natural timidity caused me problems each time I entered a new school. Invariably, boys would test me. In my first schools I had managed to avoid having to fight, but that turned out to be impossible at Banks. Shortly after my arrival there, three boys trailed me after school, taunted me, and ripped at the straps on my denim overalls. I turned tail and raced home. That night I tearfully told Daisy and Clair of the episode and said that I was afraid to return to school the following day.

"You will go to school," Clair ordered. "Now that they've made you run, they'll hound you even more if you let them. What you better do is stand your ground and forget that stuff your mother has told you about letting the other guy get in the first punch. What I want you to do, Sonny, is hit any boy who looks like he's going to lay a hand on you. If you don't, you'll regret it."

Sure enough, the next day the trio tagged behind me again, waiting until we were out of sight of the schoolmarm. Then the largest boy blocked my route. "Wanna fight?" he challenged me. Instead of begging off, I hit him flush in the face and shoved him down. To my surprise, the three of them ran away. I had no further trouble at Banks School.

My grandmother Daisy was a disciplinarian, and I resented the new way of life she imposed on me. She required obedience and an explanation for every move I made. Thus, I was happy when third grade ended in the spring of 1939 and I was free to return to Boise to stay with my father, Grandmother Isabelle, Uncle Jack, and Aunt Margaret, all of whom lived in the same house. Crowding several family members into one household was common during the Depression, and this was the situation with both sides of my family.

Freed of Grandmother Daisy's scrutiny, I roamed Boise at will that summer, running family errands, prowling alleys in search of discarded soft-drink bottles (which I returned for deposit money), and collecting old rags and selling them to the *Idaho Daily Statesman*, which used them to clean ink off its presses. For this, I earned ten cents a pound.

I spent my earned pennies mostly on movies. I once stayed to see four consecutive showings of a Tarzan movie that introduced Johnny Weissmuller as King of the Jungle. Young Johnny Sheffield made his Tarzan series debut in that movie, portraying a character called Boy. When I finally reached home around midnight, I learned that my concerned father, fearing a kidnapping, had every cop in town searching for me.

The Depression was no easier on my dad's side of my family than it was on my mother's. My father worked sixteen-hour days at the bakery, earning around twenty-six dollars a week, and he was thankful that he had a job. Employers had workers over a barrel and could force them into long hours without fair pay. Uncle Jack, also a baker, had been laid off several times, and he quaked whenever a boss came near him, fearful of another layoff. Aunt Margaret long had been a hostess and cashier at restaurants, but, like Uncle Jack, she, too, had been laid off from jobs.

"My father worked sixteen-hour days at the bakery, earning around twenty-six dollars a week, and he was thankful that he had a job."

Rusty Does it Again
"What About Spuddy?"

Emmett, ID As time drew near for Brownie and me to enter second and fourth grades, my mother began dating a man named William Marrs. I never knew how they met, but she told us that this was "real love." They married late that summer, whereupon I left my father and rejoined mother and our newly constituted family of four.

Bill Marrs moved us to Emmett, a nearby Idaho community known primarily for its fruit orchards. Now that she was again married, mother no longer worked outside the home. Thus, she was free to sew clothing for Brownie, me, Bill, and herself.

Our stepfather was out in the fields each day, laboring with WPA (Works Progress Administration) co-workers. His income must have been slim to none, because one day a week the four of us would visit a downtown site where foodstuffs were dispensed to the needy. There were plenty of people in need. We would fall into lines that stretched more than a city block, waiting for a weekly allotment: canned goods, potatoes, loaves of day-old bread, coffee, and bottled milk. I was not familiar with the term "welfare," but that's what we were on.

My personal joys were going to "Pal Night" movies with Brownie (ten cents for the two of us) and playing with my lovable little puppy, Spud—so named because his brown-on-white markings resembled potatoes.

Radio was our link to the outside, and in the fall and early winter of 1940, there were incessant reports about the Roosevelt versus Willkie campaign. Within my family

Rusty Marrs in Emmett, Idaho, in 1940.

there was rejoicing when President Roosevelt was returned to office for a third term, and by a landslide vote. "Now we know he'll get this damn Depression over with," Bill and Mother told each other.

About the time that school ended in June, 1941, so did Mother's marriage to Bill Marrs. She never really told us the details, except to say that "Bill's a good man, kids, but if he drank less, we'd all be better off." Brownie and I were saddened by mother's decision, because we had come to like Bill Marrs very much. I never saw him again.

Mother sent me by bus from Emmett to Boise to rejoin my father for the summer. "What about Spuddy?" I asked.

"Don't worry, Sonny. Brownie and I will be coming back to Boise in a few days, and we'll bring him with us."

I was excited when mother returned to Boise shortly afterwards. She had found a rental home, and I would rejoin her that autumn to begin fifth grade. But when I asked about Spuddy, mother's voice broke. She said, "I'm sorry, son, but we gave Spuddy to our neighbors in Emmett. He was just one more mouth to feed. We couldn't afford to keep him." I never saw my dog Spud again.

WORLD WAR!

Hobo Boy Fires Shot Heard 'Round Rialto

Boise, ID Mother would threaten me as though she were a judge passing sentence. She endlessly promised to wash my mouth out with soap if I didn't stop swearing. (I never did, and she never did.) She would also tell me that if I wasn't good, she would send me to live with my dad. My fate thus defined, I would feign sadness.

I was already spending my weekends and long school vacations at grandmother Isabelle's home, where Father, Aunt Margaret, and Uncle Jack lived. (Brownie always stayed with Mother; my absence made one less mouth to feed.) While with mother, I was locked in an orderly life of rules, perimeters, curfews, and table manners. Living with Father, there was the joy of participating in his family's two cherished pastimes: eating and gossiping about the other side of my family. The Meltons ate, and I eagerly matched them, bite for bite. They talked, and I was all ears; but inwardly, I winced at their belittling of my mother, my grandmother Daisy, her husband, Clair, and my mother's other kinsmen. I told myself, "This is behavior that I don't want to imitate when I grow up."

My life in the summer of 1941 was one of uninterrupted happiness. As I ran errands for Isabelle, I cruised the aisles of the mom-and-pop grocery stores that dotted the neighborhoods; and at Hinkey's All-Night Grocery, I was a familiar shopping figure on behalf of the Meltons, who lived at 205 N. Thirteenth Street.

I swam each day at the Boise natatorium. My speech was peppered with contemporary childish witticisms: "Ink-a-bink, a bottle of ink; finders, keepers, losers, weepers;" and "Who do you think you are? Clark Gable?" I talked the marbles talk: "moon aggies, pee-wees, puries, knuckles down." I'd walk across town to visit mother and Brownie and torment them by bragging about a luxury enjoyed at Isabelle's: a flush toilet. At the movies, there were usherettes bearing flashlights. In the grocery stores were my favorite reading materials: comic books.

Then summer was over, and back to Mother's I went. She still wasn't on Easy Street, but by this time she had taken waitress work, which paid a mite better than scrubbing Warm Springs Avenue mansion floors and making the beds of the rich. In between her long restaurant shifts, she maximized her time with Brownie and me. Mother was a marvelous singer, and together we were a trio, crooning old and new songs. She adored Bing Crosby and scoffed at the newcomer, Frank Sinatra, as "a temporary nuisance." She harbored a mammoth dislike of Rudy Vallee, a popular singer of the day. "Vallee is enough to puke a post hole," she told us. Her description always got us laughing.

We were always just a few steps ahead of landlords demanding the rent. They would be closing in even as Mother packed us up and fled elsewhere in the dead of night. She rolled her own cigarettes to save money; when the hapless newspaper carrier crept to our door to collect, she stalled him; she badgered our father for child support, and he in turn stonewalled her; but through it all, Mother kept Brownie and me scrubbed, and our clothes were as tidy as her limited income could make them.

Mother swore up a storm but confessed it was wrong, and when I would pop a profanity, her wrath was swift and to the point. "Shut up!" she would roar. And her handwriting was beautiful. Reading her letters much later made me aware that here was a woman with a sixth-grade education who was nonetheless a logical thinker who wrote most gracefully.

By the time I was ten years old, I had become aware of the momentous events unfolding in Europe and the Orient. Weekly "March of Time" movie briefs invariably spotlighted a strutting Adolf Hitler and his goose-stepping storm troopers. London had been pulverized by German air raids in the blitz of 1940, and England remained in danger of invasion. The British, led by Prime Minister Winston Churchill, were begging for help from the United States. In the Far East, Japan was running amok, forcing the surrender of defenseless cities and peoples. But in the Isabelle Melton home, life went on serenely, as if no evil could ever touch us. Each adult in the household was working, and matriarch Isabelle appeared oblivious to world events.

One Sunday in December of 1941, I went to the Rialto theater on Boise's Main Street to see a movie. The main feature had scarcely begun when a message flashed across the bottom of the screen. The words have remained indelibly etched in my mind:

"All military personnel report immediately to Gowen Field." Half the men in the crowded Rialto Theater bolted up and hurriedly left.

The significance of the urgent flash was lost on me at the time, and I remained at the movie, which ended in midafternoon. Returning home, I found Father and Uncle Jack crouched beside grandmother's mahogany upright Philco radio. They were straining to hear every word from the announcer.

The radio report was sketchy, but the adults told me that we would one day look back on that Sunday and remember precisely where we were when we learned that the Japanese had bombed Pearl Harbor. Previously, my father had always called them "Japanese," but his language that day changed, and his voice was charged with anger: "The damned Japs have hit us at Pearl Harbor. They'll pay for this, Sonny. It's going to be war, but we'll win this within a week."

Across America there was a mad dash to military enlistment offices. My father tried to enlist, but he was ruled out because of serious eye problems. My paternal cousin, Charles Robert Forkner joined the Seabees. Mother's brother Wilbur signed up with the U.S. Marines.

Uncle Jack enlisted in the U.S. Navy a few days after Pearl Harbor, and when he told Isabelle, she collapsed, wept uncontrollably, and lapsed into a nervous breakdown. By day, she shuffled silently through the house, shredding the daily *Idaho Statesman* and leaving tattered newsprint in her wake. (I scooped up the scraps when I was around the house.) She refused to enter Uncle's bedroom during the war, and the only thing that seemed to rouse her from the breakdown were the few minutes she would spend reading and re-reading his V-Mail letters.

Uniformed men and women were the toast of Boise, and everybody tried to contribute to the war effort. You could be branded a traitor if you fudged on gasoline rationing, failed to buy war bonds, lit a match during a blackout drill, or didn't observe Meatless Tuesday.

Johnny Sheffield, who portrayed Boy opposite Johnny Weissmuller in the Tarzan movies, visited Boise midway through the war, hyping the sale of war bonds. I joined the swarms who surrounded the army tank on which he rode. I was able to actually brush his hand. Much to my disappointment, Tarzan did not visit Boise.

During the war, there were shortages of everything except resolve to defeat the Axis, but the Great Depression had become a distant memory. Every adult who wasn't wearing a uniform seemed to have a job. In 1942, mother took a waitress job at a restaurant at the ammunition depot at Hermiston, Oregon. As usual, Brownie went with her. I sent her a Mother's Day card and enclosed my handwritten letter. It said:

Dear Mom did you get my letter the other day. I am getting along in shool very much better. Mom, My teacher, Miss Amick, asked me if you would send my report card right away because we have only four mour weeks of school. how is Sis getting along in school? fine, I bet. Mamma Dee (with whom I was boarding in mother's absence) has a nice bed four me to sleep in. I sleep out on the porch at night and by golly I sleep good. Sam and I have los of fun togeather. Sam is the boy I stay with. Yesterday, Sam choped of a big limb on the tree. well I will have to hurry to school. 8 tons of love your Son Sonny."

Two weeks later, mother sent for me. I boarded a bus, was in Hermiston late the same day, and finished the fifth grade there.

> Boise Ida
> 1021 D 2 St
> May 1 1942
>
> Dear Mom
> did you get my letter the other day I am getting along in skool very much better Mom, My teacher Miss A. mick asked me if you would send my report card right away because we have only four mour weeks of school how his sis getting along in school? fine I bet.
>
> Mamma Lee has a nice bed four me to sleep in I sleep out on the porch at night and by golly I sleep good Sam and I have lots of fun togeather sam is the boy I stay with yesterday sam choped of a big limb on the tree. well I will have to harry to School
>
> & Tons of Love
> your Son
> Sonny

Sonny's letter to his mother on Mother's Day, 1942.

In 1943 my mother was hired at a restaurant at Gowen Field, where she worked the day shift and never uttered a complaint about "lousy tippers." Her happiest day at Gowen occurred the day actor and air force officer Jimmy Stewart visited the base. "They let me wait on Jimmy," she said, "and he shook my hand. Sonny, I swear, I'm never going to wash that hand again."

By then I could claim bragging rights for the number of schools I had attended—nine by age eleven, and counting. Some people laughingly called me "the hobo boy," but I saw myself becoming a war hero. If only the fighting would last till I came of age, I could be a marine. I would be brave. I would fight well. I would be famous among my countrymen.

Alas, I was to fire just one shot in anger during World War II. In 1943 I went to a war movie at the Rialto. It starred a grim, brave John Wayne portraying an American naval commander who courageously, and against enormous odds, faced the entire Japanese navy and won big-time. My friend Jim Fritschle was with me that afternoon. Much to his surprise, and that of everyone else, especially the theater management, I arose in the midst of the screen fighting, raised my BB gun, and fired a pellet straight at the movie enemy. A gruff yet amused usher hustled me out to the street, as my movie-going countrymen cheered me.

When at last victory was ours, Uncle Jack returned home safely. Grandmother Isabelle's nervous breakdown ended the moment he stepped back into our lives.

Sonny's Dad Jailed

Boise, ID While his fellow Americans were fighting in the air, on land, and sea, my father was fighting his own personal war. From that harrowing time when I was six and saw him beat my mother, I had known that his personal demon was alcohol. Then in 1941, before the start of World War II and while packing for an impromptu move that Mother, Brownie, and I were taking to outmaneuver a frustrated landlord, I came across a small envelope containing information that confirmed my father's weakness.

The envelope bore the printed notation, "Emmitt Pfost, Commissioner of Law Enforcement, Boise, Idaho." Inside, I found two *Idaho Statesman* news stories that my mother had clipped and saved. One clipping, dated March 19, 1937, was a news roundup from police court. It recorded Municipal Judge T.B. Chapman's admonishment of Rollan Melton, who had been arrested for drunken driving: "Look at you—aren't you a fine sight?" the judge said to him. (The newspaper reported that "The defendant's face was covered with a two-day growth of beard, his clothes were wrinkled and soiled, his hair mussed, his eyes bloodshot.") The judge went on: "You love your wife and babies, don't you?"

"Yes," my father answered.

"Then why don't you act like it? My boy, I hate to do this—I wish I could show leniency in your case, but the seriousness of your offense allows me no other course but to fine you $100 and revoke your driver's license. I hope this proves the futility of drink to you; and that when you pay your fine and are released, you will be ready to become a better father to your children, and a better man."

A smaller item in the same issue of the paper reported that Rollan Melton pled guilty

> **To Serve Fines For Drunken Driving Offenses**
>
> Keith Seman, 908 Krall street; R. Melton, 205 North 13th, and Wm. C. Griffin, who each pleaded guilty to charges of drunken driving, were sentenced in Monday police court to remain in Boise jail until their $100 fines are paid or served.

From the *Idaho Statesman*, March 19, 1937.

to charges of drunken driving and was sentenced in police court to remain in Boise jail until his $100 fine was paid or time was served. I had witnessed my father's alcohol-induced humiliation, and the stories took me back to that day:

My parents were separated, and Mother, Brownie, and I were living in our chicken-coop home in South Boise. One day my mother said, "Kids, your dad's in trouble. He's been arrested, and he's in jail. He wants to see you very much. We need to visit him."

Brownie began to cry, and I asked, "What's Dad done? Maybe the police have made up some lies about him."

Mother walked us downtown to an imposing stone building. Inside, she told the person in charge, "We're the family of Rollan Melton, and we're here to visit him."

Someone led us to the cell where Father was held. When he saw us, he began to cry. He reached through the bars, held our hands, and told us, "I've done a bad thing, kids. I drank too much, and I have learned my lesson. I won't be drinking again." My mother remained silent, but Brownie and I assured our father that we loved him.

Someone came and told us that the visit was over, and we said our goodbyes and walked out to the street. I remember Mother saying, "Your father is a very good man, kids. Maybe it's good that this has happened. Everything happens for a reason. I hope your dad means it when he swears that he won't drink anymore."

Mother knew from the accumulated defeats handed her since they had married that the odds were against my father being able to rehabilitate himself. After seeing Father in jail I vowed that I would never be a drinker. I felt that Father was a good man who would be even better now that he had decided to give up alcohol forever.

Seven days after the Boise municipal judge found Father guilty of drunken driving, my mother was granted the divorce and given custody of Brownie and me. Father was still in jail. His brother Jack was trying to get together $100 to pay his fine so he could be released.

Murder in Hermiston Camp

Hermiston, OR During our brief stay in Hermiston, Oregon, I learned for certain that drinking could be immensely dangerous to one's health. We were living in a tent, one of many occupied by civilian war workers. One evening while Mother was working the night shift as a waitress at nearby Umatilla Ammunition Depot, Brownie and I were awakened by a commotion. We peeked outside, saw police cars and many people milling around, and knew something very exciting had happened. We left our tent, hoping to find out what was going on. There was conversation in the growing crowd: "Two fellows doing a lot of drinking. . . they got in a bad argument. . . one took a knife to the other. . . they say somebody probably got killed."

I strained to see along a row of tent homes into the area where the most people had collected. It was lighted by the headlights of parked cars, and several policemen were standing over a sheet spread on the ground. A man's foot stuck out from under the sheet. Sister and I, chilled by the sight of a murder victim, hurriedly retreated to our tent.

The next morning, Mother shook us awake, got us ready for school, and listened patiently as we told of the mysterious events of the night before. "I know, kids. There was a fight, and a man was murdered. That settles that—we're getting the hell out of this place!" She left us briefly, and when she returned, she said, "I phoned my boss and told him I'm quitting. Right now, we're gonna pack and catch the next bus to Boise."

A couple of days later, back in our home city, Mother found a small house for us, and Brownie and I entered still another new school. It was early 1943, and the daily conversation of Boise's citizens was dominated by war talk. The city's two newspapers, the *Statesman* and the *Capital News*, were regularly filled with stories about the Allies and the Axis, including maps of various combat theaters. There were also frequent stories about war bond drives and what people on the home front were doing to help beat our enemies, and there was news about Idaho's soldiers and sailors home on leave. The saddest stories told of the wounding or death of Idaho servicemen.

On weekends, especially, the military of which Idaho was so proud seemed to concentrate in Boise. Everywhere, there were spitshined shoes and beribboned uniforms. In the windows of many homes, Blue Star banners were displayed, indicating that a member of the household was serving in the military. A gold star displayed in a window indicated a death in combat.

Mrs. Barnhart Takes Pity
Sonny Passes 8th Grade

Idaho, Oregon When the *Idaho Statesman* reported my father's brush with the law, my grandmother, Isabelle Melton, ranted about "newspaper unfairness against the little guy." Her animus rubbed off on me, but not to the degree that I would turn down an opportunity to make some money, and when I was about ten years old, I became a carrier for the afternoon *Capital News*. I had about thirty customers on my route near Lowell School.

As the story of the war, with all its drama and action, unfolded in the pages of the *News*, I became a serious reader for the first time, one whose interests went beyond the comics and sports pages. Even so, I did not then suspect that in the future, newspapers would be the consuming interest of my life, giving me excitement and pleasure and providing me a passport to adventure and opportunity.

In the early 1940s a career in journalism was unthinkable to me. In fact, a career in anything was unthinkable. I was a schoolboy who consistently received failing grades—one who despised school and who dreaded transferring from one to another, because that meant entering a student body of total strangers. I would never ask a question or volunteer an answer in a classroom. My burning desire was to escape the tedium of school as quickly as possible so that I could enlist in the military and become a war-hero headliner.

My father told me, time and again, "Sonny, I didn't make it through the seventh grade. You must get through the eighth. When that happens, you will be the best-educated person ever in our family." I wanted to live up to his expectations—especially because I had had quite a bellyful of formal schooling, and I looked forward to terminating the painful experience following the eighth grade.

Father had still another wish: "You should never become a baker like me. That's not a good way to get ahead. Look at me, bouncing from place to place, not earning enough money to make ends meet. Son, you just complete all eight grades, and you'll always be happy you did."

Getting through school would have been easier for me if my father and mother had led more conventional lives. In the summer of 1943, my father announced that he was going to remarry. My future stepmother's name was Dora Miller. She also had been married before, but, according to Father, this was to be a marriage made in heaven. My mother greeted the news indifferently, telling Brownie and me, "Well, I wish your dad's new wife a lot of luck, because she's sure in hell gonna need it." Mother had steady waitress work at Gowen Air Field, but she thought it best that I rejoin my father for awhile: "Times are still rough, and until I get to earning better money, I'm asking that your father let you stay with him."

Father remarried and almost simultaneously quit his bakery job at the first Albertson's grocery store, located on State Street in Boise. "We're on the road again, son," he said. That road led us to Bend, Oregon. Our traveling Melton show consisted of Father, his new wife, Dora, grandmother Isabelle, and me. At Bend, located in central Oregon, I enrolled in the seventh grade in September of 1943. "Look, Dad! In just a couple more grades, I'll hold the family record for years in school."

Meanwhile, only a fool would voluntarily have been in stepmother Dora's place. Dad drank excessively and abused her verbally, if not physically. His mother, Isabelle, was "anti-Dora" from the start. As for me, I rooted quietly for a divorce. Dora was a disciplinarian, and I didn't need someone who insisted that I live my life *her* way.

I staggered through seventh grade at Bend. The school year had just ended when the most thrilling story of World War II started to unfold. The long-awaited Allied invasion of Europe began on June 6, 1944. I read all about it in the *Bend Bulletin*. By then, I was paying attention to reporters' bylines. The first-day account of history's largest invasion was written by an Associated Press war correspondent, Wes Gallagher. (Twenty years later, when I was a young editor, I would become his friend. Later we would be colleagues together on a newspaper invasion: the birth of *USA Today*.)

We remained in Bend the rest of the summer. Then, out of the blue, Father was out of work again. He took me aside and confided that his drinking had led to dismissal from this job, and that, in fact, it was the chief reason why he had been fired from so many other jobs over the years. I was thirteen, and this was the first time he had leveled with me. Fortunately, it didn't take him long to find new work, because there was a shortage of manpower with so many Americans away to war.

Dad found a job in Gresham, Oregon, near Portland. We moved there in September, 1944, and I enrolled in the eighth grade. "At long last," I thought, "I am close to breaking my family's all-time education record." There was another record I could then claim: Gresham was the eighteenth school I had attended. This utter lack of continuity and stability was a principal reason why I was hopelessly behind in learning.

My performance didn't improve at Gresham. One day shortly before the eighth grade graduation ceremony, my teacher, Mrs. Barnhart, asked me to remain after school. She told me, "Rollan, you have been unable to keep up with the others, and I am not going to recommend you for promotion."

I spoke up for the first time in the entire school year: "Mrs. Barnhart, please, please give me a chance. Pass me on. I promise to work hard in the future." She took pity on me and promoted me on to my freshman year in high school.

Of course, I had no intention of "working hard in the future," at least not in any classroom. With the eighth grade behind me at last, I was through with school. Now I was free to do whatever I pleased . . . . Then my mother called. She and Brownie were living in a town I had never heard of in a state that I had never visited: Fallon, Nevada. She got straight to the point: "I've got steady work in Fallon, son. You'll be coming back to live with me. Next fall, you'll go on to high school here."

Hobo Kid Visits Fallon

Fallon, NV On a hot, mid-June day in 1945, I rode into the Silver State on a Greyhound bus, glumly staring out at a vista that the comic book hero, Flash Gordon, might have encountered on an alien world. All that could be seen was an ocean of sand, rocks, and sagebrush. Dust devils swirled in the shimmering heat. In Idaho and Oregon, I had lived amidst beautiful forests and rivers and lakes, and this bleak landscape left me feeling blue. Mother had cautioned me, "Nevada may take some getting used to." She was so right!

To start my trip, my father had driven me from Gresham to Portland and put me on the bus—he had booked me night fare, the cheaper ticket. I had enjoyed my last two years with him, except for stepmother Dora's presence. In truth, Dora had been given a very hard time by the Melton troika. My father told me just before I began the journey to Nevada that Dora was shortly to become history—he intended to divorce her. The news made me sad in a way, because deep down I realized that she had done her best to shape me into a respectable young man.

As the bus pulled into Reno's Center Street depot, I spotted Mother, who had taken a Hiskey Company stage in from Fallon to greet me. She kissed me, and I hugged the mother I hadn't seen in two years. I let her know right off that the Nevada desert was ugly, and that even the jackrabbits seen en route appeared underfed. She told me, "If you're gonna live here son, you've got to give things a chance."

I grabbed the small cardboard box that passed for my suitcase. It held all that I owned. Across the street stood the Golden Hotel, rising fully five stories. It was the tallest building I had ever seen. Everything was new and different, but there wasn't time to walk around, because our Hiskey stage connection to Fallon was soon to leave. The Reno depot was crowded with many servicemen, and it was noisy. I pointed to a row of mechanical devices and asked Mother, "What are those things?" She laughed. "They're slot machines, Sonny, and they make a lot of money for the guys who own the casinos."

In 1945 Nevada's population was only around 125,000. Reno was by far the state's largest city, with more than 30,000 people. There was a lot of empty country between Reno and Fallon, sixty-three miles to the east, and our bus bounced along on a lightly-traveled two-lane road, passing rural mailboxes and occasionally stopping to drop off passengers or pick up new riders. Along the way we made scheduled stops in the small towns of Sparks, Wadsworth, Fernley, and Hazen. The cars and trucks that we passed looked worn out, and no wonder! There hadn't been a new car built since 1942, as manufacturing had shifted to production of essential war materials.

As we approached Fallon, which had a population of about 2,000, we began to see green fields. "They grow a lot of food out here," Mother said. "Especially cantaloupes, alfalfa, and cattle." I was indifferent. This town was sure to be like the other stopovers in my life. Everybody would be a stranger;

school would alternately bore and scare me; there would be nothing to do. I could no more imagine being a permanent resident of Fallon than I could imagine joining the Lone Ranger on a trail ride.

Brownie, the little sister I hadn't seen for two years, was waiting for us in Fallon, and she was cuter than ever. Mother still had never owned a car, so we hiked from the bus station to my new home, the Hart Apartments on LaVerne Street, near the Volunteer Fire Station. There I met the tenants of the other seven rooms, including a sailor who, Mother explained, had rescued a working girl from the local house of prostitution by marrying her.

I had no money, and I couldn't ask mother for any—she barely had enough to keep us fed and housed. As summer glided by, I scouted for a job, with no luck: I wasn't big enough to buck hay bales; and although I had been a bowling alley pin-setter in Boise, in Bend, and in Gresham, Fallon had no bowling alley. Mother asked her bosses at the Owl Café-Casino, the Louie LaTossa family, if they could use me as a dishwasher. They hired me at fifty cents an hour. I had just turned fourteen.

One day, much to my delight, the dishwasher who was to work the shift following mine called in sick. I jumped at the chance to work an additional eight hours. After I had done the double shift, I was handed eight dollars in cash for the sixteen hours of work. It was the biggest payday I had ever had.

I cashed the eight silver dollars into quarters and, when no one was looking, bellied up to a slot machine, confident of winning big money. Within ten minutes, I had lost it all. I was depressed, and I was mad at myself for being so stupid, but I had learned a lesson. In the decades since, knowing that it is the house that always ultimately wins, I have not gambled.

Grandmother Daisy and her husband, Clair Lenz, lived seventy miles away in Babbitt, a small community next to Hawthorne, where Clair was a mechanic at the military ammunition depot. My mother had weekends off, and she and I would hitchhike to Hawthorne to visit. On one such weekend a truck driver hauled us as far as Schurz, the location of a Paiute Indian reservation some distance from our destination. We were standing alongside the road at Schurz, trying to hitch a ride on in to Babbitt, when I suddenly blurted, "Mom, I'm not cut out for school. I have gone through the eighth grade, and that's enough. I won't be going on to high school."

My mother turned on me angrily. "Like hell, you're quitting! I don't give a good goddamn what your father has told you, you quit now and you'll always be a quitter! Get your head on straight—you're going to high school."

I sulked the rest of the trip, but that was a galvanizing event in my life. In the blazing summer sun on the shoulder of a little-traveled Nevada highway, a mother who cared had laid down the law. She would not allow her son to be a failure—I would continue my education.

On August 6, 1945, the *Reno Evening Gazette* reported the dropping of an awesome weapon on Hiroshima, Japan. Three days later, a second bomb was dropped from the belly of an American B-29 bomber, and the city of Nagasaki was incinerated. The newspaper said the weapons were atomic bombs. The nuclear age had begun, and the world would never be the same.

A week later, Fallon's tranquility was pierced by the shriek of the volunteer fire department's siren, which was used only to signal the arrival of the noon hour or a fire. It blasted unceasingly, making a sound as if every hand in the community was pressed to a car horn. We ran out to learn what was going on. Was the whole of Fallon being consumed by flames? A radio news flash had announced that Japan had surrendered unconditionally.

There was great joy in Fallon that day. Billie Huckaby rode her horse into the Owl Club; bottle of beer held high, she toasted victory. The little town cheered those who had brought us through the world's greatest peril, but reactions were muted in thirty-six Fallon area homes. In them, families and friends gathered to pray for the souls of the fathers, sons, brothers, uncles, and cousins who had been killed in the war.

School opened in September, and I enrolled and went out for football. The coach, Wes Goodner, would become one of my role models, but I didn't then know what "role model" meant. What I did know was that through football I could get acquainted with boys my age, and that going to class was "the pits."

I lasted just six weeks at Fallon High School. The end came when mother was suddenly laid off from her waitress job. "I've got enough savings to limp along for awhile, son," she told me, "but you'll have to go live with your dad again until I get back on my feet. Brownie will remain with me, as usual, but you must go."

I shed no tears. It was time to be a gypsy again. My record of never having gone to the same school in back-to-back years would remain intact.

Mother and Brownie walked me over to the Sagebrush Café to catch a bus to Reno and thence to Bend, where my father was again living after having divorced Dora. We hugged and kissed goodbye, and I hoped it would not be two more years before I again saw them. As the bus pulled out, I looked back—they were still waving.

I had thought that Fallon would taste like castor oil and go down harder, but I actually had come to like it a little. Too bad that I'd never see the place again. I was the young hobo kid, off to see what I could see.

Daisy Takes Charge, Raises Hell

Twin Falls, ID I re-entered high school in Bend, but regularly skipped classes. I believed I didn't need further schooling, and my father didn't force me to attend. The teachers seemed indifferent to me, and little wonder, for they must have regarded me as just another transient kid who soon would be gone. They were right about that. Not only was there no pressure to go to school, which bored me, but I was raking in ten dollars a week in walking-around money from my nighttime job as a bowling alley pin setter.

Just nine weeks after I arrived, we were on the move again, with Father repeating one of his favorite sayings: "Son, I've found greener pastures." We returned to Boise, where I didn't bother to re-enroll in ninth grade. Thus, at age fourteen, my formal education was finally over. Or so I believed.

What wasn't over was the nomadic life. Three months passed, and then Father broke his vow not to drink. He went on an alcoholic binge, missed several shifts, and was terminated by the Albertson's store in Boise. In January, 1946, the two of us moved north to Twin Falls, Idaho, where he had lined up a bakery job.

Life's highway intersects with many roads of chance. Timing and luck can lead one to an unmapped destination. In Twin Falls a single event, charged by anger, was to change my life in a positive way. The odds on what happened were surely very long:

My father and I arrived in Twin Falls at the same time that Daisy and Clair moved there from Babbitt, Nevada, where the end of the war had led to layoffs at the ammunition depot. Learning that we were now living in the same city as my maternal grandmother disturbed me. Daisy was the only family member whom I feared and disliked. She was the one who early in my life had told me I was setting myself up for failure. She was the one who monitored my every move, insisting on accountability. She was the person who questioned me endlessly about school and what I was learning.

My father and I were living in an old Twin Falls apartment house. Grandmother Daisy got our address from my mother, and one morning she paid us a surprise visit. I answered a knock at the door, and there she was, greeting us warmly but preparing to ask the sort of aggressive questions that could be so intimidating.

Although Father despised her, he was all sweetness and light at first. Then the conversation turned ugly. Daisy had a gift for asking questions that put people off balance. Her conversation went pretty much like she was interrogating witnesses in a courtroom:

"And what school are you enrolled in, Sonny?"

"Sonny's not in school anymore," my father explained. "He quit."

"Well," she exploded, "for God's sake! You can't let this boy go on without learning."

"Daisy," Father said meekly, "Sonny's already got his eighth-grade diploma, and that's farther than anybody in the family has ever gotten."

"That's crap, and you know it!" she fired back. She was just warming up.

Daisy resembled a comic-book character, almost gnome-like, cigarette dangling from its holder, her fired-up complexion matching her auburn hair. I cowered at the edge of this exchange, afraid she would turn on me. But she didn't. All her salvos were aimed my father.

"Sonny's just a boy. He don't know why education is so important. Now, damn it, get him back in school or else!"

"There's no law says he's got to stay in school beyond eighth grade," said Father. "Besides," he declared, his voice now quaking, "he's my kid. I have a legal right to help him decide."

"To hell with you!" she roared. "His mother is the legal custodian, and you damn well know it. She wants him in school. She wants him back with her when summer comes. In the meantime, Sonny's going to get back in school right now."

Father went into full retreat. "Well, Daisy, you're probably right. I'll take him to the high school next Monday and tell them that his family wants him admitted."

"To hell with Monday," she bellowed. "He's going to school right now, and I'll take him!"

My grandmother held out her hand, led me outside to her car, drove to the school, found the principal, and explained to her that I had virtually dropped out the previous mid-

THE HOBO KID 27

" 'Sonny's going to get back in school right now.' " Rollan Melton with Grandmother Daisy in 1950.

October. The principal said, "Your grandson has missed five months of his freshman year. That's too much for him to catch up. We'll admit him, but there's no way we can promote him to tenth grade at the end of the year. Next fall, wherever he lives, he'll have to start high school over again." My heart sank.

Back to school I went to finish ninth grade, knowing that I was so far behind that I could never catch up. How I wished that the adults who were ruining my life would get off my case and let me do what I wanted!

Two months later the school term ended, and my mother sent for me. She wanted me back in Fallon. There, I knew, I must face the of repeating my freshman year—I would again have to put names to faces; I might again have to fight my way into acceptance.

Growing up in a dysfunctional family had gotten me off to a very shaky start in life. I loved my family, and they loved me, but my parents' divorce had consequences that extended far beyond the court's granting custody of us kids to our mother. Although I was never an unhappy young boy, never hungry, and never thought of myself as deprived, we were dirt poor.

Moving rapidly from city to city had at first seemed to me to be just one adventure after another, but transiency exacted a toll. The constant parade of schools was the most difficult part of the experience. With every move, I was thrown in with a new set of strangers. I knew that my fellow students would be in and out of my life in a short while, and so would my teachers, who would quickly decide that I was so far behind that it would be impossible for them to help me catch up, no matter how much help they gave. The number of educational fundamentals I was missing began to multiply.

Time after time, I found that the new student is treated with wariness by the other kids. Only those students who are permanent are among the "in" crowd. To get in, it is necessary to stick around and win acceptance, and through my first nine years of school, including my aborted freshman year, I never felt that I belonged or that I was worthy of measuring up to other students or to teachers' expectations.

I couldn't catch up in my learning, and I was pained by the embarrassment of always being the only person in the classroom who was ignorant. My schooling hadn't been the positive experience that youngsters need. I felt inferior, and I was turning into a kid who needed an attitude adjustment.

With that shaky underpinning, in the summer of 1946 I returned to Fallon a second time. I was filled with anxiety, for in the fall I would return to Fallon High as a dropout who had to re-start school. I was certain to be humiliated by the other students. I felt that my grandmother Daisy had caused this misery, and I deeply resented her for it.

Fallon Freshman Returns

Fallon, NV In September of 1946, with a large chip firmly affixed to my shoulder, I re-enrolled as a freshman at Fallon High School. I scarcely remembered students in the sophomore class, to which I then should have belonged. Now I was stuck in the midst of students who had graduated from eighth grade the prior June.

I approached my studies in a blaze of adolescent defiance. Certain that I wasn't liked by other students or the teachers, I was sullen in the classroom. So indifferent was I in my first-year Spanish class that veteran teacher Hattie Brown awarded me an "F."

"In September of 1946, with a large chip firmly affixed to my shoulder, I re-enrolled as a freshman at Fallon High School."

(That would be the only failing grade I would earn in high school.)

My second "first" year was spent quietly sizing up other students and the faculty, registering in classes that were said to be the easiest, and ignoring school social events that would have better acquainted me with the general student body. There were only about three hundred students, so it would have been possible to get to know most of them had I tried. However, I wanted no part of joining up socially.

Involvement in sports was quite another matter. Athletics required brawn, not brains, or so I believed. I went out for football, and consequently began developing the first solid friendships I had ever had. I loved the body contact, the competitive aspects of the game, and the potential of being noticed and appreciated.

Just past my fifteenth birthday, I was still growing up and out. At five feet, eight inches tall and weighing about one hundred and eighty pounds, I was assigned to both offensive and defensive guard positions. This didn't satisfy me. "Too bad they didn't name me a running back," I thought. "That's where I could really shine." Coach Wes Goodner knew better. I was quick as an interior lineman, but a plodder as ball carriers go.

The season was my first in any organized sport, and I did not play a single down in a varsity game—all of my playing was in practice scrimmages. However, I learned a great deal that later would be part of the foundation needed in leadership roles. I discovered that one-man shows and miracle plays don't produce victories. Coach Goodner schooled us in the fundamentals of blocking and tackling, and the strategies of offense and defense.

Coach Goodner repeatedly schooled us, "If you ever expect to do a thing right, you must practice, practice, and practice." Even riding the bench provided a lesson in patience. The coach counseled us younger players, "You need to learn to wait your turn."

Unfortunately, I did not carry football lessons over into my academics. I was behind the learning curve, still content to remain quiet in the classroom and never volunteering a question or an opinion out of fear of revealing my ignorance.

With Mother working day shifts as a waitress, it was easy for me to routinely skip a day of class. My sister, Brownie, was then an eighth-grader, and one time I asked her to write me a phony excuse and sign Mother's name to it. She happily complied. Unfortunately, I did not read "Mother's" note before I handed it over to the vice-principal. He read it in my presence, then handed it to me and asked, "What's this?"

I read the note, which said, "Please excuse Rollan Melton's absence of yesterday. He played hooky."

After my first football season ended, I found part-time after-school jobs. At Al Powell's Sagebrush Café, I was a nighttime dishwasher, reporting to an exacting boss, Shorty, who scolded me if dishes and utensils weren't cleaned perfectly. There was a weekend job jerking sodas and taking food orders at Kick's Fountain on Maine Street. Al Burdick was the easygoing owner-manager who taught me to treat each customer as though he or she was the most important client in Fallon.

My first true boyhood friendships were formed in the 1946-1947 school year, especially with my best friend, Arthur Farrel, and with fellow freshman football players Don Ferguson, Ralph Powell, Del "Jugger" Steve, Wayne Weaver, Bill Strand, and Oscar Moser. Midway through the year, it dawned on me that it was unlikely that the next school year I would be hitting the road again. For the first time in my life, I could be attending the same school in two consecutive years. On the home front, my mother had steady waitress work, and I was bringing a few dollars into the family coffers with my part-time jobs.

In that freshman year, despite poor study practices, I slipped by with mediocre grades, which I regarded as a huge academic victory. Except in Spanish. Miss Brown was exasperated with my lack of aptitude and my indifference. She gave me an "F" and told me, "It would be wrong to give you a passing grade. I might have, but you didn't try." I was stung by her bluntness. Yet, I knew that she was honest, and that she had done me a favor by not rewarding slipshod performance.

Journalism Class Gains A Convert

Fallon, NV After a summer of hauling alfalfa bales on fellow student Don Ferguson's parents' ranch, I signed up for sophomore classes. In the options on electives, I saw that journalism was offered. I added it to my class list.

There were eight students in journalism teacher Anne Gibbs's class. During the spring semester, I found myself writing brief news stories about school events. I struggled to compose them in an understandable manner, and I found that reading the daily Reno newspapers gave me some insight into news-story writing techniques. I had not taken a typing class, but my primitive hunt-and-peck system got me by.

My journalism class stories, mainly about sports, began appearing in our mimeographed school newspaper, the *Greenwave Flash*. Although student reporter bylines weren't published, being able to shape news for student body consumption was heady stuff. I took a real liking to the class, and especially to Miss Gibbs's patient, knowledgeable teaching. She had taught me freshman English, and now, in addition to journalism, I had her as my sophomore English instructor.

In journalism class one early April day in 1948, Miss Gibbs told us that later in the week we would have a guest speaker. "Mr. Smith owns the *Fallon Standard*," she said, adding that he would speak to us about his profession, and that the eight of us should then be prepared to ask questions of him.

Claude H. Smith was a spellbinder. Physically small, graying, and bespectacled, he wore a necktie and a coat, and he sat on the edge of Miss Gibbs's desk while he talked. I wanted to know how he and his newspaper colleagues could be individuals, yet also work as a team. Although it was out of character for me to ask questions of an adult, that day I did, and he responded thoughtfully. Then he invited us to visit the *Fallon Standard* office.

A few days later, the class met at the newspaper office on West Center Street. We were greeted by Mr. Smith and his wife, Ethel, who was office manager. I stood out among the student visitors because I was the only boy in the class and the only person wearing a varsity letter sweater.

About a week later, I was summoned out of a classroom and told to report immediately to vice-principal and coach Wes Goodner's office. I was seized by fear. All of my earlier summonses by school administrators had been of a disciplinary nature. However, Coach Goodner greeted me with a smile and introduced me to a visitor: "Rollan, this is Ken Ingram of the *Fallon Standard* staff."

I was wary of the short, slender, balding Ingram, unsure of what was coming, but he was cordial. Sensing my nervousness, he quickly put me at ease: "Well, Rollan, I remember you recently coming to visit the *Standard* with Anne Gibbs's journalism class. We hope you enjoyed being around the newspaper."

I paused and finally stammered, "Yeah, it was really interesting."

Ingram then made me an offer that would change my life forever. "The girl who has been our newspaper apprentice is leaving to enroll next fall at the university," he said. "We need someone to replace her. Mr. Smith and I remember you from your visit to the paper, and Mr. Goodner says you are a responsible person. Are you interested in a part-time job as an apprentice printer?"

I started to blunder in with a question about pay, but Ingram, anticipating me, added, "You would start at fifty cents an hour. If you worked, say, a twenty-hour week while going to school, you'd make around ten dollars a week. Of course, in the summertime we would want you to work full time—forty to fifty hours a week. You may want to think this over and let us know."

I didn't even know what "apprentice" meant and wasn't about to ask, but I blurted, "I'll take it. When do I start?"

"Would tomorrow be too soon?" Ingram asked. "You can come to our office, and we'll explain the things the apprentice does and answer any of your questions."

As he talked, I was thinking of the money I might earn, multiplying fifty cents an hour by as many as fifty hours during the summertime. "God," I told myself, "I might earn as much as twenty-five dollars a week." To me, the poor fifteen-year-old, it was a staggering sum, too good to be true.

Standard Takes on Apprentice Printer

Fallon, NV Thanks to Claude Smith and Ken Ingram, I was beginning a love affair with newsprint and ink, with interviews and writing, with the stories of cities and their citizens. The addiction came on swiftly, and it was irrevocable.

My *Standard* and high school schedules were quickly worked out. There was plenty to do. Printing foreman Richard "Rap" Pedersen and his assistant, Thomas Lusk, showed me how to operate the small commercial printing presses. Soon I was running off the weekly *Standard* on Monday nights on a flatbed two-page cylinder press. Tom Lusk schooled me in hand-setting type out of the California portable type case. In between printing lessons, Tom gently counseled me on proper English. I would mangle the language, and Tom would promptly re-state my expressions in a grammatically correct way. He taught by example rather than admonishing me.

The staff was of the lean size common among Nevada weekly newspapers. Claude Smith was incredibly versatile. He was an artist turned newspaperman and publisher, and the only person I ever saw who could compose an editorial straight from his head onto the Linotype keys. Ken Ingram was a driven professional who had been educated in

The Fallon *Standard* staff, 1949. Front, l. to r.: Thomas Lusk, Ida Gibson, Ken Ingram, Marlene Plummer, Rollan Melton; Rear, l. to r.: Marguerite Lima, Claude Smith, Richard Pedersen, Ethel Smith.

journalism in Montana. He was easily the most versatile *Fallon Standard* staff member, writing most of the straight news and selling both advertising and commercial printing. Mr. Smith's wife, Ethel, was the leader of the business department and the greeter of customers and visitors. She also wrote a popular local column and sold classified ads to office visitors.

Ida Gibson was the paper's only Linotype operator, and she could set an incredible two galleys of type (some forty column-inches) an hour, with hardly an error. There wasn't enough work to employ her full time, so she worked part of each week as a typesetter at the office of our rival, the *Fallon Eagle*. Our chief rural news columnist was Marguerite Lima, who did her writing at her home in longhand, for she couldn't type. Each week she delivered her column copy to Ethel Smith at the *Standard*. Mrs. Lima had a marvelous personality and a penchant for loading her column with names and what, to an outsider, would probably seem trivial news items. In Fallon, this approach was welcomed: it helped people keep track of friends and introduced readers to newcomers.

Mrs. Lima's style, and that of every other writer at the paper, reflected Claude Smith's philosophy. He would say, "These names we're printing ... they aren't just names. They are people who count a lot, who grew up here, who have their homes and families here." Mrs. Lima, like her country correspondent counterparts, wrote about a specific community but tried to present news so that it would have broad appeal.

Ken Ingram was my foremost role model at the *Standard* and one of the great teachers in my life. After a few months there, I asked him if I could begin writing local sports stories. He agreed to let me show him what I could do.

In the beginning I loaded up my stories with an endless stream of sports cliches—hackneyed phrases that I had seen in other newspapers and that I falsely believed to be good writing. It wasn't long before Ingram put a stop to that. His technique of teaching was both gentle and firm. In editing my stories before publication, he would begin by saying, "This is a fine approach. You've done a good interviewing job. You've put many facts in this." Then he would systematically attack errors of fact and language usage, without ever putting me down. I invariably escaped without loss of self-esteem, but I was learning that there was a better way than my way. I also learned that Ken's style of constructive criticism works best.

Cub Reporter Learns Ropes

Fallon, NV My job at the newspaper was fulfilling, and I felt that I was putting down roots in the community. For the first time in my life, I attended the same school in consecutive years. I could feel myself steadily growing in knowledge of what was right about me instead of what was wrong. At Fallon High School I came to know virtually every student, and I made a special effort to get acquainted with those who were just starting high school.

I tried many varsity sports, including boxing, basketball, and track and field, but I was best suited for football, and it was in this sport that I excelled. Football (and one football coach) taught me what would serve me so well for the rest of my life: It requires team effort to win; one shining star can be one too many; allow all players to maximize their worth; develop bench strength; one day,

"I tried many varsity sports, including boxing, basketball, and track and field, but I was best suited for football, and it was in this sport that I excelled." Rollan Melton in 1949.

if properly developed, the reserve may be a starter.

Wes Goodner, my Fallon High football coach had starred as an end on Jim Aikin's vaunted University of Nevada teams of 1940-1941. These were ball clubs that featured the great running back, Marion Motley, who later became a National Football League Hall of Fame fullback with the Cleveland Browns. Goodner was a gifted leader as well as a superb athlete, and Aikin had him calling plays from the end position—Motley had trouble memorizing plays, but when told what to do, he did it superbly; the teammate who told him how to execute before each play was Wes Goodner.

On the playing field at Fallon High, Coach Goodner kept saying, "If you work at it, you'll get better." The Fallon High faculty, especially Anne Gibbs Berlin and the taskmaster civics teacher, Byrd Sawyer, seemed to be talking directly to me when they lectured students: "This is why it is important to learn." At the *Fallon Standard*, Ken Ingram and Claude Smith were more direct. In essence, they told me what Truman Capote would say about the work of another writer years later: "That's not writing. It's typing." But they added that with lots of practice and a commitment to succeed, I could improve.

To me, these critiques of my work meant that my role models believed that I was worthy of their time and their teaching. Thus, my schoolboy excitement about competitive football and newspapering steamed along undiminished. Before, as a migrant boy, I had treated real work as if it were a contagious disease against which I had been inoculated. Now I felt a seismic shift occur. I was becoming a schoolboy workaholic—anxious to learn, eager to earn, and especially desiring recognition of athletic, academic, printing, and newspaper achievement. This yearning for recognition was something I had not known in my early life. I had become ambitious.

During football season, I would awaken at 5 a.m., be at the *Standard* by 6:00, work a couple of hours, and then walk to school. During the noon hour, I'd go back to the *Standard* or home to have lunch, then back to school. After school I'd go to the football practice field and then back to the *Standard* office to work into the late evening. That sort of work load became routine, a welcome companion as I convinced myself that to be as good as I could be, I must learn more and work harder than anyone else.

I found myself in a state of constant competition, competing for varsity sports letters, for football all-state recognition, for a pat on the head from Ken Ingram for having done acceptable work. There also was heavy competition between the *Standard* and its rival down the street, the *Fallon Eagle*.

The *Standard* versus *Eagle* combat was sometimes got ugly, as each went after all the news that was fit to print, plus the dominant position in display and classified advertising and in paid circulation. The leader at the *Eagle* was Robert Sanford, a competent and persistent adversary. He was not journalism school-trained, but he could write with the best, was a printer by trade, and managed to publish a sprightly, newsy issue each Friday.

In those years, near mid-century, newspapers battling for dominance in the same market could accurately be characterized as at war with each other. This was certainly true in Fallon. Each weekend Smith and Ingram carefully studied what the rival *Eagle* was doing: who its chief news sources were; what it failed to cover newswise; which advertising opportunities it exploited or overlooked; how well it covered news from the courts, city government, police and sheriff's departments; the Truckee-Carson Irrigation District (TCID); education, farming, and ranching; water matters; the weather; sports; rural news via country correspondents; and myriad other subjects that affected the Fallon area.

That Sanford and his *Eagle* colleagues also were analyzing the *Standard* was patently clear. Knowing your rival as well as, or better than, you know yourself enhances your chances for survival and success. John Stuart Mill summed up the need for competition when he wrote that soldiers fall asleep at their posts when there is no enemy in the field. Thus did my *Standard* roots instill in me an unshakable belief that, in journalism, all-out competition is best for readers, advertisers, and assuredly for those who report and write.

Becoming a proficient reporter and writer requires years of experience and maturing, but there must be a beginning, and the *Fallon Standard* was my starting point. At night, after my co-workers had gone home, I would sit at a typewriter at Ingram's or Smith's desk, slowly pecking out my crude stories. Sitting behind the big desk of the great Claude Smith gave me chills, for he was among the most respected men in Nevada journalism—a community power and a man who had served as an assemblyman in the state legislature. He also was a chain smoker of Camels. At night, when I turned into the *Standard* janitor, it was my job to empty his overflowing ashtrays and sweep away the discarded matches and cigarette butts he left in his wake.

Ingram let me focus mainly on sports writing, the majority of which followed Fallon High School teams, the athletic territory I knew so well because I was part of it. But given my inexperience, he monitored my work carefully, schooling me to avoid composing in a novice's voice. "Something to avoid in writing," he admonished, "is coming off as timid, self-conscious, lacking in confidence, or tentative." He also knew that neophyte reporters need counseling on how to interview effectively, how to use the telephone, and why it is of paramount importance to be as accurate as possible. Ingram began listening in on my in-office interviews and those done by telephone. Afterwards, sometimes days later, he would bring up important points. "Rollan, your story was fine. Indeed, it shined in places. However," (his favorite teaching word) "you might have done even better had you asked this question, and this, and this."

Mother Defeats The Marines

Fallon, NV In my third year of high school, with the support and encouragement of my teachers, my coaches, and my *Standard* colleagues, I began to feel that going to college was an achievable dream. No one in the Melton family had ever risen to higher education, but that didn't mean that there could not be a first, and that first one might as well be me.

My prospects did not seem good, however. Even if I got the necessary grades for admission to college, how would I pay the tuition and fees? Mother didn't earn much, and I had been giving her most of my weekly pay to help with our living expenses, so I had no savings. We couldn't expect help from my father. My grades, while they had improved, seemed to make me a long shot for an academic scholarship. My only options appeared to be earning a football scholarship or doing as generations of students before me had done--working my way through. The latter seemed the more likely path, and I was eager to travel it if other options failed to materialize.

The summer between my junior and senior years I came to the conclusion that the best way to get a paid education might be to join the U. S. Marine Corps, serve three years, and then be eligible for the GI Bill. I told Mother that I wanted to join up. She gave the idea enough of a nod to cause me to take the bus into Reno to visit the marine recruiting office, where I was impressed with the dress blues worn by the two recruiters. They just saw me as a warm body, someone they might add to their monthly quota.

I filled out the official papers, took a physical examination, and was told by the marine in charge, "Look, we notice that you are two months short of your eighteenth birthday. You will have to have your legal guardian's consent to join."

"No problem," I assured him. "My mother says this is all right."

The sergeant replied, "Well, we will need her consent in writing."

The marines said that they would drive over to Fallon in a few weeks to have my mother sign for me, and that I would then be sent to Camp Pendleton, California, for boot camp.

Home I traveled with what I felt was happy news. However, my fiery mother, her Irish at full tilt, hit the roof: "Son, I never dreamed you were serious. This is a very bad idea. You are soon to be the first in your family to graduate, and you have a good job. If things work out as you want, you may get a chance to go on to college. I am not going to sign for you."

I pouted for a few days, then told Ken Ingram my sad story, expecting sympathy. He took my mother's side: "She is thinking right on this, Rollan. You've got a lot going for you. Don't screw it up by making a wrong move."

I had been loath to listen to Mother, but now I was hearing the same advice from a non-family member whom I respected highly. This was sobering. By the time the recruiters arrived to fetch me, I was happy to let Mother, my guardian angel, do the talking.

When the two crew-cut marines rolled up to our home in their immaculately turned-out Jeep, wearing their imposing dress-blue uniforms, Mother and I were waiting for them. They introduced themselves and produced the papers for Mother to sign, but she resisted:

"Hold on! I ain't signing away my boy. After he's eighteen, he can do as he pleases, but now he will do as I please."

The marines protested. They began to list what they claimed were the many benefits a young man could enjoy as a Leatherneck. Mother didn't like what she would later call their back talk. She told them plain out, "Goddamn it, I said no, and you guys better listen to me! Now, I want you to climb back into your Jeep and get on back to Reno."

They were barely out of sight when I hugged my mother, kissed her, and said, "Thanks dear. You did right for me."

Her judgment was proved good two years later when North Korean troops invaded the south, and the United States entered the Korean War. Before the fighting stopped in 1953, some 58,000 American fighting men were dead, a heavy percentage of them marines. Those killed in action included Carl "Bucky" Johnson, a Native American from Schurz, a two-time all-state football lineman with whom I had played. Johnson was also a Golden Gloves heavyweight boxing champion. I had admired him as a superb, seemingly invincible athlete, but in war, no fighter is safe from harm.

Movers and Shakers Visit *Standard*

Fallon, NV I had grown up in a dysfunctional family. Now in Fallon—at school and especially at the weekly *Standard*—I had become an integral member of an extended family of supportive teachers, employers, and townspeople. I began to see that everyone I knew was, in a sense, a role model, whether his or her actions were to be emulated or avoided.

Late in the summer of 1949, as the start of my senior year approached, my mother began drinking heavily. Early one morning the police came to our house, awakened me, and told me that my mother was in jail. The charge was public drunkenness. I scraped together fifteen dollars and bailed her out. Mother was embarrassed and contrite, but her reputation was badly damaged by the episode, and her employer, the Keystone Restaurant, fired her. Unable to find a new job in town, she called Brownie and me together and told us she was going to leave Fallon. She had accepted a job in a restaurant in Santa Cruz, California. Brownie would remain with Mother, as was the custom.

Mother said, "I hate to leave you behind, son, but you are so close to finishing at the school you love, and you have your *Standard* job." I was pleased to remain behind, and I told her that I would stay in our small rental house, pay the modest monthly rent, and carry on through my final high school year. I knew the situation could work to my advantage. After all, I would have the total personal independence that so many teenagers believe they want. With that, Mother and Sister left, and I happily stayed in Fallon, which had become my true hometown

I was performing better in the classroom, including in an elective that Ken Ingram insisted I take—typing. I resented his intrusion. After all, I could produce up to thirty-five words a minute with my hunt-and-peck artistry. But, of course, Ingram was again right. When the course ended, my touch-typing speed was up to ninety words a minute, tops in the class.

My senior football season was my best. Although mother had never seen me play, she had asked that I tell her the outcome of each game. She had no telephone, so whether the Greenwave played at home or on the road, I would wire her a Western Union telegram: "Mom: We beat Carson City, 36-21. I had no injuries."

Coach Wes Goodner had taken a personal interest in me. One weekend he phoned me at the *Standard* and invited me to visit him and his wife, Helen, at their home. When I arrived, Mrs. Goodner had some men's suits and shoes laid out in the living room. Coach explained, "Rollan, I've bought some new things to wear." Pointing to the displayed wardrobe, he said, "My old clothes are a little bit worn, but we would like you to have them if you want them." I was bowled over by his generosity. The three suits and the two pairs of shoes fit perfectly. I left before Coach could change his mind. Reaching home, I examined the suits carefully. There was not a worn place to be seen.

I was named to *Nevada State Journal* sports editor Ty Cobb's all-state second team at center, behind Reno High School's powerful Don Fife, who went on to be a Big Ten Conference all-star at Purdue University. I felt that my solid season might give me a chance to earn an athletic scholarship offer. I was on a roll—or as I later would term it, I was enjoying winner's momentum. At about the same time, Claude Smith had raised my pay to sixty cents an hour from the starting level of fifty cents.

Fallon's movers and shakers were regular visitors at the *Standard*. They included people in local politics and government, business people, educators, and farmers and ranchers. Newspaper leaders from around the state also showed up regularly at our *Standard* office. They came mainly to visit Claude Smith, discuss state politics, and learn where he felt rural Nevada was headed. Smith and Ingram made certain I

"[Mother] had no telephone, so whether the Greenwave played at home or on the road, I would wire her a Western Union telegram...."

was among those who met each important visitor. I was delighted to make the acquaintance of these men I had read about or whose work I had read.

Jock Taylor, publisher of Austin's *Reese River Reveille*, came by each week to shepherd the printing of his paper on the *Standard*'s press. I operated the press, and Taylor would peek sternly over his glasses, inspecting sheets as they spewed from our machine.

Charles H. Russell, of the *Ely Daily Times* and a state legislator, came by frequently, and he and Mr. Smith would huddle in political conversation, usually out of earshot of the young apprentice Melton. Russell later was a two-term Nevada governor.

Other contemporary weekly newspaper publishers who popped in, often unannounced, were colorful Jack McCloskey of Hawthorne's *Mineral County Independent-News*; Jack Carpenter, who earlier had worked at the *Standard* and then moved on to the *Mason Valley News* in Yerington; Paul Gardner, feisty chief executive of the *Lovelock Review-Miner*; Arthur Suverkrup of the *Gardnerville Record-Courier*; and Neal Van Sooy, of the *Nevada Appeal* at Carson City.

I met Professor Alfred L. Higginbotham for the first time in the outer office of the *Standard*. He was the legendary chairman of the University of Nevada journalism department. Mr. Smith introduced me as "a young man who graduates in June and who hopes he can study journalism under you, Al." That piqued Professor Higginbotham's interest. He looked at me, wearing my ink-stained, thigh-length printer's apron, and he asked, "Rollan, do you know how to handle hand-set type?" I replied that I did it every day, and the professor said, "Good. We can use you in our department."

The most intriguing visitors were the widely-known public figures, most of them elected officers. Mr. Smith usually told his staff when the celebrities were coming. Initially, I was reclusive, hiding out in the composing room at the rear of our office, but our boss, knowing the value to a young man of learning to meet well-known elders, invariably drew me into introductions and conversations. The most prominent of such visitors was easily U. S. Senator Patrick McCarran, the Nevada Democrat and a power in Washington, D.C. The co-author of the McCarran Immigration Act was friendly in person and not the physical giant I had supposed he would be. He was shorter than me, was portly, and he had a mane of thick, white hair that enhanced his noble presence. McCarran's greetings always began with a practiced handshake, followed by a friendly, light touching of whomever he was talking to. I saw in him a mastery of turning conversations around, so he seemed always to be listening rather than pontificating.

Senator McCarran usually appeared alone at the office, but occasionally he would be accompanied by his longtime top aide, Eva Adams, who ultimately was appointed by President John F. Kennedy to be the director of the U. S. Mint. Miss Adams was quiet, letting the light shine on McCarran while she soaked up each spoken word and detail.

Nevada's governor at that time, Vail Pittman, always was greeted warmly at the *Standard*, for he also had been a newspaper leader in Ely. Alan Bible was a hometown boy who had made good. A former Fallon High School student body president, in those years the future U. S. senator was Nevada's attorney general. By example, I learned from

Bible to get people's names and use them over and over until you know them forever.

At the *Standard* my feeling of being a vital part of a loving family grew. In 1949, Carol and Ken Ingram honored me by asking that I be the godfather of their infant son, James. Ingram, despite his own hectic work schedule, continued to counsel me personally, trying to help me launch a career. If Ingram was like a slightly older brother to me (he was fifteen years my senior), then Claude Smith was my father figure. He would offer wisdom disguised as mere little sayings: "You've made another step. Remember, every step is a new beginning." Or, "At the *Standard*, failure is not an option."

Mother and Bronna returned to Fallon as the new year of 1950 began. Mother had lined up another waitress job in town. Shortly after her return, on a bleak, icy January day five months before our class would graduate, my best friend and football teammate, Arthur Farrel, asked me to go ice skating with other kids that night.

"Sorry, Art, but I have to work at the *Standard* tonight. I'd like to go next time."

But there would be no next time. Art and the others went skating at a reservoir near Rattlesnake Mountain, northeast of Fallon. Returning to town late that night, they missed a sharp turn, and the car plunged into a frozen drainage canal. Art Farrel was killed. So were classmate William Jeakins, Edith Swenson, who had graduated the previous year, and a young sailor from the Fallon navy base.

Farrel's family asked me to be among the pallbearers. Before I left for the funeral home, Mother suggested, "Better take a handkerchief, son. You don't know how you'll react." I spurned her advice, but the moment I took my place near my friend's casket, I began to cry uncontrollably. The tears didn't stop until an hour later, when the graveside service was over.

I had been spared my friends' fate only because of a work commitment. Their deaths and Art Farrel's funeral were my first lesson in the contingent nature of life—how quickly and unexpectedly it can be taken away, and seemingly without reason. I was consumed with grief, but I have learned that we have to accept reality and move on with our lives.

Sonny Wins Scholarship
Heavy-Drinking Father Misses Ceremony

Fallon, NV There was a lot of speculation about which graduating senior would be selected as the Harolds Club Scholar of the Year from Fallon. The scholarship program had been created by the Raymond I. Smith family, the owners of the internationally known Harolds Club in Reno. The program was the largest in Nevada, annually providing one student from each Nevada high school a full ride scholarship to attend the University of Nevada in Reno. The recipients received $4,000, a considerable sum of money in 1950.

Although I applied, I held little hope of being the scholarship recipient from Fallon. My grades had improved, but they were only average at best, and I was competing against the seven top scholars in my class. I felt that a football scholarship to some university was more likely, and indeed, offers did come, the most attractive being one from the University of Oregon.

The freshman football coach at Eugene was Robert McClure, a former Nevada Wolf Pack star and professional player. He corresponded with me and made an offer. I would be on a full ride athletic scholarship. It sounded good, but as my counselor/friend/boss Ken Ingram pointed out, "If you're injured, that will be the end of your grant-in-aid; and even if you are never injured, you have to be good enough to make the squad, year after year." I replied politely to McClure that I appreciated his offer and would keep it in mind.

The Smith family let each high school's faculty determine who its Harolds Scholar would be. In Fallon, the guidelines simply were: "Must have demonstrated ability to do college work. Consideration will be given when there is special financial need." Added to the votes of the high school's seventeen teachers would be those of principal Pat Smith and vice-principal and football coach Wes Goodner, both of whom had considerable influence. As the time for a decision drew near, my chief hope was that financial need might work in my favor.

One day a few weeks ahead of our June 5 graduation, I was at the *Standard* running off an issue on our two-page flatbed press. Someone stepped into my field of vision—there stood Charlotte Sanford, of the high school faculty. "I'd like to talk to you a minute, Rollan," I heard her shout above the din of the press. I shut it down and greeted her, not expecting the news she then delivered: "Rollan, the faculty has voted you the winner of this year's Harolds Club scholarship." We both broke into tears.

As the recipient of a longshot dream come true, I bellowed my joy, hugged Mrs. Sanford, thanked her profusely, and let every colleague within the sound of my voice know of my good fortune. Then I sprinted home, just a block away, and told Mother: "I've won the Harolds scholarship. Mom, can you believe this? I'm going to go to college."

I wrote every faculty member a thank-you note, even though I knew that there had been one dissenting vote. (I later learned that Hattie Brown was the teacher who had voted against me. I could understand her reluctance to take a chance on me—she had flunked me in Spanish when I was a freshman. Years later, as my career in journalism progressed, I thanked Miss Brown by letter, never telling her I knew how she had voted way back in 1950.)

Dana Coffee, the local jeweler, had a major drinking problem, but when sober he was town cheerleader, doing supportive things particularly for the "underserved"—a word not then in the public's vocabulary. My mother had told him when I was a junior that I would be a candidate for the Harolds Club scholarship. He had responded in his gruff voice, "Well, damnit, you tell Sonny Melton that if he wins it, I'll buy him a brand-new suit for his high school graduation."

Sure enough, after I was named the Harolds recipient, Coffee strolled to the *Standard* office and told me, "Sonny, get over to The Toggery store and pick out a suit, shirt, tie, and shoes. Hell, if you need underwear, get that, too. Have (owner) Harold Bellinger bill me for everything."

One of my favorite teachers, Jenny Johns Yasmer, accompanied me to The Toggery for the suit fitting. She would later declare, "Although Rollan was thrilled with the new clothes, he was very embarrassed at having to model for a young female teacher. He took a ribbing from his contemporaries. Confidentially, I thought he looked quite dashing."

As for Dana Coffee, he at last was rescued by Alcoholics Anonymous. He became the community leader in pushing AA rehabilitation programs that helped hundreds of persons (including my mother and my sister) get sober and stay sober, one day at a time.

I wrote my father in Boise, telling him the great scholarship news. He called, saying he was coming for the graduation ceremony to see me receive the school's top academic scholarship. The afternoon of the graduation, he phoned again, told me he was in Fallon, and asked the time and place of the event. I invited him to come to our house so we could all attend together, but Father said, "No, your mother would be uncomfortable with me hanging around. I'll just meet you there and see you afterwards."

Father was not in sight that night. I supposed he was shy about making himself too visible. As prizes were awarded, mine was saved for the finale. Principal Pat Smith told the audience, "Rollan is the winner of this year's Harolds Club scholarship. He is one of the most outstanding leaders in our school . . . honest, dependable, entirely trustworthy. He plans to study journalism at the university in Reno this fall."

I was filled with pride, but my father never appeared. I later learned that he had been drinking heavily at a Fallon bar that afternoon and had missed the biggest event of my life up to that time. As for me, I was moving on. After another summer's work at the *Fallon Standard*, I would begin a great new adventure.

Police Rescue Lifeguard from Rowdies

Fallon, NV In the summer of 1950, before enrolling at the University of Nevada, I kept piling up work hours at the *Standard*. I also took on a second interim job. Our rental home was across the street from the Doris and Lloyd Whalen family. Lloyd was the Fallon city engineer, and his responsibilities included managing the Fallon Municipal Swimming Pool, where he needed a second lifeguard that summer. He knew that I loved to swim and that I had passed a water safety course in 1949, and he asked if I'd like to fill the open guard job. I told him I wanted to keep my job at the *Standard*, too. He said that was fine. So, for the next three months, I strutted around the pool, my whistle at the ready.

During that summer, I worked 6:00 to 9:00 a.m. at the *Standard*; then I walked across town to the pool, adjacent to Oats Park School, hosed down the complex, washed towels, and opened at 10:00 a.m. for a swarm of kids. There was a lunch break, a reopening at 2:00, and we would close the pool at 8:45 p.m.. My co-lifeguard was Mary Lou Kent, a

"For the next three months, I strutted around the pool, my whistle at the ready."

collegian who came home in the summers to work.

While to the uninitiated, lifeguarding might seem a breeze, I found that from a mental-stress standpoint, it was the toughest assignment I had ever had. So afraid was I of the prospect of losing a swimmer that I became a practiced pacer, carrying on conversations while nervously watching the crowd and the water. I was becoming more responsible, and the pool job was an important part of my growing-up.

Occasionally I had to be assertive, and one day I ejected a young sailor from the premises for pool-side rowdiness. At quitting time that night, I stepped outside to lock up and noticed four sailors waiting in the darkness. They were there to teach me respect for navy blue. For certain, I couldn't handle that crowd, so I stepped back inside and bolted the door. Rather than spend the night cowering in the shower room, I decided to summon reinforcements.

I phoned the Fallon Police Department and talked to Sergeant Larry Fister, the father of Don Fister, who had been a two-time, first-team all-state football tackle for Fallon. Sergeant Fister and two other officers soon arrived to rescue me. The incident convinced me that, indeed, law enforcers wore superior blue. Many months earlier Larry Fister had hauled my mother to jail for drunkenness. By rescuing me from the navy, he helped me become more tolerant of lawmen.

I reflected a lot that summer on how blessed I was to have found Fallon. Arriving there four years earlier, I had known no one except my mother and sister. I had been rudderless and without a navigator to show me safe passage. Since then, my self-confidence had risen steadily. Though I was shy and socially retarded, fellow students had gradually accepted me. The faculty and administration had seen me as an underdog who needed encouragement, and they had convinced me that I could and should learn. Journalism teacher Anne Gibbs Berlin had even appointed me editor of the school newspaper, the *Greenwave Flash*, my senior year.

I had been a loner, but I learned to appreciate the importance of teamwork, both in my job at the *Standard* and through my participation in high-school football. I hadn't stayed long enough in other cities to make any friends, but in Fallon my football, basketball, and track and field teammates became my pals.

My two closest friends in high school had been Arthur Farrel and Stanley Ferguson. Art's death taught me early how important it is to make each day count—for any of us, there might not be that many days available. Ferguson, though two years younger than I, was a powerhouse football player, and we shared similar upbringings. Each of us had been reared by a single mother and was from a poor family. Each of us had a very strong work ethic.

Before I left to study at the university, Ken Ingram accepted my recommendation to hire Ferguson to be my successor as the *Standard* apprentice. A few months later I was hearing that Ferguson was an even better *Standard* worker than I had been. I wasn't surprised. He later went on to be the University of Utah's top freshman football lineman, then had a successful career as a classroom teacher.

Choosing Journalism
Sticking With It

Rollan Enrolls at University
He Struggles In Journalism and English

Reno, NV In the late summer of 1950, just before I enrolled at Nevada, Claude Smith asked me to drive him in his car to Reno for a meeting at the *Reno Gazette-Journal* office. I took him to the newspaper building on Center Street. The four-story structure seemed immense compared to our one-level *Standard* office. "Wait out front; I won't be long," Mr. Smith said. About four hours later, my boss returned to the car accompanied by someone I didn't recognize. I stepped out of the car to greet them.

"Rollan, I'd like you to meet a special friend," Mr. Smith said. "Say hello to Senator Joe McCarthy of Wisconsin." I didn't recognize the senator's name. At that time few people, outside of Washington and Wisconsin knew who he was. He would soon lose his anonymity.

Although I was just a teenager, dressed casually in Levis and a t-shirt, Senator McCarthy pumped my hand joyously as though greeting a long-lost pal. He gave me a playful tap on the back. He was a toucher, in the Senator Patrick McCarran and Molly Malone mold. Mr. Smith finished the introduction: "Senator McCarthy, Rollan is our printing apprentice in Fallon. He was all-state in football last season, and he is soon to study at the university here in Reno."

McCarthy was lightning-quick on cue. He pumped my hand anew. "How'd you like to play football for Wisconsin? We have a great university there, and it needs strong players like you. I can fix it for you to get a scholarship."

"Well, sir, I'm already committed to school here and have a good academic scholarship. Maybe I can play football for Nevada, as well."

Going home, Mr. Smith said he believed we'd be hearing a lot more about Senator McCarthy. Indeed, within eighteen months, the Wisconsin senator was known world-wide as a headline hunter, a Communist-hater, and a red-baiter.

I enrolled at the Reno campus in early September. An orientation for first-year students was conducted by the university's registrar, Clarence Byrd. I remember only one thing he said, and it had a huge impact on me: "Look to your right and to your left," Byrd said. "Four years from now, only one out of three of you will be around to graduate." I was determined to be among the one-third.

Ken Ingram had told me before I left for Reno that fraternities would put the rush on incoming freshmen. "Don't be hasty. Get tethered to the books and to campus routine, including football," he had cautioned. "You'll know what suits you. Maybe you can consider a frat later."

I was assigned to Hartman Hall, the men's dormitory above old Mackay Stadium. I tried out for the football team as a walk-on, and the first few weeks were a blur of academic, athletic, and social activity. Indeed, fraternities were recruiting hotly. There were parties at each frat house, and I saw photographs of freshmen "to be especially nice to" posted at the Phi Sigma Kappa, Alpha Tau Omega, and Theta Chi fraternity houses. My high school graduation mug shot was among them. My reaction was "Thanks, but no thanks, for now."

I registered to take fifteen credit hours, a normal freshman academic load. Five of my Fallon classmates were also enrolled at the Reno campus: Dixie Fritz Rueda, Ruth Fitz Pintar, Stanley Schank, Cecelia Schmitt Powell, and Elaine Teel Shields. Each of them was a true scholar, among the smartest in our class. I wasn't.

Freshmen had to take an entrance examination to measure basic English competency. I feared that I would fail it and land in the remedial class, "Bonehead English." That would be an embarrassing fate, but the six of us from Fallon did well on the test, and we were passed directly into English 101.

Our small achievement was big news in Fallon. I wrote a story reporting that 100 percent of Anne Gibbs Berlin's English students had "sailed" (my editorialization) through the challenging test. I mailed it home, and Ken Ingram played it in the *Standard* as page-one news.

To my chagrin, freshman journalism majors could take only one J-course that first year, and it had to be Journalism 101, which acclimated students to the nature of news. There was no basic text. We studied *Time* magazine each week and stood for planned and "snap" quizzes on its contents.

The professor was Keiste Janulis, who had a foreign correspondent aura about him, because he had been one. He had covered the German invasion of Poland (1939), the Battle of Britain (1940), and the Allied D-day invasion at Normandy, France (1944). His motto was "Tell the people what's going on!"

Janulis had arrived on campus to teach in 1946. His specialty was news gathering and writing, but his chief mission in the freshman course was to help students define what was important in the world and relate its importance to our lives. He also used the first-year course to assess journalism majors and to weed out the weak ones. One of his devices was to visit each of us on a one-on-one basis. I was no more than a week on campus when he summoned me for the introductory session.

At his office, I found Janulis wearing his trademark tweed jacket with leather elbow pads. He was cordial, shook my hand, invited me to sit, put down his omnipresent pipe, smiled, and said, "I have just this question. Tell me, in the order of their importance to you, what your three chief reasons are for enrolling at the University of Nevada."

"Well, that's easy," I blurted. "First, I came here to play football. Second, although

"The professor was Keiste Janulis, who had a foreign correspondent aura about him, because he had been one." (*Gazette-Journal* photograph.)

I've already worked three years on a weekly paper at Fallon, I think it's important to learn some more about journalism. Finally, I didn't have time for much social life in high school. I am hoping to meet some girls here."

Professor Janulis picked up his pipe, sucked on it, glowered at me, and spoke: "Football is a waste of time. Anyone who picks it above learning is doing himself and the journalism profession a big disservice. After you end your studies, do you intend to spend the rest of your life earning a living playing football?"

I tried to answer. Janulis cut me off: "So, you worked part-time on a weekly for three years. It may have helped you, granted. But let me tell you something—you could live as long as Methuselah and not come close to knowing all there is to know about being a newspaperman." He continued, "I am thirty-three, and while I have many friends who are women, I am not married. There are those of us who put journalism first, ahead of a bunch of social experiences."

I stammered, "Thank you. I have to be going now. Goodbye."

Away I raced, trying to get out of his sight quickly. I realized what a ninny I had been—an overconfident ignoramus. I would try to make amends, but it would take time. Professor Janulis gave me a C-minus in the course.

I encountered Professor Alfred L. Higginbotham in my first week. He remembered me from our *Fallon Standard* meeting. "Good to have you aboard, my boy," he said. "I remember you. You're the one who can hand-set type. We can use that skill around here." Higgy, as he was known to two generations of journalism majors, pushed on. "We own this Washington hand press from Colonial days. Occasionally we print some fliers. We've got Franklin job-type cases downstairs. I hope you will give us a hand."

Clearly, my printing experience could help me ingratiate myself with the chairman of journalism. "Of course, I can work that in," I said.

We were in Higgy's office, which had a long table for students. The walls were covered with signs that said things like, "Get the news first, but first get it right," and "Let freedom ring." One read, "The Newspaper: Freedom's Guardian." Higgy, without any modesty, revealed, "I wrote that one myself. It was recently judged the best press motto in America." I was in awe. Imagine writing a nationally acclaimed slogan! This was heady stuff!

Higgy made his first "freedom of speech" appeal to me. I would hear it hundreds of times from him in the years ahead: "There is no single gift more precious or more important than the freedom to speak and to be heard." He was idealistic, and as a young student, that quality rated high with me. I was happy I was to major in journalism and thrilled that Higgy was to be my leader. Further, he surely would ask me to hand-set his type. The more he liked me, the better off I would be.

In my freshman year I learned that I wasn't the polished writer I fancied myself to be. Most of my Fallon newspaper writing had been about athletics. I had mastered myriad sports cliches and was passing off such weasel phrases as acceptable language, but I was pulled up short by one of the great professors on campus. Robert M. Gorrell, my English 101 professor, was a taskmaster, a pitiless critic of inferior composition. I waltzed into the course not knowing his lofty expectations and believing that I was an accomplished essayist.

Gorrell shoved home the truth. Years later, the renowned author and professor recalled:

Rollie Melton turned up in 1950 in my freshman English class, eager and ready to push Grantland Rice and Red Smith off the front page. Rollie had absorbed all the bad sports writing he could get hold of in Fallon. Blood was "claret." A baseball was "the old apple." A basketball was a "casaba"—he hadn't yet heard that a football was an "oblate spheroid." But my lack of enthusiasm for his style didn't dampen Rollie's enthusiasm for writing. He kept at it, and kept getting better at it.

If that was true, Robert Gorrell had much to do with my improvement. His red-pencil teaching struck a responsive chord with me. Professor Gorrell let me escape with a C-minus. I felt blessed getting off that easy. He had raised me to a marginal level of competency.

At the men's dormitory word filtered out to my fellow Wolf Pack football players that I was a Harolds Club scholar. Thus, they assumed I knew good writing. Some stroked me, asking, "Can you take a look at my English theme and maybe refine it a bit?" Soon I fell into rewriting some of their work. However, the pleas for help turned to howls of dismay when my writing produced C-minuses for them too.

I had arrived on campus thinking I knew something of the history of journalism. This was not so. One evening when I was eating dinner in the dining commons an older student, a returning war veteran with a worldly air about him, sat down beside me. Curious about my attitude towards the state of journalism, he said, "So, Rollan, tell me what you think about William Randolph Hearst."

I fixed him with a glazed stare and asked, "Who's William Randolph Hearst?"

Such embarrassments sharpened my determination to improve. In my freshman year, I was accepted on the staff of the student newspaper, the *Sagebrush*, for which I would write mainly sports for four years. I also heard that *Nevada State Journal* sports editor Ty Cobb needed help in handling high school sports results on Friday and Saturday nights. For those part-time roles, he leaned toward hiring journalism majors who were athletes. He called them his "Journal Jocks."

Soon after starting my studies, I called Cobb and re-introduced myself, reminding him that years before I had phoned him results of semi-pro Sagebrush Baseball League games. Cobb, who had a prodigious memory, instantly remembered, and he said, "I'll send you out to cover a prep game and see how you do." I did well enough to be signed up as one of Cobb's Journal Jocks, joining such other weekend writing warriors as N. Walter Ryals, Dean C. Smith, and Ronald H. Einstoss, all of whom I eventually would have on my Speidel Newspapers executive teams. But that was far into the future. As one of Ty Cobb's young writers, I benefitted from working under intense deadline pressure and from Cobb's excellent critiques of my work after each issue was put to bed.

I was having great fun, and I learned something each day. As Professor Janulis had observed, one could reach Methuselah's age and still not know all there is to know about writing and journalism.

Campus and Community Described

Reno, NV After the Second World War, in which Fallon lost thirty-seven young men, we prayed with the rest of

America that there would be no more fighting. But in 1950 North Korea invaded South Korea, and the United States sent troops to defend the south. By the time I checked in at the Reno campus, several university men had enlisted in the military, and a number of students who had fought in World War II were being recalled to active duty.

That autumn there was steady talk among male students of the need to keep their grades up, because it lessened the possibility of being drafted. There were sixteen hundred students on campus. To many, the Korean War seemed a remote nightmare, but its cruel nature was to hit me head-on within a month after I began my university studies:

Carl "Bucky" Johnson had been an amazing Fallon High School athlete in the late 1940s. A two-time all-state football star, he had taught me much in head-to-head scrimmages. I was younger, and he steered me through my football apprenticeship. He was the most powerful high school football player I ever knew, and he also was a Golden Gloves heavyweight champion in an era when boxing was among the top individual pro sports in Western Nevada.

Johnson, a Paiute lad from Schurz, seemed indestructible. Surely, after his U. S. Army duty in the Korean War, he would come home, begin his university education, and continue his sports stardom. However, it was not to be. Johnson died in combat a few months after the Korean War began. The government's labeling of Korea as a "conflict" was cynically euphemistic. In this terrible war, Walter Class, another young man from Fallon, would also fall.

Ours was a serene campus, beautiful in its autumn colors. The elegant, elm-lined quadrangle was the Jeffersonian center of the campus. It was surrounded by imposing buildings which were flanked to the west by lovely Manzanita Lake. Hollywood had discovered the University of Nevada in the 1940s, when film makers began shooting campus footage for such movies as "Apartment for Peggy" and the Andy Hardy films, starring Mickey Rooney.

From the start, I appreciated the university's beauty. Students and visitors entered from the downtown side, the south entrance, passing the great old stone gate that was a gift of Nevada's class of 1898. Parking was not a worry, because not many students owned cars. Some rode bicycles, but walking was the most convenient way of getting around. Downtown Reno was but a ten-minute walk away; and to a youngster from a small town, what a downtown it was!

With a population of over thirty thousand, Reno seemed like a great metropolis to me and to other students from small towns. The city was exciting, and it wasn't simply the large, showy gaming palaces that beckoned. Downtown there were small clothing stores, pharmacies, movie houses, and cafes. Popular watering holes included Leon & Eddie's, the Big Waldorf, Colbrandt's, the 116 Club, and the short-lived Buddy Baer's Bar, owned by the brother of former world heavyweight boxing champion, Max Baer. Mom-and-pop shops sold groceries—the Santa Claus Market, the University Market, Sewell's Market, and the Akert Family Market on East Fourth Street. At the heart of the city was a popular store, Armanko's, which offered all manner of fare, from new books and art pieces to dinnerware.

A favorite nightspot of many collegians was the Little Waldorf in the 300 block of North Virginia Street. In the neighborhood also was Welsh's Bakery, where you could buy bread hot from the oven; the Grotto Bar;

Chet and Link Piazzo's sporting goods store; and Hudson Lee's drive-in restaurant. South of there you could dine at Tiny's Waffle Shop, and at the Wigwam Café you could savor hot apple pie smothered with owner Les Lerude's famous sauce. At the Tower, Crest, Granada, and Majestic movie theaters, admission was just twenty-five cents. You could buy popcorn for ten cents a bag and add butter for an extra nickel. The university bunch bought ice cream cones at Hale's Drugs for five, ten, or fifteen cents. We picked up our records at Stampfli's and our apparel at Gray Reid's Store.

Southern Pacific trains came right through downtown Reno, the famous "City of San Francisco" streamliner, the "Overland," and the "Gold Coast" stopping at the mid-town station to take on and discharge passengers. Not everybody took the train. In the wintertime, some students from California would drive home on Highway 40 over the Sierra Nevada, and if there was a blizzard, they could count on a seven-hour journey.

Reno was the divorce capital of the world. University students would see the visiting six-week residents hanging out at the famous Riverside and Mapes Hotels, then the entertainment meccas of the Far West. The Wertheimer brothers brought celebrity singers and orchestra leaders to the Riverside stage. A few yards north, across the Truckee River, Charles Mapes was doing the same in his charming Sky Room. The Mapes then had been open little more than two years, and at ten stories, it was Nevada's tallest building, towering over the earlier record "high rise," Reno's El Cortez hotel, which stood six stories tall. Not a soul could envision that one day the Mapes would stand empty, a silent memory of something once grand.

You could buy a beautiful, spacious home in Southwest Reno for $30,000 in 1950. There were two daily newspapers, each owned by Speidel but competing intensely. KBET Radio featured the community's best broadcaster, Robert Stoddard. In a short while, the city would have its first television station, KZTV. Later, KOLO-TV would begin broadcasting daily at 3:00 p.m. Watching the static test pattern on the screen before the broadcast began was an exciting pastime. Reno had an airport with a tiny air terminal building and only one runway, and the big airliner of the times was United's DC-3.

Two blocks north of the Truckee River on Virginia Street stood the world's most famous casino. Harolds Club was the first gaming company to advertise itself globally and the first to hire female dealers. Additionally, Raymond I. "Pappy" Smith, patriarch of the family that owned it, was the first to admonish customers, "Don't gamble more than you can afford to lose."

I owed Mr. Smith so much—in 1946 he had launched the Harolds Club scholarship program that was paying my way through the university. Two weeks after arriving on campus, I set out to pay Pappy a visit. A phone call to his office gained me an appointment. His secretary reminded me, "Under-age Harolds Club scholars can't frequent our premises except on official business."

I was nervous as I entered Mr. Smith's unpretentious office, but he looked more like an ordinary senior citizen than the world's sharpest casino operator, and he quickly put me at ease. He was tall and graying, and his eyes twinkled from behind his spectacles. He glowed like Santa Claus.

I thanked Pappy for what he was doing for me. He brushed off the praise, explaining that no thanks were necessary, but that he expected me to do my best in school. My visit lasted no more than two minutes, and each of us stood during our conversation. Mr. Smith's parting advice was, "Keep those grades up, and you will be able to keep your scholarship." We shook hands.

(Twenty-five years later I would win the Greater Reno-Sparks Chamber of Commerce's Raymond I. Smith Civic Leader of the Year award. I was the only Harolds Club Scholar ever so honored, and it was very satisfying; but my feelings that evening did not approach the excited gratitude that came over me when I shook Pappy Smith's hand. His gift had changed my life.)

At the University of Nevada, Malcolm Love was the respected president. The student body president had a surname that resembled an optometrist's eye chart—Ted Klimasezwsk would one day be an FBI agent. Our freshman class president at the outset was Paul Vietti, out of Reno High School, but when he entered the military for Korean War duty, we welcomed William Kottinger as his successor. In not so many more years, Kottinger would be among Reno's best-known stockbrokers.

Bull-Like Rushes
Rollie Melton Makes The Team

Reno, NV I had not spoken the truth when I cockily told journalism professor Keiste Janulis that football was my top university priority. Indeed, journalism was first. Football was a close second, though. Meeting women was a distant third.

At Fallon High School I had played football for four years, was the starting center in twenty-four games over three seasons, and was a co-captain. I had earned enough notice to receive two athletic scholarship offers, but no word from Nevada. Apparently, the coaches "up on the hill" had not read my press clippings. Well, I would have to show them.

I enrolled for my fifteen credit hours, then, as a walk-on, turned out for fall football practice to prove my manhood in the adult sports world. This was to be heady stuff, for I had supposed that instead of being an obscure lineman, I would evolve into Saturday's hero. However, reality set in quickly. I was no longer lining up against high school players.

In that era freshmen weren't eligible for varsity competition, but Coach Joe Sheeketski had walk-on, non-scholarship first-year players scrimmage nightly against the varsity. We were fodder for the rough, tough, big boys. Others who were scrimmaging regularly but were ineligible to play on account of the freshman rule were all-state quarterback Floyd Vice of Elko and Lloyd Austin, an all-state lineman from the 1948 state prep champion Sparks Railroaders. Bill Afflis, a mean-spirited, low-slung blond gorilla who already had played two seasons at Purdue University, was a special case. He was sitting out the 1950 season because of the transfer rule. (Later he would become a top offensive lineman with the professional Green Bay Packers.)

The varsity players were mature grownups who shaved regularly and were mostly serious students. They enjoyed feasting on freshmen who had the gall to call themselves real players. The offensive stars included quarterback Pat Brady, a sensational kicker who that year against Loyola University in the homecoming game quick-kicked a punt ninety-nine yards at Mackay Stadium, a record never matched in college football. It was the first orbiting object before the Russians launched Sputnik.

At afternoon football practice I banged heads hour after hour with the varsity's tough, experienced linemen. The centers were veterans Al Matteucci, from Las Vegas, and the starter, Carmel "Crusher" Caruso, from Pennsylvania. Caruso tutored me on the art of long snaps to punters and holders of extra points.

The squad's most memorable character was Bill Afflis. In my first-year student *Sagebrush* sports-writing days, and still falling back on athletic clichés, I wrote that "Afflis was noted for his bull-like rushes." This outlandish phrasing brought instant criticism from my journalism student buddy, William W. Eaton, whose rejoinder was, "You make Afflis sound like something out of a Moses chapter."

The campus's ROTC commandant, army lieutenant colonel James C. Smee, was briefing assembled cadets, myself included, one afternoon at Mackay Stadium. Smee glanced up and spotted one cadet who wore no uniform. He challenged the cadet, "You, up there! Why aren't you in uniform?"

It was Bill Afflis. He leapt to his feet, all 250 pounds of him, flexed his muscles in his white t-shirt, adjusted his trousers around a minuscule thirty-two inch waist, and roared back at the colonel, "Because your staff hasn't found me a shirt with a twenty-one inch neck!"

Afflis earned side money as a bouncer at Harolds Club, a common night job for football players during the non-litigious days when troublemakers could be flung from casino properties onto their drunken heads. Afflis was also a wrestler and hung out at the Reno YMCA, manhandling barbells and anyone crazy enough to get in the ring with him. One of his favorite pastimes was inviting underclassmen, myself included, to toss ten-pound medicine balls at his face from about two feet away. He said with pride that this toughened his hide. Afflis did make it big-time with the Green Bay Packers, but his greatest fame came when he changed his professional name to "Dick, the Bruiser," and became one of the sourest of theatrical wrestler villains, and one of the most handsomely paid.

Nevada had had powerhouse teams in the late 1940s, with Coach Sheeketski profiting from the talented players recruited to the Reno program by the previous coach, Jim Aikin, who left to be head coach at the University of Oregon. With less talent and a harder schedule, the 1949 team's record fell to five wins and five losses. Sheeketski, who had been a halfback for Knute Rockne at Notre Dame and then the head coach at Holy Cross University, could coax only one victory out of our ten-game schedule in 1950. As losses mounted, fan support withered at Mackay Stadium and at away games.

Two games into the 1950 season, Coach Sheeketski called me to his campus office and delivered an unexpected, but most pleasant, surprise. He said he was impressed with my play and my promise, and he said he'd like to offer me a football scholarship. I felt like jumping over his desk and hugging him, but he had more to say.

"I understand you have a Harolds Club scholarship," he said, "so I assume you have plenty to live on. Therefore, your football scholarship will be for room and meals only—no books or other remuneration."

I was almost mute with gratitude. I mumbled, "I'll take whatever you want me to have."

Sheeketski added, "Jake Lawlor recommends this for you." Lawlor was our line coach, the one who knew my performance best, and he was one of three assistant coaches, Hugh Smithwick and Richard Evans being the other two. Smithwick also was track and field coach. Evans, an excellent judge of talent and a teacher, wound up in the pro ranks as an assistant coach.

I waltzed away from Sheeketski's office, envisioning dollar signs, realizing that I was the only student athlete then on campus who had both academic and sports scholarships. Now I must study harder than ever to build a grade point average that would enable me to keep both.

FOOTBALL CANCELLED!
Melton Named Starting Center

Reno, NV Campus enrollment, which fell sharply during World War II, had rebounded to about two thousand in 1950-1951 as military veterans, financially buoyed by the GI Bill, kept streaming in. Further education was their ticket to a more prosperous life. Many were married and lived in a converted Army barracks complex called Victory Heights, where the National Judicial College would one day be located. The families were having so many babies then that campus wags renamed the complex "Fertility Heights."

University life was broadening and exciting. I felt as if I were part of a huge family, one enriched by the presence of students from abroad and American students of diverse backgrounds. The student body included my African-American football teammates, some Asians, a few American Indians, many California students, and a number of rural Nevadans from towns I formerly believed to be hostile because of our high school sports rivalries. That nonsense went away as we became a unified student body.

The distractions of men's dormitory living notwithstanding, my grades were OK the first semester of my freshman year, with five C's and a B. In the second semester, improving my academic focus, I pulled two C's, a B, and two A's, including an A in the basic military course.

ROTC was compulsory for freshman and sophomore men, but a year into the Korean War I had begun to tinker with the idea of voluntarily entering advanced ROTC as an upperclassman. It was a combat standoff in Korea at that time, and no one had a clue as to how long the war would last. If I had to go, I hoped to avoid the draft, preferring officer's rank and perhaps a public information assignment to gain more media experience.

But first things first. Because first-year journalism majors weren't eligible for news writing courses, I had joined the *Sagebrush* staff and reported to sports editor Myron Leavitt, a Wolf Pack teammate and the last person on the planet I would have predicted would become a Nevada supreme court justice. (The carefree Leavitt was the life of parties, and he was thinking then of a newspaper career.)

After my freshman football season, I wrote sports part-time for Ty Cobb at the *Nevada State Journal*, taking late-night calls from coaches who gave us results of Nevada high school basketball games. We compiled box scores and composed brief game stories, and in the process, I became acquainted with most of Nevada's active prep coaches. The incomparable Cobb was always around to provide sound critiques of our efforts. His humor well never ran dry, even in the most pressure-cooker times.

I returned home to Fallon for the summer of 1951 and lived with my mother and sister Bronna. Again I had a busy three-month work schedule at the *Standard* and the municipal swimming pool. I was doing lifeguard duty on a hot July afternoon when a blockbuster news story broke. Someone came up to me and said he had just heard on KOH, the Reno radio station, that Nevada was dropping its organized football program. It was a stunning development.

The following morning, Ty Cobb spelled out the who, what, why, and when in the *Journal*. The university's board of regents had decided to close down the football program because costs had run amok. Debt was close to $50,000, an enormous sum in 1951, and there was no prospect that downtown athletic boosters would pay off the bills. Pure and simple, there had been extravagant spending, and there was no money to pay the rising costs.

The board of regents—chairman Silas Ross Sr., and members Sam Arentz, Louis Lombardi, Newton Crumley Sr., and Roy Hardy—had no other option, and they voted unanimously to kill Nevada football. Every football scholarship was dropped.

If my Wolf Pack teammates were to continue their football-fueled pursuit of academic degrees, they would have to move quickly. Some of the best players were promptly offered scholarships by other schools, but about half the 1950 squad remained at Nevada.

I was in comfortable shape financially, having saved some money from my summer jobs and being able to rely on the wonderful Harolds Club scholarship. In the autumn of 1951, I again reported for football. With the scholarships gone and the scheduled season canceled, those of us who showed up for football that year were strictly volunteers.

We practiced each afternoon after class under Glenn "Jake" Lawlor, who had been named coach after Joe Sheeketski's job vanished along with his high-powered program. Lawlor drew the biggest laugh of the semester, appearing at a student rally and proclaiming that "Now that the great white father (Sheeketski) is no longer with us . . . ." Indeed, with his handsome gray hair, Sheeketski more physically resembled a diplomat or a senator than an athletic coach. He stayed in Nevada, and for years was a popular greeter at Lake Tahoe and Carson City casinos.

There was just one football game for us that season. I was the starting center on the student pickup squad when we met the Wolf Pack alumni team. The old men's team, comprised of some of the stars from the late 1940s and coached by former all-America lineman Robert McClure, faced off against us upstart undergraduates. Offense did not rule that afternoon at Mackay Stadium. The game ended in a scoreless tie.

Higgy Preaches Integrity

Reno, NV The fall term of 1951 my studies included a class in news writing under Professor Janulis. He directed the Journalism 221 class from behind an oval copy desk, the type I had seen only in Hollywood films glamorizing newspapers. Janulis was a ruthless critic of student news copy, which we cranked out of the arthritic typewriters in the news lab. He stuck to basics: "You need to go back and ask your source some additional questions . . . Write simply so that any reader, of any age, can understand . . . Here's the way you use quotation marks . . . I've circled your misspellings, which are many . . . If you mangle a person's name, he'll never trust a newspaper again, if in fact he did in the first place."

Janulis, who had a slight stutter, would say over and over, "Let's get . . . what you must remember is that . . . huh, you're going to rewrite this. I won't . . . can't be the one who, huh, who does your work . . . You won't learn, won't pick it up if someone is always doing things for you."

The chairman of the two-man journalism department was the venerable Alfred Leslie Higginbotham, who reputedly had been a crack reporter with the *Cleveland Plain Dealer* before joining the University of Nevada as an English instructor in 1923. He introduced journalism courses to the curriculum and established a formal journalism department in 1943. "Higgy" had suffered multiple sclerosis in his early years. He wore leg braces and walked slowly and shakily, but he was a pillar of strength in the classroom. He knew how to draw out students, then back off and let them debate, as he did in 1951 when the nation was arguing whether convicted spies, Ethel and Julius Rosenberg, should be executed for leaking crucial atomic bomb secrets to the Soviet Union. Neither side prevailed in our hotly-debated classroom exchanges. The Rosenbergs were executed.

Higgy loved teaching the history of journalism, and I loved learning about the historic giants of American newspapers and their roles in perpetuating our constitutionally-guaranteed freedoms. He lectured unceasingly about the essentials of safeguarding those cherished freedoms and the paramount importance of press freedom and why it was urgent that we not be compelled to reveal confidential sources. From his professor's pulpit, Higgy preached the virtues of accuracy, of timely reporting, of publishing objective news stories, and of taking strong positions on opinion pages. He emphasized that the most essential single element in journalism was integrity: "Stand for what you believe in. Be honest. Protect people's rights. Eradicate wrongs."

Edward "Ted" Scripps was a senior journalism major who went out of his way to talk to me. He was an heir to the Scripps Newspaper Group and had been a student intern at some of his family's larger properties. Ted came across not as a spoiled rich brat, but as a salt-of-the-earth, pragmatic newsman. I then thought only in terms of a single newspaper, but Scripps, by his upbringing and varied experience, saw publishing chains, or, to use a euphemism, "newspaper groups." It did not occur to me that I could become a leader of such an enterprise.

Melton Hits Social Scene
Dates Marilyn Royle

Reno, NV Before I met the woman who would be my wife, my experience with the opposite sex had been slim and nearly none. In high school I was absorbed with my *Fallon Standard* job, with study, and with sports; and though I would sneak a look at girls and fantasize about them, I was too timid to let them sense my interest.

My first date was in 1948, my junior year, when I cranked up enough courage to ask sophomore Betty Harper to go to a high school dance. The days before picking her up at her home were difficult ones. There was plenty to be anxious about: I feared being alone with a girl; I barely knew how to drive, and I didn't own a car; I didn't know how to dance; and I didn't know what to wear. Worst of all, I didn't know what a corsage was. I knew a florist, George Slipper, but I had never ordered flowers. This was to be a prom, and a corsage was mandatory. My mother told me so.

My mouth was as dry as cotton when I asked my boss, Claude Smith, if I could borrow his extra car, a '37 Chevy sedan, for the date. "Of course!" he said.

My mother, thrilled that I had finally gotten up the gumption to start a social life, gave me a crash course in dancing, hauling me into our little kitchen and waltzing me between the stove and the ice box. "This we will call the Fallon two-step," Mother said. "It is the basic step you will always use."

Mother cautioned me: "It is rude to sit outside and honk for your date. You walk right up to her door and let her parents take a look at you." That was what I did, trembling at the possibility of rejection, but Betty's parents were cordial. I had a good time at the dance and delivered Betty safely to her door no more than two hours later.

My second date was a disaster. Like me, Marlene Plummer was a student employed at the *Standard*, where she was an efficient part-time clerk. The dark-haired beauty would greet me warmly in the school halls, and I took that to mean that she had a real interest in me, in my sports aptitude, and maybe even in my neophyte journalism goals. With heart aflutter, I asked her to a school dance, anticipating rejection. To my shocked surprise, she said yes.

Again, I borrowed Mr. Smith's Chevy. I picked Marlene up, and we reached the small gym just as the little music combo struck up. We danced one dance. Then Marlene went to her side of the crowded gymnasium, and I drifted to the boy's side. I pouted there, watching her having the time of her young life dancing with other fellows.

I stood frozen, lonely; I couldn't ask anyone else to dance. I thought, "She doesn't want to be with me, so I'll go home." I did. This was a bad mistake, one my mother and sister lit into me for making. "Have you ever heard the old saying, "Nothing like a woman scorned?" asked mother, who answered her own question. "Well, Buster, you'll learn the hard way."

Marlene didn't wait to waylay me at school. She came to the *Standard* before the first class Monday, for she knew my work schedule. She came straight at me, angered, and she shouted, "I'll never speak to you again." She broke her promise just once. It happened at our thirty-fifth high school class reunion. I recognized her and thought she'd surely have forgiven me after so long a time. I offered her my hand, and in my most courtly manner said, "Hi, Marlene. I'm Rollan Melton. So nice to see you again."

She gave me one of those "If-looks-could-kill" faces and said, "I don't know you."

After the disastrous date with Marlene Plummer, there followed a movie with Marjorie Andrew and a couple of dates with Lorna Jones, a movie date with Gloria Andreini, and a roller-skating adventure with Patricia Edwards. Then I graduated, dated no one that summer, and then high-tailed it to the Reno university campus.

After Coach Sheeketski's football grant gave me some walking-around money, I tried again. I took Janie Strickland to the movies. She was a freshman from Portland, Oregon. Janie was terribly anxious for the movie to end, saying she had to get home to Artemisia Hall, the women's dormitory, to study. She had blonde hair and felt that football was just a loathsome way to hurt others, and that boxing was even worse. By then I was boxing, too.

I escorted Janie to the door of Artemisia Hall, and for some reason, I felt it would be good manners to ask her mother's name. She replied, "Dorothy." She must have been relieved that we never saw each other again.

In the spring of 1952, my fourth semester, I made eye contact at Stewart Hall with a pretty girl with a blond streak in her long hair. I was bouncing up the stairs, and she was coming down, and when our eyes met, she smiled and sort of nodded. What a pretty and serene face she had. I kept moving, and she did also, but I felt a hormone kick in, the first time I had had that feeling. I didn't know her name, where she was from, what she was studying, or whether she loathed football, boxing, and perhaps even male journalism majors.

Weeks passed. One day fellow journalism major Marie Nielsen of Sparks invited me to go for a drive. We were cruising on the southern perimeter of the campus when she pointed out a young woman walking west. They exchanged waves, and I said, "Marie, I saw that girl recently over at Stewart Hall. Do you know her name?"

"Yes, I do. Marilyn Royle is a Tri-Delta sorority pledge, and I'm a member. Marilyn's a freshman and real nice. The Tri-Delts have been trying to line her up with a date for our traditional Shipwreck Dance."

The following day, Nielsen and I were at the *Sagebrush* office in the student union, a few yards south of the campus's main north entrance. I asked again for the Tri-Delt freshman's name and said maybe I could be a candidate for her sorority dance date. Marie gave me one of her cat-that-ate-the-canary smiles, looked in the phone directory, dialed 7447, and said, "This is Marie. Have you got a date yet for the dance?"

Seven-four-four-seven said, "No. But that fellow who was driving with you in your car—I might like to ask him."

To which Marie replied, "Well, his name is Rollan Melton, he's in journalism, and for heaven's sake, he just came into the *Sagebrush*. Here he is now. Ask him."

I took the phone and said, "Hello. Marie says you wanted to ask me something."

Marilyn spluttered that there was this dance coming up, and by tradition Tri-Delts were to invite dates. She asked, "Would you be free to take me?"

I gulped and paused and finally stammered out, "Well that would be fine."

Marilyn gave me the date and her address and said, "Just come casual. I'll fix some simple costumes. How'd it be if we went as bartenders?" She had a soft, lovely voice, and a guy would have been mentally defective to have refused to be her co-bartender.

I had joined Theta Chi fraternity the previous October, and I was living at the frat house on University Terrace. The Tri-Delt with the serene voice lived at 329 West Sixth Street, five blocks away. The dance was in early May. I still didn't own wheels, so fraternity brother Hans Mohr loaned me his little Studebaker, and I tooled over to fetch my date. As my mother had trained me, I rang the doorbell, and Marilyn's mother welcomed me in: "This is Marilyn's father, Bill Royle, and these are our friends, Sarah and Harold West, over for a visit."

I was just short of my twenty-first birthday, and Marilyn's parents and their friends each looked the age of my parents—meaning, to me, quite mature. My date's mother giggled, "I need to introduce myself, too. I'm Dorothy."

Marilyn entered the living room, flashed that great grin, smiled with her hazel eyes, and said, "I've made these bartender arm bands for us." She slipped two of them onto my arms, and we were set to go.

One rarely knows when fate comes knocking, and I certainly didn't. The only thing I was sure about was that Marilyn's mother was different; really different! We were about to leave for the dance, and Dorothy Royle said, "Rollan . . . may I call you Rollan? Marilyn said you play football up at school."

"Yes, I do," I told her.

Mrs. Royle said, "Do you mind if our guests and I pinch your biceps and calves?"

Before I could say yes, my future mother-in-law was feeling my calves.

Meltons and Royles: Nothing in Common

Fallon, NV My sophomore year at Nevada was over. I left the campus, returning to Fallon for what would be my final summer with the *Standard*. City Engineer Lloyd Whalen hired me a third straight time as a municipal pool lifeguard. The next three months were very busy. On Mondays, the day the pool was closed, I would drive to Emerald Bay, Lake Tahoe, where Marilyn Royle was employed as a maid at a resort. By then, I had acquired my first car. The 1939 DeSoto sedan came right off a Fallon used car lot, and for $250 cash, it was mine. It was the last time I would buy a car outright until the mid-1970s.

At the *Standard* that summer, Ken Ingram had me covering news at the Churchill County Court House, the Truckee-Carson Irrigation District, and the police and sheriff's departments. He justified ordering me not to write sports exclusively by telling me, "Athletics is fine, but there's other stuff in life, too, and somebody's got to cover it. Someday you'll be a lot better off in your career because you'll know how to do many things." At the *Standard* those final three months, the other stuff in my life included early morning hours, laboring at printer and janitor duties, errand-boy journeys around town, and an unanticipated venture into advertising.

Midway through the summer, Ingram decided to leave on a two-week vacation.

"I'd like you to handle my ad accounts," he declared. I was terrified at the prospect of having to ask a business to purchase advertising space, and I so advised Ingram. He had an answer for everything. "Just think positive," he said. "Think of yourself as the person who posts messages that help businesses win more customers, make their cash registers ring, assure their prosperity." But I wasn't cut out for sales, and I took my discomfort and lack of success as signs that I should remain on the news side of journalism. I was convinced then that writing always would be my exclusive mission.

The Monday visits at Lake Tahoe with Marilyn were my summer delight. I'd chug to the "Lake in the Sky" in my little green DeSoto with the twin mud flaps and twin aerials. Marilyn seemed to care not an ounce about the car, which had a tired engine that pooped out and stranded us a few times, but she liked me so much that she affixed a Tri-Delt sticker on my windshield, right next to my Theta Chi sticker. Side-by-side. Royle-and-Melton. I began to feel that being together was a good idea.

Marilyn was an excellent swimmer, but that's where her athleticism ended. She knew not a stitch about football, baseball, or track and field. I quizzed her gently about basketball: "How many players on a team?"

She shrugged, "You mean the whole squad, or those playing?" Clearly, sports conversation wasn't my route into her heart.

Marilyn was majoring in education. She didn't want to teach, but her mother had insisted, "Study something that will assure you of a job after college." Marilyn wanted most to be a superior artist. My knowledge of art paralleled her zest for sports, which is to say that I didn't know Michelangelo from a straight line. But from Marilyn, the artist, I was to learn.

Marilyn and I were proving that opposites do attract. Her father, William Royle, had held such jobs as state labor commissioner and Nevada war manpower commissioner, while my father was an alcoholic, drifting from town to town. I saw myself as coming from the "wrong side of the tracks." Marilyn's family was stable and owned their own home in an attractive "right side of the tracks" neighborhood. Her sister, Patricia, and brother, William, were collegians. My sister, Bronna, had decided that high school was as far as she'd go. Marilyn was Catholic; I was wedded to no church. I was from little Fallon; she was from big Reno. I boxed and played football; she disliked violent sports. In my family, every marriage had failed; except for a black-sheep uncle, all Marilyn's relatives had stuck with the same spouse.

So many differences, but so much in Marilyn Royle to love. She was such fun. So artistic. So pretty. Unstuffy. Genuinely interested in people and issues. And glory be, she was a regular reader of newspapers! She admitted that she had seen my byline in the campus *Sagebrush*. She quizzed me on my *Fallon Standard* experiences, and if she wasn't genuinely interested, then she was deserving of a best-actress Oscar.

Boise Man Joins AA, Turns Over New Leaf

Boise, ID Shortly before school resumed in September 1952, I heard from my father for the first time in two years. His letter revealed why he had not attended my high school graduation: "I did an awful thing, son.

I got to drinking in one of Fallon's bars that afternoon, and I couldn't show up at your graduation drunk and embarrass you and Brownie." When he awoke with a hangover the following morning, he had been afraid to call and apologize. He had headed north to Boise and home, but his car had broken down between Lovelock and Winnemucca. He had left the stranded car and hitchhiked to Winnemucca, arriving broke. There, he had worked a week at a bakery, raising enough money to keep him in liquor and to buy a Trailways Bus ticket home.

My father's letter closed on an optimistic note: "I'm getting married again, son, and this time it's to a woman who'll help me get completely straightened out." (I had heard such tales from him earlier about girlfriends he planned to settle in with.) "Martha is good people. We worked in the bakery together at the Albertson's store in Boise. She says that I'll have to quit drinking or there will be no marriage.

"Martha told me that I've hit rock-bottom, and that I had better admit it and go somewhere for help. She says that Alcoholics Anonymous has saved lots of people like me. Well, I've gone to some meetings and heard people's stories of self-imposed trouble, and I've been standing up and admitting that I've screwed up my life and other lives."

I had heard a ton of dead-end stories from father, but this time he sounded sincere, as though Martha had thrown him a lifeline when he was going down a third and last time. I felt empathy, and for the first time as a young adult, I believed he could rescue himself.

Indeed, he did. He was forty-seven when he found AA. He married Martha, the divorced mother of four sons, and until his death twenty-two years later, he never took another drink. My relationship with him swung around 180 degrees, and no cross words again passed between us. Father's marriage to Martha, his savior, was most pleasant—he had found the right woman. I was feeling then that I had found the woman of my dreams too.

This is the only picture ever taken of the entire Melton family.
l. to r.: Brownie, Rusty, Rollan Sr., and Rollan Jr.

Football Is Back
Melton Again a Starter

Reno, NV Going into the academic year of 1952-1953, the University of Nevada had a new president, Minard Stout. Stout had succeeded Malcolm Love, who had resigned. The university's thirteen hundred students elected Procter Hug, an athlete and scholar from Sparks, to be our student body president.

Social headquarters for students continued to be the venerable Little Waldorf Saloon on North Virginia Street, adjacent to the Southern Pacific Railroad tracks. The Wal, as it was called, was owned by Lance Morton. He handpicked his bartenders from the students who applied, and he had a sixth sense for spotting future leaders. Tending bar that year were Bruno Benna, who had been recruited from New Jersey to play basketball for the Wolf Pack; Dean C. Smith, a journalism major and feisty varsity basketball player under Coach Jake Lawlor; and David Ryan, one of my football teammates and closest friends, later a standout stockbroker in California.

The five-man board of regents had voted to eliminate the football program in the summer of 1951, between my freshman and sophomore years. We had had only a student pickup team in 1951, but in 1952 football was back, with basketball coach Jake Lawlor doubling as head football coach.

Lawlor's assignment was very difficult. After their scholarships were jerked in 1951, many seasoned players fled to athletic programs at other universities. Lawlor had to rebuild from scratch, with few veteran players, with an anemic budget, and in a new setting—the small Far Western Conference. The team did have some worthy non-scholarship performers, and I earned a starting role at offensive center after spirited competition with three others.

We were an underdog outfit, and there was a special bond among us because of talk that we would be Far Western Conference doormats. In the abbreviated season of 1952 we wound up winning two and losing two. We defeated Chico State 34-2 and the Cal-Davis Aggies 26-13, but we were overmatched against non-conference opponents Fresno State University, which defeated us 59-32, and Idaho State College, which got an early jump on us at Pocatello and whipped us 33-13. My father went up to Boise for the game, and, inspired by his presence, I played the full sixty minutes. At season's end I was named first-team center by Idaho State on its all-opponent team. (The Idaho State Bengals had a 10-0 record that year, winning the Intermountain Division title.)

It was to Jake Lawlor's great credit that we did as well as we did. He was a fiery, competitive coach, and a demanding leader—one who had contempt for players who accepted defeat as a suitable outcome. Lawlor taught us not to accept anything less of ourselves than our best efforts.

I continued to date Marilyn Royle. I hung out in some of her art classes, watching her execute her admirable drawings, watercolors, and oils. I was around so much that art department chairman, J. Craig Sheppard, accused me of ranking art above journalism. That wasn't so, of course, but I did rank Marilyn as number one.

In addition to playing football, I went out for the boxing team, coached by Jimmie Olivas, a legendary figure who had been a top

"In addition to playing football, I went out for the boxing team, coached by Jimmie Olivas...."

amateur fighter and had enjoyed a modestly successful pro career. My skills were minimal, but I reported for sparring sessions to stay in shape for football.

My two fights that season were not pleasant experiences. Gordon Surber, with whom I had played football in 1950, was the first-team heavyweight, and I was matched against him in an intramural bout in the winter of 1952. A powerful body puncher, he knocked me out in the second round. The following spring, Olivas entered me in the heavyweight division at the Pacific Coast Intercollegiate championship tournament. A Cal-Poly fighter, Jack Shaw, made short work of me, knocking me out in the second round. Sports editor Ty Cobb later joked, "Rollie, who knows? You might have been a champ had you only been able to get through a second round."

Our band of journalism majors was small, and we came to know each other well through time spent together in classes, on the *Sagebrush* staff, and in the campus Press Club. The department's reputation was good, and newspapers – especially the *Reno Evening Gazette* and the *Nevada State Journal* – were hiring many University of Nevada journalism graduates right out of school. It was my hope that I would join them after an obligatory two-year U. S. Army commitment following graduation. Failing that, I planned to return to the weekly newspaper field, hopefully in my hometown of Fallon.

Local Couple Elopes
Royles Not Happy

Minden, NV Marilyn Royle and I were growing closer and closer, and by the New Year we had decided we should marry. We told Marilyn's parents of our wish, but Dorothy and Bill Royle, while they were cordial to me, balked at the idea. They said it would make a lot more sense to wait until each of us had graduated. "Then see how you feel about marriage," they counseled. In their presence, we agreed; out of their presence, we grumbled.

Marilyn and I took the prospect of marriage very seriously. I had seen how much grief divorces had caused in my family, and Marilyn and I felt certain our marriage would be for keeps. Marilyn's parents continued to try to dissuade us, but we decided to go against their wishes. On Wednesday, March 25, 1953, her mother and father left for an overnight visit to Sacramento. Marilyn and I went in a different direction: I had no money, so we broke into her piggy bank and found fourteen dollars. We took this small sum to a Reno pawnshop and bought her a cheap wedding band. We were eloping.

Two of our closest friends agreed to stand up for us at our marriage. Marilyn chose Sue Casey Baker, a Nevada classmate who had gone through all the grades with her, and my best man was Bill Griggs, my good friend and fellow athlete. The four of us drove to Minden, south of Carson City. There, we obtained a marriage license, then went to the home of the Douglas County Justice of the Peace, Bert Selkirk, who also was owner and publisher of the Gardnerville *Record-Courier*. The ceremony was performed at the Selkirk home.

When we told Marilyn's parents that we were married, her father managed to hide

"As for us newlyweds, we agreed that while dating had been heavenly, marriage was divine." Marilyn and Rollan Melton's wedding photograph.

his pain until we were out of sight, and then he cried. Her mother, however, hid nothing. Dorothy Gray Royle's face flashed red with Irish fury. She was not happy. "You deprived our daughter of a church wedding!" she snapped. (Years later, Dorothy would admit that given the cost of church weddings, perhaps Marilyn and I had done the right thing.)

As for us newlyweds, we agreed that while dating had been heavenly, marriage was divine. Many years later, on the occasion of one of our wedding anniversaries, I asked Marilyn what she remembered most clearly about the Minden ceremony. I believed that she would say something about the euphoria of exchanging wedding vows, but she replied, "I remember that Mr. Selkirk was wearing his bedroom slippers."

Mr. and Mrs. William Royle
announce the marriage of their daughter
Marilyn Ann
to
Mr. Rollan Doyle Melton
on Wednesday, the twenty-fifth of March
Nineteen hundred and fifty-three
Gardnerville, Nevada

Marilyn and Rollan Melton's wedding announcement.

Pres. Stout Attacks Freedoms
Melton Speaks Up

Reno, NV Those of us who lived through the 1950s at the University of Nevada laugh when people refer to us as the "silent generation." It was a loud, brassy period, and a perilous one for those who were passionate about any infringement of our freedoms.

Minard Stout came to the campus as president in 1952, and the welcome mat was barely put aside before students and faculty began to feel uneasy about him. The former Iowa educator got to talking tough early, pushing to drop student admission standards to a level so low that any high school graduate would be eligible to enroll. It didn't take him long to gain the support of the five-man Board of Regents, which voted unanimously to lower entrance requirements.

Stout had pushed the change through without consulting his faculty, many of whom opposed the action.

One unhappy professor was Dr. Frank Richardson, chairman of the biology department, who reacted to the lowering of requirements by circulating a copy of a University of Illinois professor's article supporting higher academic standards in general. Richardson was a respected, tenured professor who had been at Nevada for twelve years. He was not well-known off campus, but that would change.

President Stout took the biologist's act as an affront to his own wisdom and authority, and he severely reprimanded Richardson for "trying to undermine him." To the faculty's dismay, Stout used fighting words, telling Richardson, "You were hired to teach biology and not to be a buttinsky...."

The authoritarian Stout then went after four other respected professors, contending that they had joined Richardson in what the president maintained was a plot against him. On the hot seat with Richardson were a biologist, Dr. Thomas Little, and widely known English department faculty members, Robert Hume, Robert Gorrell, and Charlton Laird. On March 31, 1953, President Stout wrote Richardson and the others letters of dismissal. The battle was joined.

Nevada's academic freedom case made news nationwide. The *New York Times* and *Time* magazine were onto the unfolding story, as faculties across the country waded in to support Richardson, who by then stood alone, because Stout, on the advice of the Nevada attorney general, had backed off on his termination of the other four professors. I was angry and appalled by Stout's assault on academic freedom. If Richardson was not well known off campus, I was much less so. My age was twenty-one, and I was just a junior majoring in journalism and doting on the frequently inspiring freedom-of-the-press sermons of my department chairman, A. L. Higginbotham. I was in my third year on the staff of the student newspaper, *Sagebrush*, for which I wrote the "Pack Tracks column," devoted exclusively to sports.

Up to the time of the Stout-Richardson episode, I hadn't written a line of non-sports copy for the campus weekly, but it was time for me to forget my sports theme for a time and to support Richardson, whom I had never met. Infringement of any American freedom was a punitive act against all. I didn't care if Minard Stout was president—what he was doing was high-handed, authoritarian, autocratic, undemocratic, and patently unfair to Frank Richardson. I delved into the facts of the case as I could learn them, and before writing my views in the *Sagebrush*, I called Richardson, asking for an interview. He agreed, and we met on campus. He told me that many other journalists had interviewed him, but that I was the only student he'd heard from.

We didn't talk long. Richardson was relaxed and very open with me, and he sure didn't come off as a sinister dissident. I told him I would write my opinion, and that it would appear in our next issue, on May 1. The column opened with verse which my journalism major friend, Bill Eaton, had written for me. Then I took off on Stout in a strongly worded denunciation.

A strong closing statement was important, and I wrote and re-wrote it, to try and make it just right. A short time later, the oppressed Richardson was to face his accusers, Stout and the regents. My closing statement said:

"Win, lose, or draw, at the hearing Dr. Frank Richardson will be able to hold his head high . . . for he would rather fail as a leader than succeed as a tyrant." Here is the column:

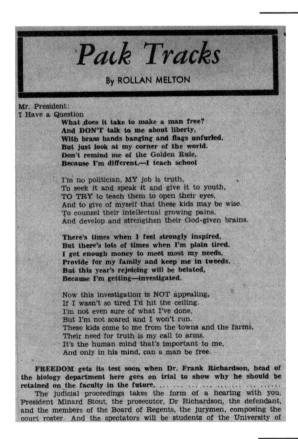

A few days later, the president sent for me. I was to come to his office said his secretary, Alice Terry. Stout was courteous, polished, and articulate. I thought at the time that "oily" would be a good word to describe him. He was facing off with me from behind his desk, and what he saw was a punk journalism kid. I was more than a little shaky.

The fact that his secretary was close by, taking down in shorthand every word we said, didn't comfort me.

I can't quote precisely what Stout said to me—in the ensuing years, I have tried to locate a transcript of the conversation, but I never could—but it was easy to get his drift. He implied that if I didn't lay off and shut up, I was probably putting my future on the campus in jeopardy. That did it for me. This guy was an intimidator, a bully, a bad actor. Of all places where freedom should ring, it is on a campus. President Stout was flying against the decent rules set in place by our forefathers. I got the unmistakable impression that he thought I was a radical, an agitator, a meddler.

I returned to our *Sagebrush* office and churned out another non-sports column, with this ending: "Freedom of the press and freedom of speech boil down to the same thing.... They are separated only by a semicolon. If Dr. Frank Richardson is guilty, then his sin has been allegiance to academic freedom. And without that freedom, how can educators seek out the truth and pass it on to each succeeding generation?"

Here is the second column, dated May 8, 1953:

Pack Tracks
By ROLLAN MELTON

—Though I disagree with what you say, I would defend to the death, your right to say it.
—Voltaire

Gentlemen of the Jury:

It should be the duty of every person interested in the controversy here at the university to make queries and arrive at his verdict on the situation. He should not shout, but ought to find out. If these interested persons will talk to faculty members, as was suggested by our administrative head three weeks ago, they may be in a position to arrive at their own conclusions.

During interviews the past week with scores of students, faculty, and downtown peoples these questions came up. A few were answered. Some may never be answered.

Can students be told that a vital question, "academic freedom," is none of their business? Can a student or a faculty member work effectively if he is afraid? Is it possible for experienced educators to suggest group faculty study of certain problems, only to be told that "to pool ignorance is to get nothing but ignorance"?

Do qualified instructors have cause to wonder when the tenure and pay increases they were entitled to on the basis of department consideration, fail to materialize? Is it a healthy academic atmosphere when faculty colleagues who have worked together side by side for years now no longer speak to one another?

From the information obtained from these queries, which were suggested by the administrative head, the following principle is found to be the essence of the whole Stout-Richardson controversy:

The primary issue at the upcoming hearing (May 25, a Monday, 10 a.m. in the educaiton auditorium) will not be to determine the moral and professional standing of the defendant, nor whether he has been insubordinate, or whether he is guilty of subversive action. Rather, it will be to learn if he, as a citizen, can exercise the right of free expression as other Americans do.

The author of this column has been commended by various persons for the essay of last issue concerning the Stout-Richardson thing. And too, he has been roundly criticized and branded as a radical, an agitator, and as "one meddling in affairs which are none of his concern."

The author welcomes these comments and interprets them as evidence that so long as people can still offer such criticism, can still voice their opinions on vital matters, can still defend without suppression the ideas they believe in, they are exercising the very rights which have caused one among us to be threatened with dismissal.

It has been argued by Stout supporters—and they have every right to argue, for the Constitution guarantees it—that the trouble at the university can be compared to dissention within a company, or coach-player trouble on an athletic team, or a riff between an employer and a lumberjack in a logging camp.

But, is it possible to make a valid comparison of the situation with anything other than a similar situation at another university?

The following are the authoritative views of a nationally known educator, Dr Monroe E. Deutsch, taken from his "Let There Be Light On academic Freedom." Dr Deutsch was a commencement speaker at this university in 1951:

"Professors are not employees of the university, but members of it. The right attitude of service in the manifold demands of the university cannot be obtained or expected from men uncertain of their tenure; neither can freedom of thought, research, or expression, especially in subjects traversed by the daily thought of the community . . . If the teacher is hampered, whose idea does he teach? Those of the regents? Of the president? Or of the legislature? But science does not follow the election returns. Within the range of the teacher's special equipment and knowledge, not as oracle at large nor as bearing an arbitrary license but in the name of his science he must be free to teach. Otherwise the university is an imitation and a sham.

"It is not as a professor he speaks or should speak, but merely as an American keenly interested in the well-being of his nation. Provided he is honest on this point, the professor should be as free as any other citizen to speak his views. And, like other citizens, he will find his protection against those who wish to silence him in that powerful document —The Constitution of the United States.

"This greatest of human achievements (a university) will weaken and perish if it is deprived of freedom. The air of freedom must blow; without it the university cannot exist. An alma mater bound and fettered could never be a nourishing mother. And there is no nobler cause than to stand in her defense."

Professors on the campus of Illinois, California, and Stanford, recognizing the danger of limiting academic freedom, have rallied to give the defendant moral support. But a newspaper editor has said that this situation should not be the concern of the faculty of these other universities. Yet, if someone were to tell this newspaperman what he could or could not print, every journalist who is worthy of the title, would rally to support him and freedom of the press.

Freedom of the press and freedom of speech boil down to the same thing . . . They are separated only by a semicolon.

If Dr Frank Richardson is guilty, then his sin has been allegiance to academic freedom. And without that freedom, how can educators seek out the truth and pass it on to each succeeding generation?

The campus was polarized. Faculty members faced off against each other, the freedom fighters versus those wishing to curry favor with their department heads, the deans, or the president. Our student body was stunned. Was this to be like Nazi Germany all over again?

Following the publication of my articles, many faculty, students, and local citizens came to the support of the beleaguered Richardson. His sagging spirits buoyed by the surging support, Richardson told a faculty colleague, Dr. John Morrison of the English Department, "I can't believe it. Melton only met with me for a few minutes." But it hadn't taken long with Richardson to confirm in my mind that he was the hero, and president Stout was the villain.

As much as I applauded the pro bono support given Richardson by four local lawyers, I began to get nervous as they urged me to write more supportive columns for their client. I had said my piece, and I told them that I would stand silent for the time being.

I felt that I needed to talk to my hero, Al Higginbotham, and seek his counsel, just to make sure my head was on straight. I called him and said I'd like to see him about the academic freedom case. Higgy said he'd love to visit, and he invited me to his home on University Terrace, near the campus. His wife, Marie, ushered me in and had some snacks for us.

I was totally at ease with the man whom I knew was a champion of freedoms. He volunteered that we were visiting in confidence. I then opened the discussion of my two columns, and he said, "Yes, yes, I've read them. They were very fine, Rollan. I think I agree with you."

I said I was troubled at this point, because I was getting pressure from both sides—get off Stout's back; write more in support of Richardson. "I feel I've said my piece, Prof, and anything else would be repetitious." Higginbotham counseled me not to write further on the matter, and I went away, aglow with the praise he had given me for my stand, and reassured by him that I was doing the right thing in now staying silent on the matter.

Towards the end of May, some two weeks after I met with Higginbotham, there were three days of hearings to bring testimony from opposing sides so that the regents could rule on whether Richardson's termination should be upheld or not. On the opening day, May 25, the turnout was so great that you couldn't have wedged another body into the Education Building's Auditorium with a shoehorn. Marilyn and I were seated about half way back from the stage. The lawyers fenced, Richardson sat calmly, and Stout perched nearby, smiling and self-assured.

One of the first witnesses to be called was my idol, Professor Higginbotham. I was thrilled and whispered to Marilyn, "Right on! Higgy will set everyone straight on what academic freedom is all about!" Instead, to my dismay, Higgy gave me the shaft. Responding to the regents' lawyer, he made

"I did feel I needed to talk to my hero, Al Higginbotham, and seek his counsel, just to make sure my head was on straight."
Alfred Higginbotham in 1963. (*Gazette-Journal* photograph.)

it clear that he was a strong pro-Stout man. "God," I thought, "I should have checked that out."

As Marilyn and I clung to each other, and my face reddened, Higginbotham took out a notebook and recited from it. He said that "student Melton" had come to his home on May 8 and professed "shame for the rumor that he had told Dr. Richardson that I was in denial of all the principles of journalism student Melton had been taught as a student at the University of Nevada."

I was in shock. Higgy testified that I had told him at his home that day, "Prof, I am ashamed of what I have done to you, and I apologize." Higgy then stuffed his notebook into his pocket, and, in concluding testimony, he said, "Student Melton said that after my teaching him the ethics and morals of journalism, he could never say such a thing about me." In his testimony, Higginbotham had invoked the name of *Sagebrush* editor Rosemary Cochran, saying he had visited with her about rumors that he "had bawled out Rollan Melton for the material in *'Pack Tracks.'*"

Higginbotham left the stand, with Stout off to the side of the stage, beaming his appreciation. Marilyn and I slunk out of the auditorium like whipped puppies. Higginbotham had made everything sound so factual, but his only truth was that I had come to his home. He did not testify that it was he who had suggested we speak in confidence. He did not testify that he told me that he liked my columns. He did not testify that he described the columns as "very fine." He did not testify that he had counseled me not to write further articles about the Stout-Richardson case. He did not testify that he used entrapment to induce me to confide in him. As far as I was concerned, Alfred Leslie Higginbotham had crash-landed off the pedestal on which I had always placed him.

I quickly went to talk to Rosemary Cochran (Girolomo), our *Sagebrush* editor, who also was the student secretary to Higginbotham that year. (Higgy had failed to testify that she was his secretary.) I told Cochran of Higgy's testimony and his assertion that she had told him that he had "bawled out Rollan Melton for things he had written."

Rosemary Cochran did a double-take. "I never had such a conversation with Prof, " she told me. Forty-six years later, in 1999, I spoke to her, and we revisited the subject of the Higginbotham testimony. I told her I had obtained from UNR's archives a copy of the 1953 testimony of our department chairman. I asked her to again react to what Higginbotham had testified. She said, "Nothing has changed. Prof was lying."

At the conclusion of the Richardson hearing during the "silent" decade, the regents (students then facetiously called them the Kangaroo Court) voted unanimously to terminate Dr. Frank Richardson—they said he was "insubordinate and uncooperative." In protest, Walter Van Tilburg Clark, University of Nevada English department professor and famous author, resigned from the faculty, stating that Stout was reducing the campus to "a manageable mediocrity."

In April 1954, the Nevada Supreme Court overturned the Board of Regents ruling, ordering that Richardson be reinstated and receive all back pay and benefits. It was a humiliating defeat for Stout. His troubles weren't over. A subsequent study showed that Stout advocates, including Higginbotham, had received unusually high salary increases during the Richardson crisis. Moreover, many of those who supported the biology professor had had their incomes frozen. More than three hundred students turned out to hang Stout in effigy from the downtown Reno Arch. In 1957, the Board of Regents, with a new cast of members, fired Minard Stout. His reign of terror, intimidation, and unfairness was finally ended.

In 1953, when I wrote my columns defending Stout, I was still a student, two years short of graduation. My faith in Higginbotham, the man I had so admired, was squashed. I would have to get my dauber up. Surely, there was a valued lesson in all of this. As a victim, I more passionately than ever believed that duplicity, subterfuge, and lying have no place in journalism, or anyplace else where freedom speaks.

Life In Fertility Heights
Melton Offered Packer Tryout

Reno, NV   For a while after the Stout affair, I was depressed and angry. I felt that the chairman of my department had betrayed me and his oft-professed principles. In my view, I was an undergraduate underdog, and Higgy held an axe that could splinter my chances of graduating with a journalism degree. Following Higgy's testimony, I returned to my study routine, but I was fearful that I'd get washed out of the program. I felt as if I had one foot on a banana peel and the other in my academic grave.

Marilyn cheered me up and helped me recognize that there was much for which to be thankful. I loved journalism and being a part of it; I loved the girl I had married; and I loved living in married student housing.

Our apartment was tiny, but it seemed much larger than any home I had known when growing up. When Marilyn wasn't in class or continuing her part-time work at the downtown Armanko's Store, she was artistically dolling up our first home. She was wall-paperer, inventive improviser, and relentless requisitioner of tired, hand-me-down furniture that her parents seemed delighted to get out of their sight.

Most tenant couples had one overriding goal: to get their student lives finished, leave Victory Heights forever, and settle into paying jobs. There were fourteen apartments in each former barracks unit and eight units in the complex. Living units varied in size and rental cost, but the charge for the Meltons' one-bedroom apartment was no more than I had paid for my fraternity house room – $27.50 a month, all utilities paid. Winter winds pushed cold drafts around the poorly-fitting doors and windows, and in the summer, dust and sand from the unlandscaped grounds blew through open windows.

The young married occupants were having babies at such a brisk pace that in our vernacular, we were living in "Fertility Heights." Each barracks was served by a cranky single-wringer washing machine, and clotheslines running behind the buildings were always drooping with diapers hung out to dry. Marilyn and I planned to delay starting our family until we graduated.

We had never had a phone in any of my family homes, but at Victory Heights Marilyn and I had one. We didn't need it to communicate with our neighbors. The barracks walls were so thin that tenants got acquainted with each other whether they wished to or not. Our apartment abutted that of Jeanne and Bill Ireland, whom I had come to know because he was student trainer of our football teams. At Victory Heights, he and I invariably visited our respective bathrooms at about the same time each morning. We would carry on through-the-wall conversations while shaving, showering, and performing other necessary acts: "Morning, Bill. Suppose you've read the *Journal* already. How did the Yanks and Mantle do in last night's game?"

The semester finally ended, and my grades were so-so. In mid-June I left Reno with other advanced army ROTC cadets for our six-week officer training program at Fort Lewis, Washington. (Fellow journalism major Willard "Red" Esplin drove us to Fort Lewis, and en route we stopped in Gresham, Oregon, where I had lived in eighth grade. The brief visit, and the memories of my time spent there, made me appreciate all the more the good luck that had been with me since.)

Being a Nevada campus ROTC cadet was one thing, but at Fort Lewis that rain-soaked summer I was introduced to the real U. S. Army. For starters I was issued two pairs of combat boots, with explicit orders to change from one pair to the other each day. This was impossible for Cadet Melton, for they had issued me three left boots and one right. My appeals to the quartermaster clerks were to no avail. I was told that they didn't have two pairs in my size, and I would have to make do until they got them. They never did.

We cadets should have brought hip waders to Fort Lewis. We had drenching rains on forty-one of the forty-two days spent there. The classes were taught by World War II soldiers who were mostly in their thirties, and who were wise beyond their years because of combat experiences. We ran five miles each morning, our helmets banging around our ears, and the NCO cadre frequently made us scrub our barracks floors with worn-out brooms, mops, and even toothbrushes, all of which had seen better days.

In the midst of sixteen-hour training days, I found myself missing Nevada and my wife. Then the grind was over. I had learned much about military leadership, but I hadn't read a newspaper in weeks.

Back in Reno, I returned to the *Journal* part-time, helping out in the sports department. There also was a new job that was full-time at the outset, and would provide me with a twenty-five hour work week after my fourth academic year began. Marilyn's father, Bill Royle, was then regional director of U. S. Postal operations in Nevada and Northern California. Bill (as by then he preferred that I call him) asked Reno postmaster Pete Petersen to hire me, and he did. Petersen said I was the first full-time student to be signed on at Reno's only post office. I was a novice clerk, given a task that I couldn't mess up very much—throwing mail into individuals' boxes.

School started again, and because I had taken light academic loads before our marriage, it was apparent that I couldn't finish my university education in four years. I would have to take one summer session and study a fifth year before graduation—providing, of course, that I didn't stumble or get tripped up by Professor Alfred Leslie Higginbotham. I never had the courage to confront Higgy with my real feelings about the shabby hand he had dealt me in the controversial Richardson-Stout academic freedom case. I distanced myself from him, although I had to take required classes he taught. I vowed to be patient, of positive mind, and to do my best to learn helpful things along my way to what I wanted—my degree in journalism.

My fourth and final football season yielded unsatisfactory results on the field. We won two games and lost three, including decisive whippings administered to us by larger, better-financed Fresno State and Idaho State. For me, the best thing about that season was my continued association with teammates of superior athletic ability and good character, and, again, with head coach Jake Lawlor. I was again the starting center. Coach Lawlor alternated the co-captains game-by-game, and my turn came in the 1953 homecoming game against a strong San Francisco State team. Mert Baxter was the other co-captain, and I deferred to this bright future army general. We were down 28-0 at halftime, had a strong rally in the final half, and almost caught up. But we lost, 28-27.

The following spring the mail brought an envelope with the return address of the Green Bay Packers of the National Football League. Eagerly ripping open the envelope, I plucked out the letter. In my athletic Walter Mitty dream world, I imagined that it would contain an offer of a contract, but there was instead a mimeographed form letter. The boiler-plate language read: "We are having tryouts next summer, and if you wish, you can attend." This gave me a laugh and confirmed in my mind that my football-playing days were over. As I have been about so many other things throughout my life, I was wrong.

Students Intern With Local Papers
Gazette and *Journal* Compete Furiously

Reno, NV Higginbotham's legacy was the journalism intern program that he had established in the early 1940s. Before then, his primary assignment had been that of instructor in the English department. The first journalism courses were offered in 1924, but until Higgy's department was formed, journalism had not had much of a presence at Nevada. Higgy convinced the administration that there should be a formal journalism department, and that he would be the best choice for chairman.

The intern program was a win-win approach. Seniors received valued on-the-job work experience while earning academic credit. No other Far West university then offered such an opportunity, and under Higgy's direction, the program got good results and unreserved praise from news and advertising professionals. Some other University of Nevada departments, in the wake of journalism's success, began implementing their own intern programs. There were then few, if any, comparable journalism programs nationwide.

Higgy was mainly print oriented, for that was the discipline he knew from his brief work experience with the *Cleveland Plain Dealer*. In the 1940s and early 1950s, the small number of radio stations operating in Reno had no news operations per se anyway. They relied chiefly on the United Press and the Associated Press, a cooperative with hundreds of member newspapers. Television did not arrive in Reno until 1952; and for many years afterwards, Reno stations offered no sophisticated local news gathering and broadcasting service.

In the Higginbotham scheme, majors in their fourth year went to non-paid, eight-hour-a-week assignments in the news, advertising, or broadcast business. A few students did tours at such weeklies as the *Sparks Tribune* and the *Nevada Appeal* in Carson City, but most interned with Reno's daily newspapers, the morning *Nevada State Journal* and the *Reno Evening Gazette*. The only daily news games in town, these newspapers were both owned by Speidel Newspapers, Inc., then with headquarters in Colorado Springs, Colorado.

Clearly, students benefitted from the hands-on experience. They forged links with professionals that led to many future full-time jobs, and in return, newspapers made good use of the interns. Ever since, newspapers and other media have regarded the intern program as an exemplary recruiting vehicle.

Since I was not going to graduate with my class, I might be able to get in an extra semester of interning. I was cautious about pitching Higgy on the possibility of letting me spread my internships over three semesters rather than two, but I mustered my resolve and got an appointment to see him. To his credit, and my ultimate benefit, he said that he would extend my interning experience over three semesters with three individual newspaper operations. He told me it was the first time any of the department's majors had suggested spreading the experience over a year and a half, but he'd let me give it a go. Maybe there was a speck of goodness in him after all.

My first internship semester was on familiar turf—the *Nevada State Journal*. I had wanted sports, but Higgy was firm. "You need to learn how to do things outside sports, which you're already passably good at," he said. The chair ruled, and events proved him right. For a four-month period I did general assignment news, including accompanying the police reporter, shadowing the guy who covered Reno city hall, and sitting in on Washoe County Commission meetings.

Combining my *Journal* internship with my academic and work loads meant that I would spend less time with Marilyn. Her schedule was hectic, too. She was taking a full academic load and was focused on her major extracurricular project, the design editorship of the 1954 *Artemisia* yearbook. Her page layout was superior, and her art, which would ultimately appear on a great many pages, was dazzling in its breadth and artistic technique.

Marilyn was also active in campus politics, and she was a vital force in Clair Earl's campaign for student body president. Earl was a pre-med major who was one of my fraternity brothers. He was not widely known on campus, and he was a decided underdog against a seasoned opponent who had already worked his way through numerous student government chairs, but when Marilyn got through advancing his campaign with her well-designed signs, placed in great number on and off campus, Clair Earl's name was widely known. The future Reno dentist won the office by a comfortable margin.

I spent many more than eight hours a week on the *Journal* internship. My motive was obvious—I wanted the breadth and number of my printed stories to be the most impressive amongst my fellow interns. I also sought to forge as much linkage with *Journal* professionals as possible, showing them by example that I had a strong work ethic. I became acquainted with the top news managers of the newspaper, foremost among them Joseph McDonald, who had grown up in Nevada's boom-and-bust mining camps in the early twentieth century and was then editor and publisher (chief operating officer) of both the afternoon *Gazette* and the morning *Journal*.

Robert Trego was the city editor of the *Journal*, overseeing local news coverage. Trego's wife, Peggy, was a leading general assignment reporter, and her specialty was producing refined historical feature stories for Sunday issues. Early on I was whistling a merry tune while writing a story when Trego stopped at my desk, glared at me, and said, "Never whistle in any newsroom. It bothers people, and I hate it personally." My whistling days were over from that moment on.

Many top *Journal* stars were products of the Nevada campus journalism program. Ty Cobb was the best known, for he had worked at the *Journal* since graduating in 1937 and was the driving force of the most thorough coverage of any sports department in the state. No serious fan would miss Cobb's morning report, including his newsy column, "Inside Stuff," which was bulging with athletes' names and deeds. Cobb labored as a one-man department for more than fifteen years, but, as the number of sports events multiplied, so did the work load. When it was clear that he needed full-time support, management authorized another sports position, and Cobb hired Len Crocker, a Reno High School and Nevada journalism graduate, as his assistant.

On the city side, the affable and competent executive editor was Paul A. Leonard, a Nevada journalism graduate and a World War II veteran. Leonard had had experience in non-newspaper management in Elko, Nevada, and he was recruited to Reno by men who realized that they must prepare successors. Leonard clearly had the sort of executive ability that Speidel Newspapers wanted in Reno.

Another journalism alumnus was a standout beat reporter who seemed destined for management opportunities. Even a cub such as myself could see that the reporter with the most potential on the city staff was James W. Hulse, a young man who had won a Harolds Club scholarship and had distinguished himself as a Nevada undergraduate journalism major. Hulse had joined the *Journal* fresh out of the university in 1953, and many believed that he could rise as high as he wished to go in the organization. I had seen him around the journalism department a few times when I was starting my studies, and he already was setting a standard against which all the rest of us measured ourselves.

I first saw Jim Hulse in action as a professional when we were both sent to the Reno Police Department to cover a breaking crime story. I was there as intern/observer and was not expected to write the story—the assignment was Hulse's. Seated next to the young reporter, I had a chance to observe his note-taking practice. I've never seen the likes of it, then or since. While other reporters strained to keep up with the dialogue, Hulse was casually recording every word in formal Gregg shorthand.

When I wandered back to the *Journal* newsroom after the press conference, I found Hulse already there. "Guess you'll be writing your story pretty soon, won't you, Jim?" I asked.

"No," he said, "the story's already done, edited, dummied on page one, and sent down to the composing room to be set." Such a performer! Unfortunately, the newspaper game couldn't hold him. Hulse went on to

Stanford University, where he earned a doctorate in history. He then returned to Reno to accept a position in the University of Nevada's department of history. He became a distinguished professor, a prolific writer, and a respected political activist.

Frank Sullivan was a veteran newspaperman and the *Journal*'s managing editor. He came from a pioneering Nevada family that was of Irish descent. Sullivan, too, was a Higgy protégé. He had once been a rising star in the business, but when I met him, he was a man who liked a drink, and he was frequently in his cups by the middle of a shift.

Sullivan was notorious for making up page one by mid-afternoon, perhaps eight hours before deadline. He would then cross Center Street to a bar and drink Scotch into the evening heedless of the unrelenting emergence of new news. Not infrequently, Sullivan would vanish completely—a newspaper Houdini. It would be left to Robert Trego or sports editor Cobb to freshen up page one before the issue went to press. Frank Sullivan was a good soul, but, like many news people of the era, he was ruled by drink.

The *Journal* press run didn't begin until after midnight, so I would never be around to visit with the printers, with whom I strongly identified because of my weekly newspaper apprentice training. But during my second internship semester with the *Gazette*, I hung out in the composing room adjacent to the newsroom and watched the Linotype operators strain to make deadline. I'd listen to the purr of their remarkable typesetting machines and watch these skilled artisans rapidly assemble news-story type and advertising and then send the finished work off to be put to newspaper bed.

While the *Journal* had been a somewhat casual news operation, the *Gazette* was more structured and staid, and it was a bastion of journalistic conservatism. Gravel-voiced John Sanford's family had owned the paper before Speidel acquired it in 1939, and he was still its editor, presiding over a small, highly competent staff. His second in command was Joseph R. Jackson, who had grown up in Sparks, the son of a newspaperman. Like Reno native Sanford, Jackson was a "Higgy grad," as his generation proudly referred to themselves.

Many of the paper's veteran reporters were Nevadans and former news interns. The most senior among them was William Friel, a Tonopah native and another of Higgy's boys who stuck around and wound up with the hometown paper. Friel was a former *Gazette* sports editor and a fiercely competitive man who delighted in occasionally beating Ty Cobb to a story, most famously one in 1948 that was still talked about when I joined the paper.

In 1948 Ty Cobb campaigned to get post-season honors for the great Wolf Pack quarterback, Stan Heath, whose heroics had led Nevada to a national ranking as high as number three. Thanks to Heath's talent and Cobb's persistent publicizing and behind-the-scenes arm-twisting, United Press named Heath to its first-team All-American major college football squad. It was the greatest honor ever given to a Nevada football player. Cobb was beside himself with joy.

United Press moved the news on its wire but embargoed it, meaning that the story had a release date of twenty-four hours later. The *Journal* subscribed to United Press and the *Gazette* to the Associated Press, but Friel got wind of what UP had done. He went with a story that said in essence, "The *Gazette* has learned that tomorrow United Press will announce that Nevada quarterback Stan Heath has been selected first-team All-American."

Friel's breaking of the story was entirely legal, for as a non-UP client, he couldn't be put under embargo. He had merely used the advance story as a tip sheet for his own scoop. Ty Cobb, beaten on his own story, was furious. Years passed before he was able to speak cordially to Friel.

Though the *Gazette* and *Journal* had the same owner, the war between the news staffs was true war. Staffs at opposite ends of the hall strained to upstage their counterparts and get the story first. Tempers were often frayed. Competing reporters ignored each other at public meetings, exchanging only glares.

By plan, each paper deliberately set out to be different from its unholy neighbor down the hall. The *Journal* editorial page was liberal, while the *Gazette*'s expounded orthodox Republicanism. The *Gazette*'s Sanford was loath to permit reporter bylines, but the *Journal*'s policy was to showcase its staff members, leading reporters to joke that "*Journal* bylines are given in lieu of pay raises."

I got on well with both sides, making friends from each camp and marveling at their vicious behavior towards each other. These guys and girls competed with an intensity that my football teammates could have learned from. It was a replay of the competition I had grown up with between the *Fallon Standard* and the rowdy crowd at the hated *Eagle*. The public had no idea of the grinding, slashing, and head-butting that went on behind the scenes at the newspapers in Fallon and Reno, but readers were all the better for it. Two distinctly different newspaper voices in a community is a good deal for citizens.

My final stopover in the internship triple play was the *Sparks Tribune*. The weekly was owned by Barbara and Carl Shelly, longtime residents of the community and civic cheerleaders. They were committed to wholesome news coverage in their tabloid weekly. Barbara had gained considerable news experience on the Nevada campus and later working for Reno's dailies, but she was busy tending to wifely and parental commitments and spent little time at the *Tribune*. Carl's involvement in many community endeavors included holding a seat on the Washoe County Commission. Earlier he had been an effective state legislator. The Shellys also owned hardware stores in Reno and Sparks.

When it came to running a newspaper, the Shellys shared Claude and Ethel Smith's philosophy: they wanted its content to be 100 percent local. Both couples believed that their weekly papers couldn't survive if they were not exclusively devoted to what was happening in their respective towns.

The Shellys' son, Bruce, had grown up with the *Tribune*. He was a great help to them, as was Robert Petrini, a Sparks native and also a product of the Nevada journalism department. But about the time that I came aboard as an intern, Petrini was in transition to another opportunity, so the Shellys officially signed me on as their city editor. I also retained the status of intern, picking up academic credit for the third consecutive semester.

While the Shellys weren't absentee owners, they were not around much in my year with them. I was pleased that they trusted me. I did most of the local news writing, as well as writing headlines, editing photographs and captioning them, and taking charge of page design and makeup. It was a heady experience, my first go at producing a paper, and I did it without much help.

My *Tribune* tour was a refreshing change from my *Journal* and *Gazette* intern experiences—I was back into community journalism. Increasingly, I was coming to believe that the chief mission of any good newspaper should be to provide readers with the information necessary to understand their community's past and present, and to give them perspective on how they fit into the life of the town.

Stork Visits Meltons
Rollie Vows to Graduate

Reno, NV In November 1953, Marilyn missed her period. At first we thought little of it, because she had occasionally missed one before. When she missed it again in December, we suspected that our efforts to delay having children might have gone awry. Was it possible that the rhythm method had failed?

The only Reno physician I knew personally was Dr. Louis Lombardi—Reno native, member of the university board of regents, and respected general practitioner. Dr. Lombardi examined Marilyn and confirmed that she was pregnant. "Congratulations," he said. "Next June we'll know whether you might have another football player in the family."

We called Marilyn's parents right away and told them that their first grandchild was on the way. They were stunned at first, but then they broke into cheers. Marilyn's mother had questions and advice:

"Do you know exactly when the baby will be born?"

"No."

"What will you name the baby?"

"It depends on whether we have a girl or boy."

"You will need a crib, baby clothes, a little pan to bathe it in. You'll need a lot of things."

"Yes, Mother."

I called my father, and I reached my mother in Fallon by calling her at the Keystone Restaurant, where she was waiting tables. This was to be the first grandchild for each. In Victory Heights, the news took on a life of its own. It was as if jungle drums were sending the word to interested and disinterested people alike, some of whom were already parents several times over.

Buoyed by the news that baby would make three, Marilyn and I maintained as normal a schedule as possible. Marilyn remained in school through the spring term of 1954. She said she'd resume her studies in due time after the baby arrived. I carried a heavy course load, trying to play catch-up on hours needed to graduate. My grades had improved since my marriage—my full agenda had forced me to learn and practice good time management. (In later years, as I progressed in my career, what I had learned while young about managing the clock, rather than letting it rule my life, was to be useful.)

We fine-tuned the family budget, trying to set aside as much as we could to pay the baby doctor, Frank Samuels. My post office supervisor, Albert Shine, agreed to give me a few additional hours every week, and so did Carl Shelly at the *Tribune* in Sparks. Meanwhile, Marilyn and I kept to our study schedules and maintained our campus civic obligations.

As part of her role in putting on the World University Service carnival, Marilyn appealed to the famous singer, Rudy Vallee, to be on the program. Vallee was appearing in the Mapes Hotel Sky Room. She pitched him on the angle that he was married to a former University of Nevada co-ed and owed it to her alma mater. Vallee was crotchety. He groused about being pestered by do-gooders, but he said he'd sing at the student assembly, and he did. His wife accompanied him to temper his temper, and the entertainer gave the students a remarkable show.

As the spring semester wore on, Marilyn changed her wardrobe to maternity clothes. She also completed the artwork, cover design, and page layout for the 1954 *Artemisia* yearbook.

June arrived, but there was still no baby. We talked about a name and had several in mind should the baby be a daughter. If it were a son, my middle name, Doyle, was considered, but I favored giving a son Marilyn's maiden name, Royle, as his first name. We began kidding around: "If it's a boy, Royle Doyle Melton has a lilting ring to it."

On June 28, Marilyn began to sense that the baby would soon be born. That night we considered two options to induce labor: take our aging car on a spin over a bumpy road or dine out on pizza. We chose the pizza. The following day, Marilyn's contractions began, and we hurried her down from Victory Heights to Saint Mary's Hospital, a block from her parents' home. Our university student friend, Ruth Fitz Pintar, joined us at Saint Mary's. She began massaging Marilyn's back.

Tipped that there was another arrival at the campus, I left Marilyn and sped to the *Artemisia* office and back as fast as our cranky old car would carry me. I had picked up a copy of the spanking new *Artemisia*, with its gorgeous kelly green cover. In her joy over its arrival, Marilyn temporarily forgot her birthing pains, but not for long. Marilyn's contractions drew closer, nurses summoned Dr. Samuels, and Royle William Melton was born that day. His health checked out good, and Marilyn, though worn out, experienced the euphoria that only a new mother can know. As for me, I was a nervous basket case, jubilant husband, and joyous new father.

I phoned my in-laws with the great news, and they visited shortly thereafter. While holding her first grandchild, Marilyn's mother advised her, "Don't let

"Royle William Melton was born that day...and Marilyn, though worn out, experienced the euphoria that only a new mother can know." Marilyn Melton with her sister, Patricia, after Royle's birth.

Royle be a bottle baby. You must breast-feed him."

Dorothy and Bill Royle were kind to let the three of us stay with them for a few days, but baby Royle kept yowling night after night, and all of us were soon sleep-starved. Marilyn took our infant to Dr. Samuels and told him about the baby's constant crying. The doctor said, "This mother's milk isn't working. You must switch him to the bottle."

Later, at the Royle home, Marilyn and her mother explained to me that Marilyn would have to dry out by using a breast pump: "Rollan, go get one and bring it back here."

My naive response became part of family lore. "Where do I go?" I questioned. "Commercial Hardware?"

Marilyn had intended to enroll that autumn for what would have been her senior year, but Royle was just two months old. She couldn't bear being away from him a few hours while I baby-sat, so her senior academic year was postponed indefinitely.

Given our expanded family, it was imperative that I complete my university education and get a job. Fortunately, one was guaranteed. I had completed four years of ROTC and would be sworn in as a second lieutenant when I graduated in June of 1955. Most newly commissioned young infantry officers were still being sent to Korea then. Although the fighting had ceased in 1953, an occupation force was still required.

I had enjoyed my infantry officer training at Fort Lewis, but I hoped that with my newspaper experience and a journalism degree from a respected four-year university program, I could contend for a military public information officer (PIO) position. That would give me more breadth of experience and enhance my chances for employment in journalism after the army. When I began looking into this, I found that regular army infantry officers held PIOs in contempt. Even Nevada's professor of military science and tactics, Major Alex Lemberes, told me, "Melton, we're training you to be an infantry leader, not a word-merchant. That's what you'd best plan on." So that was that; I was resigned to it.

Before I did anything in the army, I had to finish my fifth and final year and earn a degree. My academic load was heavy in my last two semesters, but my grades were the highest they had been. Earlier, I had avoided taking classes that I felt were beyond my intellectual ability or were in subjects that I believed did not apply to my career goals.

In my concluding two semesters I tried to plan my studies better, follow through promptly, and manage several tasks simultaneously. My most critical need was focus. In athletics I had learned that if you stay focused, you'll save yourself a heap of trouble. Now I was determined to apply that lesson to my studies. My final year at the University of Nevada was one of the most draining years of my life, but also one of the most satisfying. Being a husband, father, and student while simultaneously holding several jobs tested my commitment and toughened me mentally.

I had read neither Dale Carnegie's hallmark books nor any management book, but, following the advice of my role models, I had come to accept that your chances of succeeding at any endeavor are enhanced if you believe in yourself and your capacity to win. In the fall of 1954 my mother-in-law asked me if I was really going to earn a degree; and if so, when? I assured her that I was close to achieving that goal. Then I would serve two years in the army before getting a real job.

Midway through my tenth and final semester, Dorothy and Bill presented me with the beautiful University of Nevada class of 1955 ring that they had ordered weeks before. Now I couldn't stop. Too much was at stake, and too many people were counting on me. I couldn't bear the thought that I might let them down.

BIOC at Fort Benning
Influence Won't Help

Fort Benning, GA Thirty of us from the 1955 Nevada graduating class would soon be placed on active duty, having been commissioned as second lieutenants the day before the June 6 commencement. We believed that our basic officer training, which would begin in a few weeks, would be a prelude to being shipped to Korea to serve in the euphemistically labeled "peace-keeping" force.

In later years, Korea would be the "forgotten war," sandwiched as it was between World War II and Viet Nam, but at the time, it was a tragic reminder to Americans that man's capacity for deadly mischief is limitless. The war had cost more than 40,000 American lives, a loss never to be forgotten by their families and friends.

In my boyhood during World War II, I had imagined myself fighting and risking my life for country, honor, and personal glory—I had myself cut out to be a hero. Now I was twenty-three, and I knew that, heroism aside, I'd be better off alive than not. As for my chances of being sent to Korea, what would be, would be.

During the next two months, I kept busy at my two jobs—clerk at the Reno post office and editor for the weekly *Sparks Tribune*. Then Marilyn and I and our son vacated our apartment in Victory Heights at the beginning of August, 1955, and motored off to Fort Benning, Georgia, and the beginning of a new life.

We secured a one-bedroom apartment on Benning Road, barely outside the main entrance of the historic infantry training site. Coming from Nevada's temperate climate, we were unprepared for Georgia's high heat and humidity. A few weeks after we reached Fort Benning, we discovered that Marilyn was pregnant with our second child. The baby was due to arrive in April, 1956. By then I would probably be in the fourth week of my tour of duty in Korea. Wives could not accompany husbands to that country, so I wouldn't be with her when our family increased to four.

It was scorching hot out on the huge Benning training reservation, where incoming new lieutenants were assigned to 200-man companies. My unit was the 111th Company of the Student Brigade. The formal description of our sixteen-week program was the Basic Infantry Officers Course (BIOC), and the army's goal was to teach us how to be soldiers and leaders. Our unit was pure all-American. We had hometowns ranging from Reno, Nevada, to Nevada, Missouri; Ohio to Oregon; Tennessee to Texas; Maine to Mississippi; coast to coast, border to border, and as far away as Hawaii.

The 150 of us who had received our commissions through ROTC and the Army National Guard were galvanized and amused by the presence in our company of fifty lieutenants who had graduated that summer from the U. S. Military Academy at West Point. There was an air of superiority surrounding these gentleman officers, as if they were saying to the rest of us, "You're here from Podunk, and we will set high standards for you." We labeled the cocky West Pointers "ring knockers." There was a determination in our non-West Point ranks to outshine the academy officers in physical work, in class, and on the playing fields.

Our schedules were heavy from dawn to far into the night. We had long hikes in the morning and spent afternoons and evenings at indoor and outdoor lectures. We saluted virtually everything that moved, addressing it as "Sir." We grew familiar with infantry-related weapons, many of World War II vintage. There were lectures in tactics and leadership.

A favorite teaching method of our faculty was to keep us alert by first posing a hypothesis and then calling out the name of a student to answer a question about it. My most embarrassing experience of the sixteen-week program came when I was called upon to respond to such a question.

Lecturer: "Our radar has detected an unidentified aircraft that is reported to be en route to Fort Benning. Based on intelligence, there is a strong possibility the incoming plane may be hostile. This aircraft may possibly carry an atomic bomb. Hypothetically, you are the commanding officer at Fort Benning. What measures do you intend to take . . . Lieutenant Melton?"

Lieutenant Melton (leaps to his feet): "Sir, I'd disperse the troops!"

The answer drew one of the largest laughs of our four-month training period. Flustered and red-faced, I sank to my seat amid BIOC snickering. I knew I must have dropped another notch or two in overall class standing.

My dismal performances in map reading and in weapons maintenance further distanced me from any possibility of military stardom. I couldn't follow a precisely marked map of Reno, let alone figure what my position was on the huge military reservation. Somehow I muddled my way to a passing grade in map reading anyway.

The same with weaponry-familiarization testing, which was a critical phase of training. As army faculty emphasized, "You cannot lead men satisfactorily unless you have an intimate knowledge of their weapons. You should be able to strip and reassemble them, even if blindfolded." One fateful day I found myself out in the field, the machine gun assigned to me disassembled in some thirty pieces, and about a minute away from the deadline for putting it back in working order. We were not blindfolded, and we had been warned that we *must* complete this task.

I was down on my knees, the parts spread in front of me, desperate, knowing that I was about to blow the assignment and be sent home to await being drafted into the enlisted ranks. Just as I reached the point of hopeless despair, a pair of combat boots moved into my field of vision. My gaze traveled up the Army fatigue uniform, from legs to wearer's torso. With dread, I looked up to see who was there to witness my failure.

A miracle had occurred: standing over me was a master sergeant wearing a name tag that read "Melton." I struggled to my feet, pointed excitedly to my own nametag, and sputtered, "Sergeant Melton, my ancestors grew up in the South. Maybe we're related. I'm really not mechanical, as you can see. Can you help me?"

Sergeant Melton answered, "No problem, Lieutenant Melton. Let me show you how to do this." He made a few easy strokes, and the weapon was whole again. Before moving on he told me that we probably were not related. "Your people came from the South," he said. "Mine helped settle Wisconsin." He was the only Melton I met during my army service.

I became friendly with a fellow lieutenant, William E. Haas, of Greenville, Illinois. He learned of my newspaper background and invited me to help create a brief record of our student brigade. I volunteered Marilyn to do art illustrations. Haas was the editor, we collaborated on the writing, and I did the layout. His wife, Laura, typed all the copy, and our mini-yearbook was mimeographed and distributed just before our class graduation. It contained pictures of each of the 200 graduates and listed their names, hometowns, and the schools where they had earned their degrees.

Marilyn and I were among a handful of Nevadans then at Fort Benning, scattered through different units. Occasionally, we visited Charles Spina and his wife, Nancy, both natives of Reno, where he had been an outstanding baseball player with Reno High School and Nevada teams. He had finished his BIOC training a short time before we arrived, and by then he was an infielder on the Fort Benning team. The other Nevadans based there were Henry "Hank" Clark, a future Reno financial officer; Donald L. Wilkerson, later a Reno business entrepreneur; Edward C. Stephens, a former Nevada football teammate who would remain in the army; and Richard M. Wiseman, a political science major.

Wiseman had been a political intern in Washington, D.C., for U. S. Senator George (Molly) Malone, Republican from Nevada. Wiseman confided to me that Senator Malone's political influence could help us avoid assignment to Korea. Wiseman predicted that duty in the United States or in Europe would be a sure thing if we used Malone's clout, but I was nervous about trying to use political influence. As an ROTC cadet, before going on regular duty, I had asked a Nevada military professor for his opinion, and he had told me that an "influence" label on one's military file could make him a potential target for any careerist who opposed influence unless it was used for him. I declined Wiseman's offer.

With graduation approaching, members of the class grew anxious. Not one new officer said, "Boy, would I love to be assigned to Korea!" Two weeks before finishing BIOC, we received our orders. Richard Wiseman, so certain that Senator Malone's power would work wonders, was already preparing for his requested assignment to Germany. He was stunned to learn that he was to spend the following nineteen months in Korea. My orders were for Fort Riley, Kansas. Marilyn and I would remain together through my army tour, and I would be present when our second child was born.

As for the final academic ranking of our 200-man class, the West Pointers were confident that academy graduates would take first, second, and third places. However, to the unrestrained glee of three-fourths of our class, a national guard officer led the academic parade. The first runner-up had gotten his commission through a university ROTC program. The academy barely averted a whitewash as a West Pointer finished third.

Our training done, it was time to vacate our interim home. As Marilyn, Royle, and I drove away, Marilyn began to cry.

"What's the matter?" I asked. "You've said for four months that you can't stand Columbus or Fort Benning or Georgia."

Marilyn replied, "Yes, but this community is now a part of our lives, and I'll never see it again."

Nevadan Gets A Break
Melton Will Be Big Red One's PIO

Fort Riley, KS For the following nineteen months, our home was eastern Kansas, near, and then at, Fort Riley, the famous old United States Army cavalry post. The First Infantry Division (Big Red One), America's most decorated military unit, had relocated there the previous year after occupation duty in Germany that had begun in 1945 when World War II ended. There had been much competition among cities to land the division, which had close to twenty thousand personnel and would create tremendous economic growth in any community. A spirited campaign, led by the Kansas congressional delegation and community leaders in eastern Kansas, had made the difference.

Upon arrival at Fort Riley we found a dramatic shortage of housing on the post, and neighboring Manhattan and Junction City could not accommodate the spillover army population. As the lowest form of army officer life (second lieutenant), I lacked the rank and the pull to secure us a home at Fort Riley proper. We were wait-listed for post housing, and in the interim were fortunate to locate a rental situation at the home of a family in Manhattan, eighteen miles northeast of Fort Riley. The family moved into its basement to make room for us.

I reported for duty and was assigned to the 29th Infantry Regiment of the First Division as a platoon leader of forty soldiers, mostly kids fresh from boot camp. I was blessed to have as my chief aide a veteran sergeant who supported me as I took my first wobbly steps in a position of leadership.

I had been cautioned never to jump the chain of command—such behavior could be the military kiss of death if you were caught. Nonetheless, I was anxious to try for a public information officer assignment. My chief aim was to prepare as best I could for a post-army newspaper career. So, without asking permission from my company or battalion commanders, I secured an appointment with the regimental leader, a full colonel.

Before I could ask my first question, the colonel asked me one of his own: "Have you cleared this visit within your unit?"

"No," I stammered.

"Well, why didn't you?"

"Well sir, I didn't know exactly what the procedure should be."

If a glare was a weapon, I would have been mortally wounded. "Well, since you're here anyway, what do you want of me?"

I was compromised, overmatched, and so scared that I almost wet my army pants. "Sir," I croaked, "I have been a newspaperman for several years, and I have my journalism degree . . . ."

He interrupted. "Don't dance me around your life story! What do you want?"

He wore a Combat Infantryman's Badge, earned through considerable fighting in World War II. I felt small in his presence and knew that I had violated military protocol, but I had to keep going. "Well, I am hoping, sir, that you will consider me, sir, for assignment to our regimental public information officer position, should it be open, sir."

The colonel looked horrified. "You mean leave your infantry leader job? The very opportunity we've been training you for? Not in a million years, lieutenant! That will be all." His angry face was red as a tomato.

"I understand, sir! Thank you, sir!" Away I dashed, certain that I would be cashiered out of the officer's ranks and spirited west to Fort Ord, California, to train with enlistees; but my company commander never mentioned my end run, though he had to have been told of it.

I quickly fell into the platoon-leader drill, resolving to do the best I could. I was certain that the rest of my army time would be spent as a platoon leader. Not that it was a bad job.... Yet, it seemed only right that I should visit the First Division information office, just to say hello and check things out and let them know of my background.

I went to the main post and climbed to the second floor of the native limestone building that had been built soon after 1853, when Fort Riley was established. The PIO office was a sprawling complex that filled the entire floor. Lieutenant Frank Manitzas greeted me. He was second in command, reporting to a Major Ahearn, a career officer with no media background. I told Manitzas of my hope for PIO experience and of my encounter with the colonel, and I sought his guidance in trying for a regimental information assignment at some point. He explained that there were four such positions in the First Division, and each man reported to the division PIO office. "There are no vacancies coming up," he said, "and there'll be nothing in our division office, because I am going to 're-up' for another three years."

That was that, except that Manitzas, a Texan with a drawl and a cordial manner, asked me about my background. I told him, emphasizing my hands-on newspaper experience. I told him that I was just twenty-four and had much to learn. Manitzas, who was twenty-six, said, "I understand. So do I."

I had almost given up my PIO aspirations, but not entirely. Not yet. Then fate intervened. The colonel who had chewed me out was reassigned, and we were told that his successor would be on the scene shortly. I thought I'd make a run up to regimental headquarters again to get a sense of who was whom.

I called and asked to meet with the interim commander. I said that I wanted to talk about a public information opportunity. The man on the other end of the line said that Major Etchemendy would talk to me. Major Etchemendy.... There were Basque people named Etchemendy back home in Nevada. I had met some when I played football against Douglas High School teams in the Carson Valley, where many Basques lived. An Etchemendy had refereed many of our Fallon games—that Etchemendy was built low to the ground and looked like a blocking back. Perhaps the major was related to Nevadans with the same surname.

As my appointment drew near, I decided to tell the major that I knew of several Etchemendys in my state. An enlisted man ushered me into the major's office. It couldn't be! The last time I had seen this major, he was wearing a whistle and a referee's uniform. I snapped a salute and said, "Sir, I am Lieutenant Melton."

"Where you from, Lieutenant Melton?"

I said Nevada. The major clapped me on the back and said, "From Fallon, right?"

I was close to fainting. "God, sir! I knew an Etchemendy at home who refereed our football and basketball games. Was that you, sir?"

The major laughed. "I'm Leon Etchemendy, born and raised in Nevada, and I remember you playing at Fallon for one of my closest friends, Wes Goodner. Sit and let's visit."

"It's great of you to give me an appointment, sir."

The major said, "Rollan, when there's just the two of us together, I'm 'Etch.'" He saw my wedding band and asked if my wife had joined me at Riley; he wanted to know if I had married a Nevadan.

"Yes, Marilyn Royle and I met at the University of Nevada. She was born in Reno."

Etch grinned. "Would she be the Marilyn Royle who attended Northside Junior High School?"

"Yes, yes. How do you know?"

The major explained that after World War II, he resumed his education, was hired in the Washoe County (Greater Reno) School District, and wound up at Northside School. Marilyn was one of hundreds of students he knew in the district, and especially at Northside. The major had been recalled by the army when the Korean War began in 1950.

At Etch's invitation, I explained my hope that I could land a regimental public information job. I told him of my visit with the departing 29th Infantry Regiment commander and how later I had introduced myself to Major Ahearn and Lieutenant Manitzas at the division PIO. Etch said carefully, "This is good to know. I hope things will fall into place for you. In the meantime, I hope you enjoy being an infantry platoon leader."

Shortly thereafter, Ruby and Leon Etchemendy had Marilyn and me to their Fort Riley home for dinner, a visit dominated by talk of Nevada sports, of Coach Goodner and his wife, Helen, and of the University of Nevada, where the major had been educated. The Etchemendys were two of the most cordial persons Marilyn and I had ever met, and we were immediately put at ease. They had three young children, and Ruby and Marilyn quickly got to the subject of Marilyn's pregnancy—it was February, and in another two months, we would be the parents of two. Neither the major nor I brought up the subject of public information, and I supposed nothing was percolating in that regard.

A few days later I was at a rifle range, overseeing training. An enlisted man walked up and said, "Sir, you're wanted immediately at the division public information office. You are to ask for Lieutenant Manitzas. The lieutenant has cleared this with your company commander, and I am here to drive you over."

En route to the division PIO office, my excitement grew. A regimental job must have come open—I would report directly to Lieutenant Manitzas. Lieutenant Manitzas got quickly to the point. "I told you a few weeks ago that there were no PIO jobs on the regimental level and that I'd be running our office for at least the next three years. Well, there still aren't any openings, but I've decided that I'll not be staying in the army. We need a successor. Lieutenant Melton, we've got some fine information officers reporting to us, but based on your earlier visit and your records, I have recommended to Major Ahearn that you be my successor." My jaw dropped. I started to answer, but he talked on. "Providing you'd like to take my job."

My God! The opportunity to move to division, take charge of the news and clerical staff of eighteen, and run the information machine of the army's famous Big Red One outfit was unbelievable. It was still another case of my tendency for being in the right place at the right time and for being the beneficiary of luck. "I accept! When do I start?"

The man I was succeeding smiled and said, "I'm practically out of here now. The division's commander and Major Ahearn want the transition to begin as soon as possible. Yesterday wouldn't be too soon. Today's Thursday. Major Ahearn wants you to take over by Monday."

Events were unfolding rapidly. "Well, I'll need to wrap up a number of things in my platoon."

Manitzas cut in. "That's all taken care of. Your company commander is freeing you immediately. This has all been cleared with Major Etchemendy you know him, do you not?" He gave me a knowing smile, as if to say, "You had the inside track because you knew someone who knew someone." I didn't respond, nor did I tell him the real bottom line. This was pure chance—a dream come true.

On Monday, Major Ahearn welcomed me to my new assignment. "We're impressed with your varied news experience, and we are especially pleased that you want, and believe you are qualified for, public information work." Lieutenant Manitzas briefed me on the mission of the office, and then he and the major walked me into the expansive newsroom. They called an impromptu staff meeting. Ahearn told everyone of Lieutenant Manitzas's decision to leave the army, and he introduced me as Manitzas's successor. Boom! Not an ounce of hesitation. It was the military way: train-plan-execute-perform.

I called Marilyn as soon as I could. "The division PIO?" she said. "That's wonderful—even better than what you were hoping for. Maybe this means we'll be able to move to quarters on the post."

I then hurriedly called Major Etchemendy and gushed my thanks. He disclaimed any credit and said, "Nevadans deserve an occasional break. You'll do great."

This was an opportunity to cherish. I fully realized for the first time what an asset breadth of experience in your chosen field can be in a competitive job market. My selection as division PIO also seemed to validate my efforts since high school to improve myself, expand my realm of experience, and develop friendships and relationships that could provide links to opportunities. It helps to let those who might have an impact on your life know that you are reaching for more responsibility and that you have properly prepared yourself to do the most with it.

PIO Takes Charge, Interviews Enlisted Killer
Wife Gives Birth

Fort Riley, KS I had eighteen months left before discharge, and I wanted to make the most of them. Fortunately, Lieutenant Manitzas had left me a fairly efficient operation. In a "small world" angle, I found that among the regimental PIOs reporting to me was my fraternity brother and fellow Nevada journalism graduate, Willard "Red" Esplin, who was career army and a reliable newsman.

Within the first week, I had interviewed each of the eighteen staff members. I learned something about each new colleague's life history and about his areas of responsibility and expertise. I also asked each what he had on his "wish list." Comments ranged from gripes about crotchety typewriters, to the need for additional dictionaries and an Associated Press stylebook for each writer, to requests for maps of the greater Fort Riley-Manhattan-Junction City area, and to other items that tied into standard news operation needs.

We sought to cover Fort Riley military news just as a full-time independent daily would have, except that as the publicity arm of the post, we would put a positive spin to news releases. Regimental information staffs funneled all their news copy and photographs through our division office. We did the final editing and transmitted news packets daily by mail to faraway newspapers, by wire to the *Kansas City Star*, and by daily personal deliveries to the *Junction City Union* and the *Manhattan Mercury*. Those area dailies made generous use of our news output. Many of their readers were military families, and the First Infantry Division's presence had a major impact on area commerce.

The management of the local papers had pushed hard to bring the Big Red One from Germany, especially the *Mercury*, which was owned by the Seaton family. Patriarch Fred Seaton was a member of the U.S. House of Representatives, and he had been especially effective in convincing federal decision-makers that Kansas should be the unit's new home.

Within three months of my joining the staff, Major Ahearn was shifted to a new assignment away from Fort Riley. His successor was Major John Swearingen, a career officer with a southern drawl, a charming demeanor, and a penchant for letting the military newshands do their work so long as they performed efficiently. Swearingen encouraged delegation, and he was quick to compliment when work was exceptional. He was just as quick to tell me if he was displeased.

I arrived at the office one morning unshaven for the first time in my military career. Major Swearingen said in his Southernspeak, "Rollan, is my eyesight going bad on me, or didn't you stand close enough to your razor this morning?" I offered no excuse, and he said, "Officers need to set a good example for the troops."

One of my chief functions was to serve as liaison between our staff and the staff of Fort Riley's commander, Major General Willis Mathews. The general's unswerving belief was that all First Infantry Division news should be good news. I was chief speechwriter for him, and I interviewed him several days before each formal speech to learn what he wanted to say and how he wanted to say it. During one such visit, he paused in mid-sentence to tell me sternly that my weight was not good news. (Despite the rigorous Fort Benning training program, my weight had ballooned to twenty pounds above the acceptable level.) General Mathews barked, "You're fat! Go on a diet. Now."

"Yes sir," I answered, silently noting that the general was himself carrying a "spare tire" and an extra chin.

I was able to reduce to an acceptable weight, but my troubles with General Mathews weren't over. When he asked Major Swearingen to arrange to have formal holiday color photos of the Mathews family made, the major passed the assignment on to me: "You take charge of this, Rollan, and don't screw things up."

I lined up a cameraman through the signal corps, went personally to the general's home on the post, and oversaw a delightful photo shoot. I ordered the photographer to make many extra exposures to cover our act. As we were leaving, the general told me that he wanted proofs of every picture taken, and as soon as possible.

The following morning, the photographer called me. "Sorry, lieutenant, but there has been a malfunction with the camera. None of the pictures turned out." I nearly croaked. In fact, I feared that the general would croak me. Major Swearingen, bless him, managed to blunt the division commander's wrath. We rescheduled the shoot, and I used a different photographer.

News in the army was not different from news in civilian life—it wasn't always happy. In the worst episode of my public information watch, a disgruntled enlisted man in my former First Infantry company brought his M-1 rifle to company headquarters and shot to death the unit's first sergeant. Our people went into action immediately, alerting the Associated Press, United Press International, the *Kansas City Star,* and the dailies at Junction City and Manhattan. We transmitted the details of the story, signal corps photos of the crime scene, and photos of victim and suspect.

The division's JAG (Judge Advocate General) lawyers advised against permitting civilian reporters to interview the suspect, but there was no prohibition against any of our staff doing an interview. I decided to interview him at the post stockade. My subsequent "follow-up" story to the wire services and general media focused largely on his upbringing and his military record.

My story led General Mathews to complain that we had given the media more than was necessary, but I countered, through Major Swearingen, that it was best to approach such a situation as if you were a staff member of the news media we served. Major Swearingen calmed the general down, and I heard no further complaints about this.

In addition to Leon Etchemendy and Red Esplin, there was another Nevadan attached to the Big Red One. Enlisted man Douglas Byington and I had played football against each other when he was at Sparks High School and I was at Fallon. We had become close friends on the Reno campus, where we were football and boxing teammates.

In April of 1956, when Marilyn was approaching full term, Byington offered to use some of his annual leave to baby-sit our son, Royle, when the time came to take Marilyn to the base hospital. On April 13, her labor pains began. We summoned Byington and sped the eighteen miles to the base hospital. Our second son arrived shortly before midnight. Ever since, we have called him our lucky Friday-the-thirteenth guy. Marilyn wanted to name him Lance. I said, "No. That sounds like he's a knight astride a charger. Let's name him Wayne." We did.

Shortly thereafter, post quarters became available for us in a World War II barracks building converted into four family apartments. In summertime our apartment was sweltering hot, and during the tornado season, we trembled in fear. The building was structurally weak, our apartment had no closets to take cover in, and there was no basement. Now hear this: No place to hide. Late in the summer of 1956, a tornado swept across the plains just half a mile from us, scarring the land and destroying buildings.

After the tornado season, we had the infamous Midwest winter to remind us of how moderate the weather is in northern Nevada. In a blizzard in early January of

1957, I was covering news of a training exercise when a soldier turned up missing. Search parties were organized, and troops linked arms and walked miles, searching for the missing GI. Ultimately he was found safe, warm, and well-fed back at the base. He had walked out to safety, and he wondered aloud to my staff interviewers what all the fuss was about.

Major Swearingen put me in charge of what he called the care, feeding, and stroking of visiting celebrities. There were many. Two of the most memorable were retired Major General Terry Allen, the great commander of the First Infantry Division during its World War II campaigns in North Africa and Europe; and Hal Boyle, a distinguished Associated Press writer and columnist who later would win a Pulitzer Prize. Boyle had been a war correspondent and a close friend of the revered Ernie Pyle in Europe.

Unlike many so-called celebrities I escorted around, both General Allen and Hal Boyle were loath to talk about themselves. Each was curious about our men and their equipment, and the land on which the post was located. Boyle had followed the Big Red One during its battles in Europe, and we were thrilled when he did a column for AP, drawing parallels between the contemporary First Infantry and the one he had covered in 1944-1945.

We were always eager to greet visitors who had served in both world wars with the Big Red One, and in 1956-1957 there were still many World War I veterans alive. As for World War II veterans, they occasionally held their unit reunions at Fort Riley. The war had ended only eleven years earlier, so those veterans were still relatively young.

(I did not then know that one of the great Big Red One heroes in the fierce European campaigns was Jack Streeter of Reno, whom I was to cover in many news stories in later years. Streeter was a captain in the First Infantry when he led his men onto Omaha Beach on D-Day, the first day of the invasion of France that was the beginning of the end for the Axis. Streeter was the most decorated Nevada soldier in the war, and he later served on the board of directors of the Big Red One alumni association.)

While I was off playing public information officer, Marilyn was doing hard duty, toiling as wife, mother, washerwoman, cook, and seamstress. We were able to put aside enough after the $100 monthly rent to buy her a sewing machine on time payments. (In the following decade, she would make all of our children's clothes and her own.)

Like so many other young army couples, we scraped by month-to-month. Marilyn came up with many creative ways to prepare (and disguise) hamburger. Eating out was a rare treat. Occasionally we would sneak our Nevada classmate, Private Doug Byington, into the officer's club for dinner.

Coach Makes Mistakes but Learns From Them
Home Means Nevada

Fort Riley, KS In the autumn of 1956, I was given an unexpected assignment. Unbeknownst to me, the First Division command staff had been perusing personnel files, shopping for someone to coach the Big Red One's football team. A full colonel asked Major Swearingen if he would permit me to accept the head coaching job if

"Like so many other young army couples, we scraped by month-to-month." Rollan and Marilyn with Wayne (l.) and Royle at Fort Riley, 1957.

it were offered. Of course, Swearingen, knowing that General Mathews was behind what was afoot, said that would be all right. The subsequent invitation both stunned and flattered me. I had no coaching experience, but surely I could rustle up some assistant coaches who could help me out.

I had missed the camaraderie and combat of football, and I felt that coaching would give me leadership experience beyond what I was getting in the public information office. The division's top brass offered to relieve me of my information officer duties until the football season was over, but to Major Swearingen's relief, I preferred handling both positions simultaneously. I continued my daily PIO work until 3:00 each afternoon, and then left for football practice.

Unfortunately, my coaching stint was an unmitigated disaster. I made so many mistakes! I functioned like a twenty-five-year-old coach with a nine-year-old's brain. But I had a great learning experience in how to survive management quicksand.

I decided to be a player-coach, although I was in terrible shape. We had no physical training program, and I had been parked at a desk job for eight months. Although I was given the opportunity to put together a squad of forty-four players, I held the number to thirty-three to "save training costs." A real dumb move. After all, these guys were paid by the army whether they were playing soldier or playing football.

We were competing in an eight-team military league. We won the opening game by a touchdown, but a number of our guys suffered injuries. "Holy Toledo, there's still eleven games to play," I worried. After the fourth game, we had guys who were banged

"I decided to be a player-coach."

up so bad that they should have been in traction.

In my eight playing seasons in high school and college, I had paid strict attention to what *my* role was and never worried about my teammates' responsibilities and health. Now, as coach, I needed to know the whole package—defense, offense, strategies, scouting, motivating players. Football is as much mental as physical, and sound team chemistry and controlled group emotion can win games when nothing else works.

As people were injured or dogged it or quit outright, we needed reinforcements, but they were limited because I hadn't foreseen that reserve strength is essential. (Later in life, when management opportunity came my way, I would use the experience gained from my coaching mistakes to minimize newspaper mistakes. The players could be broken into two types: those who followed me and those who didn't. The chief management task in later "real life" would be to determine how to motivate non-followers or remove them; how to reward achievers without playing favorites; how to prepare reserves to take over.)

As our losses multiplied, tension began to mount on the squad. I overheard grumbling from the team about "Coach's mistakes." I also endured second-guessing by the bird colonel who had first offered me the "opportunity" to coach. He would call me, suggesting sitting one guy and using another. It read like a horror movie script, but this was non-fiction and sometimes comical. I concluded that the brass wouldn't give me a court-martial for ignoring their golden advice, so my assistants and I kept making the decisions that we felt were best. We won three games, lost eight, and tied one.

Our most glorious afternoon came against a sadly overmatched federal prison team at Fort Leavenworth, Kansas. We won by fifty-five points, and we were feeling and acting like big shots that night in downtown Leavenworth.

I asked players and coaching assistants to return from their dinner to our military bus by 8:00 to begin the ride home to Fort Riley. I was the first to step aboard, and there were just a few of us on the bus when a fistfight erupted out on the sidewalk. I scrambled out and saw that one of my players was in a battle with a stranger. Forgetting Nevada boxing coach Jimmie Olivas's advice from years earlier, "Beware of the sucker punch," I bravely rushed in to break up the combatants.

The civilian hit me flush in the face, and I went down like a rock. As I struggled up, he hit me again. By then, my returning players had begun to arrive at the scene. The other guy seemed to pick up allies, too, and for awhile it appeared that there would be a riot in downtown Leavenworth. I was still weaving around, trying to clear the cobwebs and sort out what had happened, when the city police swarmed in.

As the police established order, my players gathered around me to ask, "Are you all right, Lieutenant?" When the "civilian" overheard that, he dashed to my side to offer an apology. As it turned out, he was a Fort Leavenworth enlisted man wearing civilian clothes. Assault on an officer by an enlisted man is a serious offense, and he figured he was a candidate for the army stockade.

By this juncture, the military police also were present, and they asked if I intended to press charges. "No way," I quickly said. "We just want to get out of here and go home."

Relieved of the prospect of doing heavy paperwork, the police vanished, and so did the guy who had dropped the Sunday punch on me. The bus headed to Fort Riley. I was going home to Marilyn to explain my swollen jaw.

One of the lessons I learned in coaching the team that season was that it is not wise to be a player-coach. Perspective is lost when the leader is in the midst of the battle. I played only in our opening game, then focused exclusively on being the coach. It was a good decision . . . not that we won any more games because of it. It taught me early that the strong leader lets others do the heavy lifting. That's why the others are there. That's what they want.

When the football season ended, I was an army short-timer, only needing to cover a six-week field training operation in Louisiana before my discharge. Major Swearingen got me aside before I left for Louisiana and asked if I wished to remain in the army. "If so, I will help you try for Regular Army status," he said.

I said, "Thanks, but I want to go back to newspapering."

In Louisiana's huge, remote Fort Polk military reservation, thousands of peacetime Big Red One soldiers waged war against a "hostile" force. I wrote the daily lead stories for transmission back to Fort Riley, and my enlisted aide, Corporal Thomas R. Ward, and I stole away occasionally to Lake Charles to seek out retired First Infantry Division combat veterans for interviews.

(Tom Ward was an intellectual, a Williams College English honors graduate who later was chief speechwriter for the chairman of the Kodak Corporation in his hometown of Rochester, New York. My chief contribution to Ward's career was that early on I forced him to learn touch-typing, just as Ken Ingram had done for me in my high school senior year.)

I never tired of learning of individual combat histories, and Ward and I always kept up the hunt for First Division alumni who had distinguished themselves in battle. In the aggregate, the individual soldiers' stories were an important part of the continuing compilation of Big Red One history.

Home means Nevada. Early one day near the end of the Louisiana maneuvers, I was in a Jeep driving down a dirt road in a remote area of the Fort Polk military reservation. The terrain was swampy. We scooted up a small hill and around a hairpin turn, and through the early morning mist I saw a roadside sign. I let out a joyful yelp that alarmed my driver. He asked, "Are you all right, Lieutenant?"

I beamed. "Nothing could be finer," I said. The sign's message was a familiar one: HAROLDS CLUB OR BUST! It was the signature of Reno's historic gaming club, then the most famous casino in the world.

"What is it, sir?" the driver asked.

"Stop here while I take a look," I said. I didn't have a camera. Into my mind came memories of the Smith family, who had paid my way through college and done so much to open the gate to opportunity. We paused while I reflected on how blessed I was. As we drove away from the famous slogan, I was more anxious than ever to put the army behind and return to what I now considered to be my native state.

Veteran Finds Work In Reno

Fort Riley, KS When we were reunited at Fort Riley, Marilyn and I had serious talks about what our options would be following my discharge. One appeared to be to take a job at Wayne,

Nebraska. Several weeklies were published there by the family of one of my regimental PIOs, James Kramer. When I neared the end of my hitch in the army, he drove me to his little town, let me tour the newspaper plant and the community, and then offered me the opportunity to work some one hundred hours a week as editor of the family's cluster of weeklies for compensation of ninety dollars a week. I wasn't intimidated by the prospect of long workweeks, but our family of four couldn't manage on that salary, so I declined the offer.

I had to arrange some kind of post-army employment, and I treasured my years in Fallon and my newspaper experiences there, so I wrote my former boss, Claude H. Smith at the *Standard*, and asked if he would hire me. Mr. Smith replied promptly. In his letter, he told me that the *Standard* had no openings; that he didn't expect any; and that furthermore, he felt that there was greater opportunity for me in the daily newspaper field. I was disappointed, but Marilyn felt that Mr. Smith was right. Besides, she preferred the city over rural life.

Along with his letter, Mr. Smith enclosed a "To Whom it May Concern" letter of recommendation in which he said, "There are few whom I have had occasion to recommend so highly." His glowing endorsement was unsolicited, and it pumped my feeling of worth.

So, Fallon was out. Soon we would leave the military, and we had hoped to have a job lined up before my discharge. I remembered *Nevada State Journal* editor Joe McDonald Sr.'s job offer of two years earlier and his stated interest in me should the newspaper have an opening after my discharge. We had subscribed by mail to the *Journal* throughout my two-year hitch, and I knew from reading it that McDonald had retired.

McDonald's successor was Charles H. Stout, who had been an executive with the corporate office of Speidel Newspapers. Speidel was the owner of eight dailies, including the *Journal* and the *Reno Evening Gazette*. (Up to then, my only knowledge of any company called Speidel was of the one that made watch bands.) If I couldn't get hired in Reno, I figured I might try to sign up with one of Speidel's other newspapers.

Meanwhile, my viable options were few. Ty Cobb earlier had praised my sportswriting, so I called him to inquire about sports openings. He had none. His was a two-man department—himself and his able assistant, Len Crocker. "Sorry, but we won't be adding a third person," he said.

Cobb wondered if I would be interested in a beat reporter job, and I said I would, so he referred me to *Journal* executive editor Paul A. Leonard. I had met Leonard when I was a student intern with the Reno dailies. I called the friendly Nevada journalism graduate, who also had been a star mile runner at the university. He was supportive. However, while he said that he knew and liked my work, the *Journal* had a full complement in the newsroom and hadn't budgeted any new hires. Leonard promised to mention my interest to his *Gazette* counterpart, editor John Sanford.

A short while later, good fortune again came my way. A former classmate of mine, William W. Eaton, by then the police reporter of the *Gazette*, phoned me to report that the *Gazette*'s editorial executives, Sanford and Joseph R. Jackson, wanted to find a new sports editor. I was excited and said I would follow up.

THE FALLON STANDARD
Nevada's Foremost Weekly Newspaper

COMMERCIAL PRINTING • LITHOGRAPHING • OFFICE SUPPLIES

CLAUDE H. SMITH, MANAGER

PHONE HARRISON 3-4022

FALLON, NEVADA

June 5, 1957

To Any Fellow Publisher or Editor,

    I am glad to be able to recommend Mr. Rollan Melton for any opening you may have in the news room. He has written me that he expects to leave military service soon and re-enter newspaper work.

    While attending high school here Mr. Melton was employed in our mechanical department where he made rapid progress in various printing operations.

    During his senior year he earned a scholarship in the University of Nevada where he studied journalism. While a student there he handled sport news for the Nevada State Journal and wrote for other publications.

    On occasional assignments for us he turned in excellent copy. Since then he has been doing journalsm work in the Army.

    Melton is ambitious. He is a young man of character, honest in every respect. I am sure he will prove faithful, loyal and industrious.

    There are but few whom I have had occasion to recommend so highly.

Fraternally

Claude H. Smith for
THE FALLON STANDARD

"Along with his letter, Mr. Smith had enclosed a "To Whom it May Concern" letter of recommendation...."

Eaton was fiery. Though we were contemporaries, he had already penetrated what he sarcastically called " the *Gazette* management inner sanctum." He told me, "What *they* are thinking, Rollan, is that they'll get you in here for a short time on general assignment, and then they'll pull the plug on the current sports guy and let you have at it." Eaton grimaced as he said "they," as if to imply that they were the enemy.

I phoned Jackson, my supervisor when I had interned for academic credit three years earlier. Now, the longtime managing editor was saying, "We've got an opening for a general assignment reporter. Something in sports may open later, but the reporter job is yours if you're interested."

This was the break I had hoped for. I excitedly accepted. I told him, "That's great, sir. I'm getting out of the army in about the third week of July. It will take me a few days to drive home. After that, I can come to work anytime you say, sir."

Jackson suggested the third week of July as my starting time. "Mr. Jackson," I said, "I can't thank you enough, sir. I'll do my best."

Jackson had been a naval officer during World War II. He said, "Around here, you don't call any of us 'sir.' Another thing, Rollan, is that my father was 'Mr. Jackson.' My name is Joe."

I asked about starting pay, and Jackson said, "We'll talk about that with the guild, and visit with you about that when you arrive here."

I told him that whatever the *Gazette* felt was fair was fine with me. (I had heard of the American Newspaper Guild, but didn't know anything about it. Before long, I was to find out more the hard way.)

Marilyn was beside herself to learn that I had at last found civilian work. We were confident that we would disprove the "You can't go home again" theory. Our new beginning was to be in the city and state we loved. We had had things good up to then, but the best was yet ahead.

Striking Opportunities

Publishers Killed in Auto Accident

Fallon, NV Marilyn, Royle, and Wayne flew to Reno shortly before my discharge so that Marilyn could be matron of honor at the wedding of her sister, Patricia, to Ronald Rose, a career army artillery officer. I stayed behind to ship our belongings home and close out our barracks apartment. I then drove west.

For nearly two years we had lived as unsettled flatlanders, ever yearning for the towering mountains of home. Now I cruised back into Nevada, loving what, as a boy, I had had the audacity to call its lunar landscape. Towering along my route through Ely, Eureka, Austin, and thence into Fallon, the oasis of my youth, were muscular and majestic mountains, draped in summer's foliage. What loveliness! How good to be home!

I reached Fallon, but Mother no longer lived there, having moved during my army years to Stockton, California. My sister Bronna had married and moved to Phoenix, Arizona. So my remaining "family" in Fallon was my newspaper family. They welcomed me as a sort of young, rising newspaper son. Greeting me were Ken Ingram, his wife, Carol, and Carol's parents, Ethel and Claude Smith, owners of the *Standard*. (They were my first and most significant bosses, my newspaper godparents, and I always called them Mrs. Smith and Mr. Smith.)

Mr. Smith apologized for not hiring me, but he justified the decision: "You are joining a fine newspaper, Rollan. Your chances of going places are greater than with us." I drove on to Reno to join the *Gazette* the following morning, cheered by their well-wishes.

Twenty-seven days later, my journalism godparents were dead. On Sunday, August 18, 1957, Ken Ingram called late in the afternoon to tell me that Ethel and Claude Smith had perished that morning in a vehicle accident in Churchill County, thirteen miles from their home. It had been customary for the couple to take a Sunday morning drive after church. Frequently, one or more of their three grandchildren were with them, but this Sunday they were by themselves. They had stopped along Highway 50, near Lahontan Reservoir, to aid a stranded motorist. Ethel and Claude stepped out of their car and were struck by another vehicle.

Nevada journalism had lost two dear colleagues, and Fallon and Churchill County two beloved and respected citizens. No one's loss was greater than Ken Ingram's. In a tragic moment he had lost his cherished employers, his beloved in-laws, and the grandparents of his children. Ingram nonetheless cleared his head. There is an axiom among newspaper people: You must get the paper published, any calamity be damned.

Ingram told me, "Rollan, we need you to come to Fallon and help us get the *Standard* out by Tuesday night.".

"Of course," I said, "I'll be there early tomorrow and stay as long as necessary."

Mr. Smith had said often that "every step is a new beginning," and this tragedy triggered a new start for me. Joe Jackson assigned a colleague to cover my *Gazette* absence, and I was at the *Standard* by dawn the next day.

Ingram had been on the phone calling for volunteer recruits, and everyone said they'd be there to help. They were. As shaken as he was, Ingram took charge, but he was in no condition to write. That would the responsibility of the impromptu team he had hastily summoned. He had me write the lead story, telling of the deaths, digging out accident facts, assembling the Smiths' biographies, and advising of funeral arrangements. I was armed with what Mr. Smith and Ken Ingram had drilled into me while I was a teenager at the *Standard*: "Get the facts, and then report who, what, why, when, where, and how."

One of the state's top newspapermen, Pete Kelley of the *Nevada Appeal*, had a significant role in putting out that first issue without the Smiths. So did Bob Sanford, who had been a printing apprentice under the couple, then their longtime competitor at the *Fallon Eagle*, and, at the time of their deaths, the manager and co-publisher of the *Mason Valley News* at Yerington. From the *Mineral County Independent-News* at Hawthorne came newsman James Pyatt. Muriel Smiley Kent and longtime *Standard* rural correspondent Marguerite Lima were in the ranks of helpers, and so were Emily Bowers and her son Don of the *Fallon Eagle*, the *Standard*'s hot rival under any other circumstances.

Ingram gave us our charge: "Do what you will on the story of this community's great loss, but let's also remember what Ethel and Claude would require—a newspaper issue that gives total news coverage of what's happened in the whole town during the past week." By Tuesday we had cobbled together a strong news package that also featured reaction to the deaths by two of Nevada's leading rural country news publishers, Jock Taylor, publisher of the *Austin-Reese River Reveille*, who that year was president of the Nevada State Press Association, and Paul Gardner, owner and publisher of the *Lovelock Review-Miner*. Gardner eloquently memorialized his lost friends: "Claude and Ethel Smith's last deed was characteristic of their lives: They were killed while helping someone else."

Much of the news appearing in the August 21 issue reporting Ethel and Claude's deaths had been written by them the previous week, on the day before the accident, but Mr. Smith had always maintained that you can't get out a good newspaper alone. For the next several weeks, I was home in Fallon, helping to get out a good newspaper.

Gazette Staff Welcomes New Recruit

Reno, NV The first issue of the *Reno Gazette* was published March 28, 1876, during the presidency of Ulysses S. Grant. Three months later, General George Armstrong Custer left his Fort Riley command in the Kansas Territory, dispatched to the state of Montana to extinguish Indian uprisings. At Little Big Horn, he and his entire cavalry unit were defeated and killed by the Dakota and Cheyenne. The *Gazette* devoted two paragraphs to the story.

More than eight hundred newspapers had been born and died in the state by the time I became the latest of the thousands who had worked at the *Gazette*. My first work day was Monday, July 22, 1957, two days before my twenty-sixth birthday.

Gazette news managers and the local chapter of the American Newspaper Guild had agreed that I should be credited with only two years of experience rather than the four that I had hoped for, and my weekly salary was set at one hundred dollars, or ten dollars more than I had been offered a few weeks earlier in Nebraska. After taxes and deductions, I would net seventy-three dollars weekly.

There was still our first home to find and to buy, but it appeared that the *Gazette* pay would be enough to squeak by on. Besides, Bill Eaton assured me, "If you do good, the guild will push *them* to give you more. A lot more."

I had gone from command of an eighteen-person news staff in the nation's best-known army infantry division to the *Gazette*, then Nevada's largest daily, where I was responsible only for myself. I was the most junior member of the news staff on the second floor of the rickety old Gazette Building on Center Street. Managing editor Jackson made me the general assignment reporter. I would be given any breaking news that Jackson or his chief assistant, city editor Bryn Armstrong, felt they could trust me to handle. I was also given any flunky work my older colleagues didn't care to bother with. I was the new kid reporter, and it was obvious that I would be watched like bacteria in a petri dish.

Jackson gave me my first major task: Look into alcoholism in the community and report on what, if anything, was being done about it. On this subject I had an inside track, having been raised by a family who had imperiled themselves by drinking too much. I worked up a four-part series that prominently featured Alcoholics Anonymous, which had done a fabulous rehabilitation of my father. (And would later help my mother and sister.)

In Jackson's judgment, my series was just OK, but coming from an editor who gave few reassuring compliments, this was tantamount to high praise. Senior staffers joked that you could write a Pulitzer Prize gem, and Jackson would reward you by proclaiming, "Well, this isn't all that bad."

My general assignment tour at the *Gazette* was brief but rewarding. At times, I tagged along with seasoned reporters on their news beats. Like a rookie waiter shadowing an experienced server, I was absorbing how to better serve up well-done stories to a news-hungry public. An aggressive city hall newsman, William Gold, took me around to municipal government offices, explaining that to the working reporter the most helpful information sources were often clerks, secretaries, and even janitors, rather than city bureaucrats. "The elected dogs want things left out. The low-paid stiffs who actually do the work know best how flawed city government is," he said.

Easygoing, blunt-talking Ed Slingland's news beat was Sparks. One evening I was with him when the council denied us access to a public meeting. I launched into my practiced "freedom of the press" yelp, an imitation of what we had heard Professor Al Higginbotham preach during our campus years.

"We can roast them for this in print," I said, but Slingland cooled me down. "First we get the story," he said. "The best way to assure freedom is to develop many sources. No matter how hard some try to hide the news, there's always an insider who will leak to you if he trusts you to keep the confidence." After the meeting ended, Slingland worked his insider pipelines, and he printed a full disclosure the next day on what had occurred behind closed council doors.

Lloyd "Punchy" Rogers was a seasoned, all-purpose reporter and gifted writer. Walter MacKenzie, who as an undergraduate had narrowly lost his race for a seat on the University of Nevada Board of Regents, was the *Gazette*'s man at the Washoe courthouse beat, and he was working diligently to cultivate his most promising news source, William Raggio, the new district attorney. William Friel had grown up in the historic mining town of Tonopah, and his rural roots helped him plug into sources around Nevada. He earlier had been an effective one-man *Gazette* sports department.

Bill Eaton was a mature air force veteran turned news sleuth who was skilled at penetrating police secrecy, especially when the cops were covering up the misdeeds of law enforcers. He would march into the offices of the police, highway patrol, or sheriff's departments, declaring, "I'm Eaton, and I'm here for news." Or, "This is Bill Eaton, boy reporter. What dirt have you got for me today?"

On my first day aboard the Good Ship *Gazette*, Eaton suggested that I join the Reno unit of the American Newspaper Guild. "Everyone in the *Gazette* newsroom is in it," he said. "None of the *Journal*'s people are members, proving how stupid those dummies down the hall are. It costs just five bucks a month in dues. In turn, when things come up to talk to management about, you won't have to take it up with the bosses. The guild will do it." I didn't want to be the only non-joiner in our newsroom. Besides, the guild sounded like a very agreeable thing. I could hardly wait to sign up.

Accidental Journalist Becomes Sports Editor
Melton Scoops Cobb

Reno, NV "*Gazette* sports department" had an impressive ring to it, as if it were a high-powered collection of newsmen, working hard to bring readers all the sports news that was fit to print. In truth, the *Gazette* sports department was one cluttered desk on the perimeter of our cramped newsroom. The department had always been a one-man operation, with such eventual heavyweights as Friel, Joe Jackson, and Carl Digino occupying the desk at one time or another.

When I came aboard, the sports desk was manned by George Umbenhaur, an agreeable chap who had only one glaring handicap—he knew nothing about sports. He was out of his element and unhappy in that department. The guys down the hall with the *Journal* were beating him to the news every day. I had been with the *Gazette* six weeks when editors Sanford and Jackson called me in to an office, banged the door shut, and said that they had given the relieved Umbenhaur a new newsroom assignment. The sports editor role was mine if I wanted it. Did I ever!

Melton, the accidental journalist, swiftly accepted the offer. It was my dream come true, and it was something I had wanted since first pecking out primitive sports stories at Fallon High School. I relished the prospect of visiting all the coaches and athletes—anyone remotely connected with sports—and writing about subjects with which I was familiar.

I also savored the chance to compete with the *Journal*. Two guys against one gave me a perfect opportunity to show that an underdog might cause more than accidental pain to the pesky rivals down the hall. I had long been in awe of my sports-writing mentor, Ty Cobb, and I respected his assistant, Len

"The sports editor role was mine if I wanted it. Did I ever!"

Crocker. Yet, the prospect of occasionally beating them to the news punch excited me.

The *Gazette* ran a brief story reporting my assignment. Well-wishers called or wrote. Sports people pledged their support. My high school coach, Wes Goodner, drove in from Fallon to congratulate me.

For years, John Sanford had witnessed sports figures come by the office to stroke new sports editors. He visited me at my desk a couple of weeks after I accepted the job and admitted that coaches and readers approved of the change in *Gazette* sports leadership. Then he poked his corrugated face close to mine and growled, "Don't get too settled in and think you're going to make a career out of this. Our sports guys never spend their lives on this beat. Remember this also: people may want you to think that it's you they need, but it's not you—it's what you can do for them."

Sanford's contempt for sports was undisguised, and he typically tacked the label "perennial sophomore" on anyone who had a difficult time forgetting his athletic past. But Joe Jackson got me aside and said, "Don't worry about John's disdain for sports. He is more aware than he lets on that it is important to cover them."

Marilyn and I had found a three-bedroom tract home for $15,500, and we were congratulating ourselves. "Just think, in twenty years we'll own this outright." Meanwhile, I was loving the excitement of covering sports. I was absorbed in journalism to the exclusion of all else except Marilyn and our sons.

Being a one-man department was akin to owning my own newspaper and being solely responsible for what was right and wrong. All local sports copy was written by me. Page layout was among my jobs, as were writing, editing, writing headlines, and learning to manage sports copy flow—the systematic, timely sending of my local news stories and Associated Press wire copy to our composing room by pneumatic tubes. Copy flow had to be on a fixed schedule by all news departments so that the printers wouldn't be handcuffed by a glut of last-minute text, headlines, and photographs.

I also enjoyed working with printers. After all, I had been one during my years at the *Fallon Standard*. The sights and sounds of the operation were intoxicating—our temperamental press, with its wheezes, groans, and squeaks. Molten lead poured into Linotype machines manned by practiced compositor-artisans, and a platoon of printers, their aprons scarred with layers of ink, hunched over page chases, filling them with ads and news. Every man and woman had specific tasks, and the urgency of their duties and the importance of getting it right contributed to the drama of each newspaper day.

I had my hands full presenting a sports section to the public each day. Actually, "section" is an inaccurate description. I was given scant space to tell my readers all that was going on in sports, near and afar.

Space for sports coverage was scarce because straight local news was given first priority, and that meant devoting more space to it. I whined that "the *Journal* gets the big breaks on sports and reports the whole story. It isn't right." My bleating didn't dent management's set mind. Jackson cooled me off: "Everyone worth his salt wants more news space. No one gets all they want." So I did the best that could be done with the news hole allotted me—I reinstituted a column called "Nevada Sports," which my predecessor had let drop. Into it, some three times a week, I loaded tightly-written items about people and events.

The *Journal* had the jump on late afternoon and nighttime sports results, so I increasingly put a features spin on our local stories. The cast of characters and events had changed in the two years I had been away in the army. Thus, it was imperative during much of my first sports year to learn who the new newsmakers were and to convince them to give me breaks on stories that formerly went first to the *Journal*.

Ty Cobb's stranglehold on sports news sources had been in place since 1937, when he joined the *Journal* straight off the Nevada campus. I was to encounter no more professional or more honorable competitor than he in my career. It was rare that I could beat the Cobb-Crocker tandem. The real fun was in trying.

Cobb's greatest loves were boxing and baseball, and so I relished attacking those areas that once had been his province alone. Slowly, I earned the confidence of Reno professional boxing promoters Buddy Traynor and Johnny Russo, and they took pity on me, tossing me an occasional news bone.

My largest boxing-news breakthrough occurred in 1958, when world light-heavyweight boxing champion Archie Moore set up a training camp in Carson City, tuning up for a ten-round non-title fight in Reno with local favorite Howard King. I got a tip that the colorful Moore was coming to town on a certain day. He would be at John Petrinovich's popular Grand Cafe, a favorite dining and drinking hangout for people addicted to sports, and especially to boxing. I

Rollan Melton Sr. with boxing champ Archie Moore in 1958. (Photograph by Dondero.)

met the champion there, did the first of many interviews I would have with him, and followed up the next day with a straight news story complemented by a personalized column about the famous ring warrior.

I had scored a rare beat on Ty Cobb, but he seemed oblivious. A scoop by a punk sports-writing pretender appeared pathetic when compared with the volume of Ty Cobb's comprehensive sports reporting.

Cobb's easy way with his column, "Inside Stuff," had influenced me for years. I had unlimited respect for him. He could briefly pout when beaten on a story, but he was a grand man, truly the "dean of Nevada sportswriters," an honorary title that both pleased and embarrassed him. "I could never be dean of anything," he protested.

Ty Cobb was the driving force in creating the Sierra Nevada Sportswriters and Broadcasters Association, which brought competing print and radio and television reporters together in Reno for the first time. Sports coverage improved as a result of our weekly meetings, which featured reports on coaches, managers, and athletes. The competing news mediums also came to appreciate each other's challenges and to learn from each other's experiences.

Reno Alive With Sports Celebrities

Reno, NV During my studies at the university, I had been deaf to suggestions that I take speech classes. In fact, no one had needed help in public speaking more than I did. In the army I was fairly relaxed when speaking to small groups if they were comprised of people I knew, meaning my news colleagues and the athletes we covered, but returning to civilian life, I was afraid to speak in public. Invitations to address sports banquets or graduations were politely turned away.

After I was elected the vice-president of Sierra Sportswriters in 1959, I prayed that the presiding officer would always show up at the meetings. Once he didn't, and I had to chair the meeting. I was tongue-tied and made a fool of myself, stuttering, stammering, and yearning for the meeting to be over. But I rationalized that so long as I stuck strictly to sports during my career, there would be no need to be a polished speaker. Ty Cobb, who was an excellent toastmaster, suggested that there might come a day when I would find speaking ability more important than it then seemed.

Fortunately, interviewing and informal conversations didn't give me the jitters. Nor did talking to celebrity athletes; and there were many chances to speak with famous sports figures, because Reno was then alive with them. Many came to participate in the Holiday Hotel's "Mug Hunt" golf tournaments, staged annually by general manager Newton Crumley. Crumley was a master at bringing prominent sports figures together with Nevada writers and broadcasters. At one time or another his guests included Dizzy Dean, Lefty Gomez, Joe DiMaggio, Jackie Jensen, Rocky Marciano, "Crazy Legs" Hirsch, and Duke Snider.

Retired superstars of sport also visited Reno. I once had a fascinating interview in a Holiday Hotel suite with sensational boxing champion Henry Armstrong, who had defended his welterweight title five times in 1939, including two defenses in five days that October. I brought along a camera loaned to me by my photographer friend, Don Dondero. As I fumbled to solve the mechanical mysteries of the Rolleiflex camera, Armstrong said, "Wait a minute, son. Let me show you how this is done." He did.

An encounter with Johnny Weissmuller, my favorite movie star in my adolescent years, was the most memorable (and saddest) brush with a famous athlete in my *Gazette* sports career. When I was a lad in Boise, I had worshipped the Olympic swimming champion turned box-office star. (He was "Tarzan.") I had hoped to meet him one day, but felt that I would never get closer to him than a seat at a movie theater.

In 1959, Weissmuller came to Reno to join other celebrities at a sports banquet for athletes and members of the media, arranged by Newton Crumley. I maneuvered myself into a seat at the dinner table next to him. He had retired several years earlier from making movies, and he was, by this time, the shill for a Los Angeles company that sold portable swimming pools.

The celluloid star I had adored in the early 1940s and the man whom I met at the Holiday were totally dissimilar. In the movies, Tarzan was King of the Jungle, fearing no man or beast. He was kind to others and spoke few words. In person, the 1959 Weissmuller was overweight, a stumbling boor, and rude to his dinner companions; and before our very eyes he got so drunk that several of us asked the hotel for assistance to escort him safely to his room.

So it also went with a few other personalities that I met in that era, but most were well behaved. Baseball star Jackie Jensen, for instance, was a classy gentleman who volunteered his time to help young people. He retired to Reno and became the baseball coach at the University of Nevada.

Reno was always noteworthy as a haven for characters. The city of the late 1950s had plenty of them in its local sports community:

Coach Jake Lawlor was quick to intimidate referees and needle any of his athletes who performed below his expectations, but his Irish disposition cooled after games or practice, and he was the epitome of thoughtful kindness. Wolf Pack boxing coach Jimmie Olivas had a notorious inability to get people's names right: Bill Griggs was "Riggs;" Sam Macias's name dribbled out as "Samuel Mercer."

In Elko late one night, a group of us were standing on a street corner following a University of Nevada match against Idaho State College. A woman spotted Olivas and rushed over and embraced him. She inquired about his wife, Mary, and exclaimed how thrilled she had been to stand up for Olivas and his wife when they were married. He greeted her respectfully, nodding agreement. She walked away, and Olivas whispered, "What was her name?"

The Reno journalists of the era were no less colorful than the newsmakers we covered. The public couldn't believe reports of how competitive the *Journal* and *Gazette* staffs were or how vindictive the sniping and insults could be. Each side took joy in unearthing the other's misstatements, poor grammar, or slips in common sense. Merriment erupted in the *Gazette* newsroom the morning that we read *Journal* city editor Frank Johnson's bylined story that "the victim had died as a result of the autopsy." Alas, poor Johnson was left coming off as an imbecile because of a dropped line of type.

Competition was also fierce in another part of the Gazette Building. The major news services, United Press International and Associated Press, had news offices there, and their staff members relentlessly sought to be first to release news. AP bureau chief Edward Olson and his assistant, Paul Finch, were matched against Bob Bennyhoff, an aggressive UPI chief, and his colleague Clark Bigler, a star reporter.

One of the toughest competitors, and one who was customarily ahead of the wire services and Reno newspaper writers on divorce news, was William Berry. He was the most prominent area ski writer, but he also was a relentless pursuer of ladies who had come to Reno for divorces. The messier the divorce, the better for Berry, whose newspaper clients included New York's sensation-mongering *Daily News* and *Post*. Berry also was a correspondent for London's *Mirror* and *Daily Telegraph*.

So immersed had I become in the huge fun of sportswriting and trying to outwit the down-the-hall opposition that I was shamefully out of communication with my own family. One afternoon editor Sanford confronted me, tittering and waving a handwritten letter in my face. "Here," he blurted, "this came addressed to 'Editor, Gazette, Reno, Nevada.' You better read it."

The writer had scrawled sentences on white, lined paper, and the handwriting looked familiar. I began to read from it, but could barely finish for laughing so hard. The letter said, "Dear Editor: I have a son who reportedly is living in your town. We heard that he may be a sportswriter with your newspaper. Is this true? Or is it a false rumor? Mr. Editor, if you happen to know such a sportswriter or know of him, please ask him to write to his concerned father." The writer signed his name and city of residence—Rollan Melton Sr., Boise, Idaho.

In those days I didn't dream that I would ever be anything but a sports reporter and columnist. It was such a fun way of earning the family's keep! I was at the heart of the action, but I hoped that the day soon would arrive when I would have more news space and a writing assistant, luxuries Ty Cobb had earned over the years.

By the end of my second year with the *Gazette*, I had learned to absorb the bad with the good. I was often criticized, especially when a coach or a parent felt that his team or son or daughter had been bad-rapped in a story I had written. I came to learn that writing for a newspaper isn't for sissies, and that you must have a thick hide if you are to remain in a profession in which you touch the lives of so many people, some of whom are quick to criticize.

Guild Threatens Strike

Reno, NV Not all news broke outside the Gazette Building adjacent to the old brick city hall on Center Street. For instance, our editor fired city hall reporter Bill Gold for stealing private documents from Mayor Francis "Tank" Smith's office. Gold had fished them from under Smith's door with a bent coat hanger.

And then there was the union. The guild chapter president, Katharine Mergen, our society editor, came to see me a few months after I had taken over sports. She cautioned me, "Start putting down all overtime you're working when you fill out the weekly time card. You are setting a bad precedent by only charging management for forty hours a week."

In truth, it *was* impossible for one person to efficiently cover all the sports in our growing town in a mere forty hours a week. In the following pay period I claimed fifty-five hours, bringing anguished howls from John Sanford, who gave his patented speech about "holding the line on payroll costs." The lecture prompted Bill Eaton to remark, "Rollan, welcome to our club. You've just been 'Sanfordized.'"

There were internal rumblings that our guild union representatives and newspaper management were having steamy negotiations about the renewal of the existing contract. There were oblique suggestions that "if management doesn't lighten up, it may have a ding-dong fight on its hands."

The local guild unit represented all non-management personnel in the *Gazette* newsroom and a few staff members in the advertising department, which was non-competing and functioned for both newspapers. Altogether, there were thirty-three members.

The major issues of contention between the two sides were salaries and management's proposed installation of automatic linecasting equipment in the newsroom. The guild feared that such installation would cost some union members their jobs. Management said that this was not so. The guild and management were suspicious of each other to the point of paranoia.

I was ignorant of the history of organized labor in the United States, and I found it beyond reason that one might actually close down one's own employer except in the most extreme circumstances. I paid no heed to guild griping. After all, Eaton had advised me upon my hiring that the guild would do all the talking for me. Anyway, I didn't have time for petty politics.

In early June of 1959, those of us who had sneered at the possibility that the guild would go out on strike against our newspaper's management were becoming unsettled by the latest turn of events. Management's lead negotiator was Charles H. Stout, publisher of the *Gazette* and the *Journal*. Negotiating for our union was a fiery American Newspaper Guild national representative and organizer, Joseph L. Campo—he had been sent in to "lead us to victory" in the negotiations.

The first time I listened to Campo speak in a group setting, I found him to be a fast-talking, emotional, persuasive leader. Heads were nodding approval as he preached the gospel according to the national guild. His high-pitched hype reminded me of the church revivalists I had heard as a child. He gave me the chills. I wanted to speak out, to question him aggressively about the issues, but I lacked the courage to say what was in my heart when the demeanor of my *Gazette* colleagues implied their approval of union goals.

As the meeting ended, it was agreed that the Reno guild chapter would continue its "refusal to bend to management's intractable stance." Most believed it could work to the guild's advantage if management found out we were contemplating taking a strike vote should talks continue to sour.

Joe Campo had earlier represented guild members in San Diego and in Los Angeles in lengthy negotiations, and he later was involved in angry discussions between the guild and management in San Jose, California, leading to a strike. He told us that there was no way that a crew comprised exclusively of newspaper executives could possibly publish two newspapers a day if we struck. "You'll find those clowns on their knees, begging you to come back to work," Campo predicted.

The larger question was whether the printers and pressmen, who also were unionized, would cross the picket line in the event of a strike. Campo didn't hesitate. "If you go out," he said, "the typographical union won't come in to set a line of type, and the pressmen won't think of coming to work.

Their international brothers will back them all the way."

Returning home that evening, I briefed Marilyn thoroughly on what had been said and told her that although the climate was tense, I was certain that the reasonable people I knew on both sides would satisfactorily resolve their differences. Marilyn said she prayed I was right, but that sometimes emotions overrule people's common sense. In two or three more months, our third child would be born, and we both hoped that the contract talks wouldn't spin out of control.

Talks continued, and on the surface, work purred along as usual. July drew nearer. Editors Sanford, Jackson, and Bryn Armstrong were exempt from union jurisdiction and kept up their cordial relationships with staff members.

My usual work hours were from 6:00 a.m. to around 5:00 in the afternoon. When the Los Angeles Dodger baseball farm club, the Reno Silver Sox, was in town for home games, I covered them at night, and I also was the club's official scorer. That moonlight job earned me seven dollars a game. I was picking up another ten dollars at each game for sending a summary of the game and a box score to the AP and UPI via Western Union. If a strike didn't screw things up, our family finances would be OK even after the third child arrived.

As sports editor, I was beginning to draw appreciative calls and mail. I gave no thought to ever doing anything else in the newspaper field. I believed that readers couldn't do without my daily reports on the sports they followed, and it was a joy to come to work each morning. Surely, the guild vs. management conflict would cool without a strike. Better days were coming.

The third week of June, all guild members were quietly told that there was an important meeting scheduled late on a weekday afternoon in a Mapes Hotel suite, and that everyone had to be present. In we filed. "Management refuses to budge," Joe Campo told the quiet members. "You know how badly management has treated you. They are sure as hell out to kill the union."

Kay Mergen spoke up: "We'll pass out a piece of paper to each of you, and on the question of whether to strike or not, just vote yes or no." She asked if anyone had any comments. I ached to question the wisdom of pushing the situation to the brink. So did a few others. None of us spoke up.

"All right, good," Campo said. "What you have is a chance to give management a hell of a wake-up call. Rattle their cage. Let them know we mean business." A strike, if necessary, was approved by a vote of 33-0.

STRIKE!

Reno, NV Surely, all this discord was a bad dream, concocted by schemers on both sides, each lunging for every advantage he could gain. Surely, my personal professional journey wasn't going to be interrupted or ended by wrong-thinking people. I reassured myself that at the eleventh hour common sense would prevail, and the warring sides would put aside their animus, smile politely, shake hands, and say, "We've got a deal that each and every one of us can be happy with."

The Monday following our meeting I got another jolt. Managing editor Joe Jackson called me in and laid the wood to me: "You're spending too much time parked at your desk, working the phone. No sports guy is going to see the big picture if he doesn't get out on the street and find out what's there, and what people are saying, and who's doing what to whom." He was correct, of course, and I changed my routine immediately. After each edition was put to bed, I would bolt out of the Gazette Building, as if fired from a rocket. I worked the gyms, the ball yards, and the coaches' offices. Then back to our office I would sprint to churn out broader and deeper sports copy.

The Reno Silver Sox were in a home stand at old Moana Stadium that week, so I covered the games for the *Gazette*. As usual, I also attended the weekly sportswriters and broadcasters meeting at the Mapes Hotel and listened to a parade of coaches explain how they had managed to win despite injuries, or how the bad breaks really killed them in the end. The information was always delivered in doublespeak, and I was learning to cut through the bromides and weasel phrases to get at what the athletic leaders were really talking about.

My working days were my idea of experiencing heaven without the inconvenience of having to die first. No one was about to deny me complete access to professional happiness! At home after each shift, I would reassure Marilyn that I had heard nary a peep about the pesky union stuff. We hoped that no news meant that the guild and management were working their way through their disagreements, and that each would come out feeling that they had picked up more yardage than they had lost.

As the week came to a close, scuttlebutt had it that the situation was growing more tense by the hour. Management was adamant: it would not accept the guild's proposal that any "agency shop" be created for the news and advertising departments. If we became an agency shop, it would mean that all non-management employees must pay dues; even non-guild members would be required to pay union dues as a condition of employment. Our union was also holding out for a top weekly salary of $200, up from the existing standard of $122.50.

On Saturday morning, June 27, the situation went from grim to perilous. Our union committee walked out of negotiations on the issue of the agency shop. From the outside, it was difficult to figure who was doing what to whom, but I was banking on the reliability and sense of responsibility of my colleagues on the negotiating committee. Our chairman was William Scales, and society editor Kay Mergen was in the thick of things as president of our local. Colleagues from the newsroom representing the thirty-three-person guild unit were Lloyd "Punchy" Rogers and my dear friend and classmate, Bill Eaton; and from the advertising department, David Uribe and Helgo Erickson.

The *Gazette* and *Journal* had been published for more than eighty years without interruption. Through fire, flood, power failures, and human errors, the news always got written and plunked down at the readers' doors. I reassured Marilyn on Sunday morning, "Look, the *Gazette* and *Journal* have a combined circulation of many thousands. Our guild and management aren't about to put aside our obligations to our readers and advertisers."

Buoyed by our youthful confidence that there were brighter family and newspaper days ahead, we spent that Sunday with Royle and Wayne. Summer heat was building, and our little house on Yori Avenue was not air conditioned. Marilyn, nearly seven months into her pregnancy, was saying, "Soon there will be five of us. Things are looking great, but gosh, it's hot!"

The union-management climate was also steamy that Sunday. At around 3:00 Monday morning, June 29, the ringing telephone awakened me. It was Bill Eaton. "Time to get up. We're hitting the bricks this morning at 6:00," he said matter of factly. "We're taking on management, and we're gonna lick them. All of us are to arrive outside the Gazette Building around 5:45. We'll have signs for everyone to carry. We'll start the picket line at 6:00 sharp. One other thing: this has to be a complete surprise to those management bastards. We'll have them on their knees, begging us to let them get back to publishing again."

So, it was to be like that . . . . The guild had made a decision on behalf of each of us trusting souls. We had empowered the unit to act, with our 33-0 vote. Now, we would have to live with the consequences. [1]

I dressed, watched the clock, chain-smoked, loaded up on coffee, and told myself, "Damn! Can't we just call this whole thing off?" The next hours were unreal, like a very bad war movie in the making, with Rollan Melton among the troops marching in scripted lockstep.

We collected in the warm morning air outside the newspaper building, and the pep-talking went on and on as we propped each other up with confidence-building cliches. "This will be the shortest guild strike on record. We're calling management's bluff, and there is no way in hell they'll get the papers out without us."

The recurring talk was also of the pledge our guild leaders said they had received from the printing and pressmen—that they would honor our picket line and not report to work. Indeed, that would be a key element. The printers' union had a storied reputation for standing firmly behind other unions. But, the pressmen's union? That was a different story. If there was to be a fracture in union solidarity, it likely would be the pressmen, we were cautioned. Yet Eaton and the others believed that the Reno pressmen truly meant it when they said, "We're behind you all the way, and you can put that pledge in the bank!" They were right. Six o'clock was the starting time for the crafts, and as that hour arrived, there wasn't a printer or pressman in sight.

The guild appeared well-prepared. Our leaders handed us picketing schedules. "We will be walking in four-hour shifts," we were told. My assigned walking tour was to be 2:00 to 6:00 each afternoon, but for appearance's sake on that first strike day, all of us remained massed outside the building, front and back, until mid-morning.

Unfortunately, management had anticipated the strike and had entered the building early without having to cross a picket line. Also among the people in the building that morning were the wire service reporters. The first story they filed was the news that the *Reno Evening Gazette* and the *Nevada State Journal* were being struck for the first time in their histories.

I returned home after mid-morning to break the news to Marilyn, but she had already heard it on the radio. "No matter what, I'm behind you," she told me. We spent the next few hours reassuring each other and rehashing the unthinkable. Money-wise, we felt we would be OK.

I told her, "Mergen and Eaton and others on our negotiating team assure us that the national guild will have fifty-five dollar strike benefit checks for each of us each week that we're out."

---

1. The Reno Newspaper Guild Local 208 was founded in 1950 as a chapter of what was then known as the American Newspaper Guild (ANG), an arm of the AFL-CIO. The strike began on June 29, 1959 and ran until October 12 of that same year.

"Our leaders handed us picketing schedules. 'We will be walking in four-hour shifts,' we were told." (Photograph by Dondero.)

"Well, that's almost half of what you make when you're on the payroll," Marilyn said. "So it sounds like we'll be covered."

"I'll keep working at the ballpark when the Silver Sox are at home, and that will be some extra bucks," I said. But surely, all such measures would soon be unnecessary. "They say management will be incapable of publishing without us," I said. "I believe they're right."

When I returned to the Gazette Building that day before my 2:00 picket shift began, I experienced a moment of truth. So did my colleagues. The *Gazette* had somehow gotten out a twelve-page edition. The banner headline, eight-columns wide in ninety-six point, all capital letters, proclaimed, "NEWSPAPER STRIKE CALLED." There were related stories down each side of the front page: "Guild Proposals Held Unreasonable," and "A Statement by Publishers of the *Gazette* and the *Journal*." Just under the *Gazette* page-one nameplate was the familiar notation, "Eighty-third year."

So here I was, unemployed for the first time in my work life, stuck on a picket line: a sports editor bereft of typewriter and printing press; a young man stripped of his cocksure attitude and filled with anxiety upon learning that somehow, some way, the management people inside the building had pulled off a miracle. Without workaday reporters and printers and pressmen, management had still put out an edition. True, it was sad-looking. Patched together. Poorly printed. Filled with stale old type from the prior day's *Journal*. Yet, it was a newspaper, and it affirmed that management was determined to prevail. They were helped by the fact that the morning *Journal*'s news-side had no one in the union, so all my *Journal* colleagues were still employed, not only producing *Journal* news copy, but writing for the *Gazette* afternoon side.

Life on the picket line could have been better. Reno was not a union town. The curious would stop and ask, "What's this all about?" Then after hearing our biased account, some would say, "Well, good luck." For the most part, passers-by ignored us. But there were some abusive remarks. "You guys are loco, trying to deny us our newspaper!" Always it was "our" newspaper, and understandably; for truly, it *was* their paper and their ten-cent-a-copy window onto the world around them.

The days lengthened and my apprehension grew, as management never missed publishing, afternoon and morning. The truth was shattering: we were not needed; I was not needed. No longer did my phone carry the voices of coaches sharing their news. Why call Melton?

As we unionists settled into a picketing routine, I asked to be taken off the afternoon march and reassigned to the midnight to 4:00 a.m. tour. Thus, I could continue to cover night baseball. Further, I asked and received permission from the guild to leave the front sidewalk beat and walk the back alley—I wanted to hide from public view.

Melton Regrets Striking
Cannot Find Another Job

Reno, NV Nothing was more important to me in my career than helping to get the newspaper out, but as much as I detested trying to shut down my own employer, I had been among the unanimous voices that had set us up for this confrontation. There was no one to blame but myself. What should I have done differently? Given another chance, would I go in to work, or would I honor the strike? I always came up with the same answer. As much as I opposed the guild battle plan and the strike, I could never see myself turning against colleagues. Since my young years as apprentice printer and rookie writer—and on athletic fields, in the army, and in newsrooms—I had always felt a compulsion to go with the team.

I was stuck with my decision, but after four weeks of picket-line marching, things began to unravel for the union. Out of the blue, the American Newspaper Guild announced that due to financial exigencies, they could no longer provide us with our weekly fifty-five dollar benefit checks. Not a single striker was independently wealthy; none that I knew of had any family wealth to fall back on.

As our purses emptied for lack of pay, so fell the morale of those of us who felt that we had been whipped from day one. Still, our union representatives would not return to the bargaining room. Nor would management. There was a total stalemate. I reached the point of accepting that there was no direction to go but down. I sank into depression.

The guild unit's writers did manage to publish our own little tabloid. It was thin, and its contents were slanted to our side of the strike story. I had a bylined sports story with the opening paragraph, "As I was saying before I was so rudely interrupted . . . ." But the strike paper idea couldn't be sustained. The only printed news in town was coming from inside the Gazette Building.

Adding to my anxiety and that of my colleagues was the appearance of new faces crossing the picket lines. They were strike busters hustled in from other places. Guildsmen for the first time took up the chant, "Scab, scab, scab," the four-letter word that would foul the air in the days and weeks to follow, but to no effect. Soon, the bylines of these "scabs" began to appear in the *Gazette*.

As the days grew into weeks, with little money coming in, it became clear that Marilyn and I must either leave our beloved Reno, or I must find a new occupation. We wanted to stay in Reno.

There is nothing so difficult as finding a new job when you've given up your old one. I picked up a report that my beloved alma mater, the University of Nevada, was in need of an alumni association director. I hastily put my qualifications down on a single page of copy, so as not to burden the reader with an over-abundance of adjectives. Nevertheless, there was so much to report that even I was impressed: printer, writer, army officer, public information officer; work at the *Standard* in Fallon, at the *Gazette* and *Journal* while a student; city editor of the *Tribune* in Sparks while still an undergraduate. Editor-publisher of a military tabloid. Sports editor of the *Reno Evening Gazette*. Happily married. (Only one wife in my history.) Soon-to-be father of three. And all of this by the time I was twenty-eight. That surely ought to sell with the campus decision-makers.

While I was confidently awaiting my appointment, fellow striker Kenneth Robbins asked me, "I wonder if you would mind if I also apply for the alumni director's job? There is no way they'll pick anyone but you, Rollan. I know that. But would you object if I stuck my name in there?"

"Of course not," I told him, but I thought to myself, "Ken is going to have his own moment of truth. When the decision is reached, I'll reassure him and wish him all the best as he tries to find something to keep him and his family going."

The time for the alumni council decision came. Our across-the-street neighbors, Joanne and Robert "Lefty" McDonough, were voting members of the council. They had encouraged me to apply, and they promised that they would speak strongly in my behalf. Then, when I was chosen, they would come break the good news to us.

We were waiting with eager anticipation when the McDonoughs arrived at our door. I expected Joanne to hug me and give us the cheery news; then we'd pop the bottles of beer and have ourselves a gala celebration. Instead, our neighbors entered our house with somber faces that gave me the shivers. I wasn't ready for what they told us:

"Sorry, Rollan, but you weren't selected. We spoke up for you as best we could, but the person they selected was the consensus choice. His written presentation filled up a whole loose-leaf notebook. Although everyone was tremendously impressed with your reputation and with what you submitted, they went the other way."

"Who did they give the directorship to?" I asked.

"Well, he has worked with you at the paper. A fellow named Ken Robbins."

The McDonoughs left us to ourselves, and as the gloom thickened, I noted that it was time to return to the only job I presently had: the picket line.

I increased my efforts to find employment in Reno, as I came to accept that I never again would work for the *Gazette* or *Journal*. Chamber of Commerce executive director Jud Allen gave me time to explain how I could apply my communications skills advancing the Chamber's mission. Then he said, "It sounds good, but frankly, Rollan, we just don't have the budget to be adding people."

At Harrah's, public relations director Mark Curtis Sr., whom I had known since I was a freshman at Nevada, listened to my brief appeal for employment. "You are the fourth person on strike who has been in here," he said. "Much as I wish you luck, we simply don't have anything available, and I don't foresee that we will."

Shortly thereafter, I learned that the public relations position at the University of Nevada had unexpectedly come open. I immediately placed a call to the office of campus president Charles J. Armstrong. His secretary, Alice Terry, made me an appointment to visit the president.

I had badly undersold myself in my earlier quest for the campus alumni director job, and I wasn't going to make the same mistake again. I prepared an outsized personal written presentation that I believed would be a job pitch that the president couldn't refuse. My confidence was high as Armstrong invited me to take a seat. I was prepared to dazzle him. Then he ruined everything: "Miss Terry has told me of your interest in the public relations position. Mr. Melton, do you have a master's degree?"

I sputtered, "Sir, I do not . . . however . . ."

Dr. Armstrong interjected, "Then, we need not discuss your interest any further. In determining what we are looking for in candidates, we have decided that an advanced degree should be among the requirements. Thank you so much for visiting me, Mr. Melton."

The strike experience was exposing me to rejection, and with each rejection, I had to re-build my confidence—sort of like the need to remake the bed each time I arose.

Thoroughly discouraged, I reported back to Marilyn that my latest "opportunity" was kaput. The end of summer drew near. Hope for a satisfactory resolution of the strike was no longer hope—it was fantasy. The guild might as well forget settlement. It had worked itself into an untenable position.

Management Was Ready
Chick Stout Led The Team

Reno, NV Throughout the work stoppage attempt, especially during the first few weeks, *Gazette* and *Journal* management had performed a virtual publishing miracle. The papers came off the press as scheduled, a total of thirteen times a week, week in and week out, without a single miss, despite onerous challenges imposed by the strike. The executives understood two important things: First, readers and advertisers rank foremost—service to them has to be as good as newspapers can make it, and it is imperative that such service be uninterrupted if a newspaper is to survive. And second, given the intransigence of the union and the immovable strength of management, the guild's strike attempt had no place to go but down.

Contrary to what those of us in the strike force had believed would be the case, either through the gospel given us by "stoppage adviser" Joe Campo or because of our own wishful thinking, management had not been surprised by the strike. Charles Stout had hoped that the guild leadership would eventually back off from its hard-line demands, but when the union's 33-0 strike vote came, he and his managers were prepared. They went into action before the picket line began to form.

Before dawn on the day of the strike, the front-line executives, their managers, and the newsroom personnel from the non-guild *Journal* were inside the building, poised to take over the positions that would go "dark" in the event of a strike. As we began the picketing promptly at 6:00 in the morning, Stout and his people were already working to get the *Gazette* to press and then distributed to homes and to newsstands by early afternoon.

Stout's superintendent of crafts, Victor Anderson, shouldered the heaviest burden on that first day, and in the difficult days that followed. Anderson had correctly anticipated that his pressmen would honor the guild's picket line, at least early in the strike. He was on his own, but he was an accomplished compositor and printer, and as management's good fortune would have it, he also had vast knowledge of the workings of the aging press located in the basement of the Gazette Building.

Charles Stout had worked his way through the University of Iowa as a Linotype operator on the *Daily Iowan*, the campus newspaper at Iowa City. Now, at his strike-hit newspaper in Reno, he returned to the work that he had mastered as a collegian, and he began setting freshly written news copy into type. A news wire service took a photo of the broadly smiling Stout, diligently at work at the *Gazette*'s Linotype—a smartly dressed publisher, complete with bow-tie, performing manual labor. The picture moved nationwide, and it was published a few days afterwards in *Editor & Publisher* magazine, the weekly bible of print journalism.

Early on the first morning of the strike, those of us on the picket line became aware of activity within the building we were trying to shutter. Advertisers went in and out. By 8:00 a.m., non-unionized staff from departments other than news and advertising had entered the building and were at their work stations. Inside, superintendent Anderson toiled alongside publisher Stout and a few other executives who were passably good at printing tasks. Column by column, the makeshift staff was able to cobble together enough fresh news pages to get a fairly representative issue off the press that afternoon. Strikers who had sworn not to read the Reno dailies until the controversy was ended were seen furtively buying a *Gazette* at nearby newsstands.

When he wasn't setting type, Charles Stout was fielding calls from other daily and weekly newspaper owners who were offering help in any form, including the volunteer services of their printers, pressmen, writers, and advertising salespeople. Stout also was taking a sizable number of supportive calls from fellow Reno-area business leaders, including those who headed banks, casinos, and utilities. Stout later acknowledged that during the strike period, businesses raised their normal advertising volume several notches to ensure that the newspapers had adequate revenues to remain in business.

With the printers and pressmen respecting the picket lines, Anderson, Stout, and business manager Clarence K. Jones arranged for replacement personnel to take over vacated crafts positions. Meanwhile, Paul Leonard, John Sanford, Joe Jackson, and Bryn Armstrong were hiring news writers anxious to work in one of the West's best news towns. As the *Gazette* kept being published without us, there was a growing sense that this strike would fail. We kept marching, but some of us felt that we were newspaper lemmings, about to plunge to group unemployment off cliffs rising from unreasonable demands.

Unfamiliar faces were entering the Gazette Building and emerging eight hours later. It didn't take a high IQ to figure out that these were our replacements. Not all the visitors were "foreigners," though. The wives of *Gazette* executives were around throughout the strike. Paul Leonard's wife, Gwen, had had some newspaper experience in Elko, where her husband earlier had worked for the daily *Free Press*. She became the interim society editor of the *Journal* when regular editor Alice Melarkey elected not to cross the picket line. John Sanford's wife, Myrtle, helped out on the *Gazette* side, as did Joe Jackson's wife, Sadie. What became known as the "Wife Corps" included Betty Jean Conton, Levina Digino, Verna Anderson, and Betty Stout.

The guild had predicted that if any affected union broke ranks, it would be the pressmen. The assumption was correct. A week into the strike, the pressmen's union voted unanimously to return to members' vacated positions. Moreover, under superintendent Anderson's leadership, outside printers began to arrive to permanently replace the members of the Reno unit of the International Typographical Union who refused to cross the picket line. The new hires included journeyman printer Donn Wheeler, who a few weeks before had been among the strikebreakers crossing the ITU line in front of the struck daily newspaper in Lima, Ohio. Wheeler was a natural leader, and before long Vic Anderson made him his lead foreman.

Those of us on the outside, speculating on what was occurring within, grew increasingly restless. National Guild adviser Joe Campo had virtually disappeared from our midst as our position grew more precarious, and a striker in a non-union town soon discovers that his pool of friends is shallower than he thought. In my case, aside from Marilyn, my support was slim. Ken Ingram, by this time having established his own commercial printing firm in Reno, gave me encouragement. So did Don Dondero, who was an independent-contractor photographer for the paper. Richard Trachok, the University of Nevada football coach, had seen strikes devastate miners' lives when he was growing up in Pennsylvania, and he always had a sympathetic word for us. Robert Nitsche, the business manager of the Reno Silver Sox baseball team, was always cordial. Few others were.

We strikers began to feel increasing pressure to find new jobs. Our stress heightened as we came to suspect that our "temporary replacements" would soon be permanently filling our positions. The people who crossed our lines to put out a newspaper each day seemed more self-assured. Their confidence was buoyed by their success in preserving the *Gazette*'s record of continuous, unbroken publication.

I believe that the Great Depression upbringing and the World War II combat experiences of many on the management team influenced the way that they handled our strike. These were mature executives.

Dealing with a strike wasn't exactly child's play, but compared to what these men had been through in the military, it wasn't much. They were up to the task.

Classified manager Carl Digino had been a combat marine. Paul Leonard had been an army officer in the South Pacific, Joe Jackson a navy officer in the Pacific fleet. As a commander in the U.S. Navy, Charles "Chick" Stout had led combat units in the Atlantic and Pacific Theaters—his assignments included supervising the building of air strips on Pacific islands.

Chick Stout had joined the Speidel corporate staff in Colorado Springs after the war. His financial and planning expertise had quickly impressed John Ben Snow. (Snow was a retired F. W. Woolworth executive who acquired the individual Speidel newspaper properties piecemeal from 1921 to 1948.) Stout turned out to be a perfect operations assistant to Harry S. Bunker, the chief executive of the Speidel corporation, and Bunker began grooming the former naval officer to succeed him as Speidel's president.

It was in the best interests of the corporation for Stout to get hands-on newspaper executive operations experience, so in 1956 he came to Reno to succeed the retiring Joseph McDonald Sr. Stout's wife, Katherine, had fallen ill with cancer the year before. The former actress and concert pianist made the move to their new home in Nevada, but in 1957 she died. Stout was left with his three children: Richard, then thirteen; George, ten; and Martha, eight. The family was still grieving when, in 1958, contract negotiations with the Reno guild chapter began to take a nasty turn.

Stout was under additional stress at the time. He had acquired land near the center of Reno on which to construct a state-of-the-art newspaper building. As the guild advised management that it had secured a unanimous strike vote from its members, Stout was reviewing architectural renderings for the new plant at 401 West Second Street, a block from venerable Saint Thomas Aquinas Catholic Cathedral.

Chick Stout would not yield to stress, nor would he lose focus. In choosing ground it believed it could win on, the American Newspaper Guild hadn't bargained on facing the likes of him. He proved at every juncture that he and his Reno newspaper colleagues could not be intimidated, would not be defeated. Stout's steady, confident stewardship led his team through.

Disillusioned Sportswriter Crosses The Line

Reno, NV Rah-rah Joe Campo, who had convinced us that a strike was our great weapon, was now the invisible man.

On the picket line the most common question was, "Where do we go from here?" Our only skills were writing news and selling advertising, but there was only one daily newspaper act in town, and we had closed ourselves out of it.

At home, Marilyn put me to work to get my mind off of my self-imposed problems. She had me trimming shrubs and grass, straightening up the garage, and spending more time with our sons. Then she came up with the ultimate demand: our one bathroom was in dire need of painting. So on a steamy August day I set to work in the closely confined little bathroom, slapping on the enamel. It was slow-going, and the heat was almost unbearable.

Marilyn's father dropped by unexpectedly. He stood silently in the bathroom entrance, watching me do my painterly thing. Stripped to the waist, bathed in sweat, angry at management, angry at the folly of the guild, cursing myself for being stupid enough to get involved, I painted on, bitching and moaning. My father-in-law listened to my bellyaching, and then he said, "Have you considered hiring union labor to do that?" What a card!

From a financial standpoint, we were almost running on empty, but we had managed to scrape together back-to-back $100-a-month house payments. Thanks to Silver Sox business manager Robert Nitsche, I still had a few dollars coming in each night the ball club played at home.

Near the end of August, Marilyn carted Royle off to school for his first day at kindergarten. At last I finished painting the outside of our three-bedroom home. The union was beaten, that was clear. New faces walked the picket lines—they had been hired to do the four-hour tours by many of my striking colleagues while those same colleagues looked for work. I couldn't afford to hire any picket replacement labor, so I did my own picketing.

Then, out of the blue, editor John Sanford called me at home and said, "I need to talk to you, Rollan. I want you to meet me for lunch today at the Holiday Hotel."

I didn't know what my boss was up to (he would always be "the boss" to me), but I replied, "Sure, John, I'll be there."

Shortly before noon I arrived at the Holiday Shore Room. John Sanford was waiting. He quickly got to the point. "Rollan, the strike is over. True, technically it isn't over, but the guild is finished. Of the thirty-three vacated guild jobs in news and advertising, thirty-one have been filled. There are two of you whom we want back—Walt MacKenzie and you. However, we have replaced you as sports editor with a young man from southern California. That means that if you come back, it will have to be in the position we still hold open for you—that of telegraph editor."

I was stunned. I could no longer be the sports editor—my beloved career/pastime that was so much fun that it had never seemed to be true work! I wavered. "Well, John," I said, "let me go home and talk this over with Marilyn. I'll get back to you . . . ."

Sanford cut me off. "There's no need to talk to her. You either do it or you don't. Come on with me. We need you; we want you. This is your chance. The strike is over—get that through your skull. There may be scattered picketing, but the whole thing is over." We walked out onto Center Street, and John marched me the two blocks to the Gazette Building.

My friend Bill Eaton was among the pickets out front. I walked through the picket line alongside John Sanford, trying to avoid my classmate's hate-filled eyes. I heard his voice. "Rollan, I will never speak to you again, you son of a bitch!" He never did.

Telegraph Editor Looks Ahead

Reno, NV After ten weeks of the picket-line blues, I stepped back into the *Gazette* newsroom. I was unprepared for the emotional impact of those first minutes in the news environment I so missed. John Sanford delivered me as if I were a human trophy. Senior editors Joe Jackson and Bryn Armstrong, right on deadline, were processing reporters' last-minute news stories. Each gave me a cordial handshake, welcoming me as casually as if I had just resurfaced from vacation.

The newsroom was largely unchanged. The desks jammed into the too-small room were cluttered, as always, with scrawled notes, copy pencils, mounds of copy paper, unread magazines, news clippings, and ash trays brimming with cigarette butts. Over everything could be heard the hurried chatter of manual Underwoods. People bustled about, straining to put together the issue by deadline. But the friends with whom I had worked, laughed, and partied were gone. I was a stranger among strangers; I was starting, once again, at the bottom of the heap.

My new colleagues stared curiously at me, perhaps wondering, "New flack from a casino, or a body bearing legitimate news?" I started to walk around the room to introduce myself, but Sanford intercepted me. "You'll meet all of them in due time," he said. "For now, go on down the hall to Chick's office. He wants to visit with you." I shuddered at the prospect. For some of the early weeks of the strike, before I had requested only night picket duty, I had watched the short, slender, intense publisher cross the picket line, slipping through the scowling, out-of-work sentinels, ignoring all of us.

In my two years at the sports desk, I had been so far down the pecking order that I had never personally met Stout. Now I stood before him and offered my sweating hand. He said in his deep baritone, "We're happy you've returned." I stuttered my appreciation, adding that I would do my best for the *Gazette*. Stout gave me a steely stare. "We hope so," he said.

After the *Gazette* was put to bed that day, Sanford and Joe Jackson coached me on my new assignment. I was to be the telegraph editor, processing Associated Press wire service copy and discussing with Jackson and Armstrong any Nevada rural or statewide news that should be considered for prominent display. They explained my new deadline requirements and said I would handle the editing and layout not only of page

---

Union Leader Slain

In the summer of 1960, shortly after the official end of the newspaper strike, Joe Campo applied for a Nevada gaming license for a lodge on Montgomery Pass, near Hawthorne, Nevada. He had become associated with Joe Conforte, the infamous whoremaster of Nevada, and he was living at the lodge, which had earlier been one of Conforte's houses of prostitution. On the night of September 19, Campo was shot and killed by his common-law wife after he smashed his way into her bedroom and threatened to kill her. Beverly Jean Harris was found innocent of any crime after an investigation proved she had acted in self-defense.

one, but also of inside pages set aside for AP stories. This was a role that had been filled by the striking George Pratt, a page-makeup whiz who had brought a refreshingly modern look to the *Gazette*. He had been adept at layout, graphics, and writing headlines. I had learned a lot from George.

I swiftly acquainted myself with each of the new reporters and with the fresh cadre of imported apprentice and journeyman printers. My telegraph editor role would put me in close contact with Donn Wheeler, who had arrived in Reno after helping break the International Typographical Union strike at Lima, Ohio. Wheeler's steady presence as day-side foreman freed Vic Anderson to reassert himself as the expert generalist who oversaw the composing room, the press-room, and the mailroom.

I grew to admire Robert Bohon, my successor as sports editor. Bohon had not been an athlete, but he was a solid sports journalist and a cordial companion beyond the *Gazette* newsroom, especially at Moana Ball Park, where he covered Silver Sox baseball games with the *Journal*'s Ty Cobb and Len Crocker. My official scorer duties, and covering for AP and United Press, kept me connected to the camaraderie of the baseball press box, but I tried not to get in Bohon's way. He was sports editor now, and although he occasionally asked me to contribute to his pages, I kept my distance. A "has-been" or "used-to-be" shouldn't hang around, shadowing or second-guessing a successor.

Within days after my return to the *Gazette,* Walter MacKenzie left the thinning picket line, rejoining the staff in his old role of Washoe County Courthouse reporter. He was our only *Gazette* veteran, and newsroom management had its hands full overseeing the new crop of reporters. Some were just breaking into the newspaper game and needed to acquire the maturity that solid coaching and experience can provide. Bryn Armstrong was an especially able copy reader, and a solid mentor of reporter neophytes.

John Sanford was less visible in the newsroom, leaving most story and news display judgments to Jackson, Armstrong, and me, but he was zealous in safeguarding the integrity of the news. Not many days after I resumed work with the newspaper, an imported rookie editor of the weekly "Entertainment Guide" (later re-named "Best Bets"), committed an unpardonable sin. Sanford had excellent community feedback, and a reliable source tipped him that his entertainment editor was mooching food, drink, and other favors at the Riverside, Golden, and Mapes Hotels, promising "the best entertainment coverage I can provide" in return. Sanford called the man to his office. The offender confessed, and in an instant his career at the *Gazette* was kaput. He had been with us just three weeks. Even experienced editors can let a loser slip through the hiring screen.

When John Sanford declared that Bob Bohon was the new sports editor and that I could not return to the job, he reassured me by explaining what had happened to former *Gazette* sports editors: Joe Jackson had moved into management following wartime service; Frank McCulloch was presently a writing star for Henry Luce at *Time* magazine and had produced many cover stories; Edward Montgomery had won a Pulitzer Prize at the *San Francisco Examiner* in the early 1950s; Harold Ross graduated from *Gazette* sports into a comparable position at the much larger *Oakland Tribune*; Carl Digino was promoted to classified manager for the *Gazette* and *Journal*, having joined the executive ranks not many years earlier; and Bill Friel had gone on to meritorious general assignment stardom at the *Oakland Tribune*.

Not many days into the telegraph editorship, I began to see that I might also be able to advance beyond sports. For the first time, I was paying attention to news of the nation and the world. By the nature of my assignment, I was learning that the sun did not rise and set with how the Yankees were doing or what was occurring in pro football, basketball, and boxing.

Other opportunities soon came my way. Sanford asked me to begin researching and writing the daily editorial page feature, "Pages from the Past." I would hole up in our darkened newspaper library each afternoon, scan microfilm files of *Gazette* issues published ten, twenty-five, fifty, and eighty years earlier, and select choice items for the re-telling. It was one of the best Nevada history educations anyone could receive.

My "news strings" were broadening, too. I occasionally wrote Nevada-related stories for medical magazines, which would pay up to one hundred dollars for some feature stories. I was fortunate to be named northern Nevada stringer for the *Wall Street Journal*. I continued my Silver Sox sideline coverage, and sports editor Bohon occasionally invited me to do a special news or feature piece for him. So, despite the fact that the wire editor position minimized my *Gazette* writing, I kept pace through my various independent contractor writing assignments. Always, I ran offers to be a news stringer past Joe Jackson, to avoid the possibility of conflict of interest.

The virtues of being on the wire desk were many. Among the major pluses was shaping the most solid relationship I had ever enjoyed with our printers. Vic Anderson and Donn Wheeler constantly emphasized steady copy flow—spreading the volume of stories sent to compositors and page makeup men so that they were not deluged by a tide of copy hitting them all at once. Deadlines varied for all departments—sports, financial, local, national, international. The last pages to be processed and sent to the pressmen were the business page (so as to include the latest news from Wall Street) and the showpiece, page one.

Altogether, my assignment was heady. It was broadening, and the experience it gave me would profit me, my colleagues, and my readers in the years ahead.

"Misfits" Films in Reno

Reno, NV The early 1960s was a glorious time for the "Biggest Little City in the World." Reno nights were alive with tourists, many of them drawn by the appearance of some of the world's great entertainers on stages at the Riverside, Mapes, Holiday, and Golden Hotels. Each property tried to outdo the other in capitalizing on the growing visitor base. Although it offered no hotel accommodations, Harolds Club was attracting the largest crowds in town by promising fun and delivering it.

The social scene had never been brighter. Every other Monday night, the Sparks Nugget, as it was then known, had a backstage hosted party for media following the two-week entertainment stand of the latest star. Harolds Club's Fun Room was aptly named, for the Smith family was attracting some of the brightest show business personalities. At the Holiday, Newt Crumley presented programs that made the hotel-casino a popular stopping place.

The premier event of 1960 was the filming of the movie, "The Misfits," with the era's superstars, Clark Gable, Marilyn Monroe, Montgomery Clift and Thelma Ritter on location in Reno, and at Dayton, near Carson City. After the conclusion of the filming, Charles Mapes held another of his gala parties, hosting the cast and scores of business leaders and media in the famous Mapes Sky Room. Visitors were agog at the celebrity guests.

Marilyn Monroe was quite late in arriving. She looked more like a lost waif than a superstar, and I would have walked past her on a Reno street and never recognized her. (Reno's outstanding freelance photographer, Don Dondero, had shot hundreds of pictures of Monroe during the filming and related social events. He called her the most photogenic person he had ever shot. "It was impossible to make a bad picture of her," he said.)

The real star of the reception was Gable—he looked in wonderful physical condition. Several of us from the media spent a good part of the party around him. I asked him whether he favored John F. Kennedy or Richard M. Nixon in the presidential campaign which was going strong at that time. He easily deflected my question, saying in essence, "Each candidate is great. Each would make a fine president. America can rest easy with either man as our leader."

The studio did its final editing of the "The Misfits," and prior to its premier at Reno's Granada Theater, editor Jackson asked if I would attend and write the *Gazette* review. I watched the movie intently, took notes in the darkened theater, and the following day wrote that the film was just all right as movies went. I had misjudged how the public would respond. After barely civil reviews around the country, "The Misfits" became a cult film, shown around the world for decades. The general public decides what is a bomb or a hit.

The modern new Gazette-Journal Building was finished not long into 1961, and each department relocated—our newsroom to the second floor. The transition was easy, and the spacious new environment dramatized how cramped had been our earlier quarters.

"The real star of the reception was Gable—he looked in wonderful physical condition." l. to r.: Rollan Melton, Clark Gable, unidentified.

When we're going at full tilt and loving every aspect of life, as I did, time moves swiftly. I had done some singing in high school with my friend, Wes Ugalde. Then during my University of Nevada years, I sang at friends' weddings for meager pay and mostly for personal enjoyment. Colleagues knew that I loved singing, and they prevailed on me to double as entertainer and master of ceremonies at staff parties and at the Christmastide company-wide holiday dinner-dance. I heard through the grapevine that Chick Stout was pleased with my performance, but I chalked up such talk to baseless rumor.

Meltons Multiply
Tragedy Strikes

Reno, NV On September 11, 1959, little more than a week after I had returned to work from my stint as a striker, our third son was born. We named him Kevin Claude Melton, giving him his middle name in memory of my beloved first boss, Claude H. Smith, of the Fallon *Standard*.

Then, in the spring of 1960, we learned that Marilyn was expecting again. The baby, if it arrived on schedule, would be with us by mid-November, about fourteen months after Kevin's birth. Given percentages, we felt that this time we surely would be the parents of a daughter; but no matter what its sex, we pledged that this fourth child would be our last.

Meanwhile, our eldest sons, Royle and Wayne, were each of school age. Kevin had been toddling for two months, when, on November 11, 1960, our family expanded again. It wasn't the daughter we had hoped to have. We gave our fourth son, Jaime, the middle name of Gray, which was Marilyn's mother's maiden name. It was obvious almost from the beginning of his life that he had inherited the abundant redhead genes from my mother's side of the family—Jaime had auburn hair and a lively personality. We were a family of six making do in a three-bedroom house with a single bathroom that two years earlier had received doses of enamel applied by a non-union laborer.

In July of 1961, for the third straight summer, Marilyn and I took the children for a vacation at South Lake Tahoe. We spent a week in a rental home at Marla Bay, and then bundled up the four boys and journeyed back to hot Reno. On the evening of July 18, Marilyn took Royle and Wayne to a "Three Stooges" movie, and I stayed back to babysit Kevin and Jaime, who had cribs in a bedroom adjacent to ours.

Late in the evening I looked in on the two little guys and then went to bed. Marilyn was home shortly thereafter and re-checked Kevin and Jaime before going to bed. She was awakened by Jaime's crying around 2:00 the next morning. She warmed him a bottle, and after he fell asleep, she returned to bed.

I awoke at my usual hour, 6:00, and as was my practice, the first thing I did was check our crib babies' room. To my horror, I saw that a corner of Jaime's bedspring had given way. The baby had slid feet-first into the resulting small crevice, and he hung suspended, limp and chalk white. I screamed, and Marilyn instantly sprinted to us. We saw no sign of life, but Marilyn immediately applied artificial respiration.

I called for an ambulance, which arrived within minutes. Leaving Marilyn crying, I rode with the ambulance crew, who tried to revive Jaime en route to Washoe Medical Center. But it was too late. Our baby,

Jaime Gray Melton, was pronounced dead of suffocation.

The *Gazette* reported Jaime's death that afternoon. The following morning I received a call at home from a woman who identified herself as a former salesperson in the *Gazette* and *Journal* display advertising department. She had been among those of us who struck Reno Newspapers Incorporated in 1959. She said she was calling from her home near Portola in northern California, and she wanted to tell me that she had seen the story of our son's death. I started to thank her for her thoughtfulness, but she interrupted and said, "This is God's way of punishing the striker who went back to work. You've gotten exactly what you deserve."

Nothing can prepare you for the death of your child. They are supposed to outlive us, but who can foresee that a nut on a second-hand crib spring will work loose? As Reverend Jesse Jackson would declare nearly forty years after we lost Jaime, nothing about our faith makes us pain-proof. It hurts, and we must dry our eyes and continue to work until our time is finished. The baby's death was a profound reminder of how fragile is life, and that it can be altogether too brief.

Following Jaime's death, I experienced as never before the emotional bonding that tragedies so often bring to survivors. The support of our families and friends was instrumental in helping us move on from grief. No gesture was more touching than the one made by my colleagues at the *Gazette* and *Journal*. They paid for a grave marker, and we wrote this inscription:

Our Beloved Baby
Jaime Gray Melton
1960-1961

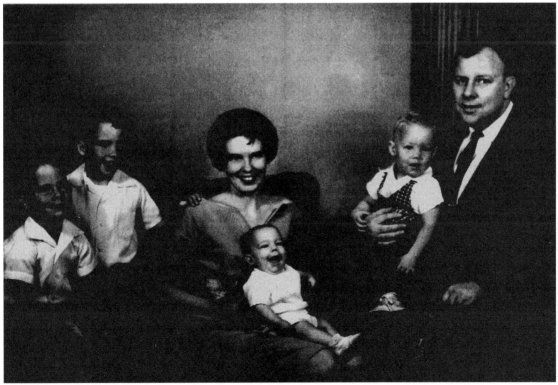

This 1961 photograph is the only picture of Rollan and Marilyn with their four sons. l. to r.: Wayne, Royle, Marilyn, Jaime, Kevin, and Rollan.

Many a couple who had lost a child earlier were among those who gave us support, and we learned of such losses only after our own. Marilyn and I were also helped to get through by having Royle, Wayne, and Kevin to care for... and in my case, the newspaper life that I had known almost every day since I was fifteen.

Novice Gets Lead in RLT Musical

Reno, NV In late 1961, a few months after Jaime's death, I heard from a special friend, Michael Schon, who was a bit older than me. Schon had been a successful semi-professional baseball player around Reno. He was now involving himself in amateur theater. He phoned and said that there were tryouts scheduled at the Reno Little Theater for a stage musical called *Take Me Along,* an adaptation of Eugene O'Neill's *Ah, Wilderness!* At first I begged off, saying that because of my work schedule, I had too few hours for rehearsal.

"Come on, Rollan," Schon insisted. "I remember you singing at friends' weddings while you were at the university, and there will be an opportunity to sing in this show if you do well at the auditions."

At the core of my reluctance, though I did not admit it to Schon, was my fear of performing in public. Singing at weddings had terrified me. Yet, Schon kept pestering me. Finally, I agreed to appear at the Reno Little Theater's Sierra Street Playhouse for a tryout, expecting that if I did satisfactorily, director Edwin Semenza and musical director Sylvan Green would give me a choral role. Auditioners were asked to sing one song, and I picked one I could belt out, the better to hide my untrained vocal shortcomings.

Growing up, I had listened to Al Jolson records on my mother's beat-up old record player, and in the privacy of our homes, I'd growl woolly imitations of the legendary Jazz Singer. At the audition, I flung stage fright aside long enough to sing *California, Here I Come,* one of Jolson's most famous. Then came a parade of others trying out, including Michael Schon with his rich baritone voice, while strait-laced Semenza and Green showed not a flicker of bias for any of us.

The evening dragged on until the last of the candidates tried out. Semenza and Green huddled, whispering, and then Semenza, who had been a leader in founding Reno Little Theater in 1935, announced, "Thanks for your efforts and for saying how we can reach you. We've got a number of roles to offer, and we'll get back to you with our decisions."

The following day, Semenza called me at the *Gazette* and told me "You did all right. We want you in *Take Me Along.*" I mumbled my thanks, preparing to be assigned to the chorus. Semenza said, "We are offering you the lead as Sid Davis, who is a newspaperman in the play."

I broke into a sweat and thought, "God, I'll be up there alone, with hundreds gawking at me and hearing me talk and sing."

Semenza hurried on, all business. "You do want the part, don't you?"

I mumbled, "Oh, why, sure."

Semenza said the cast would begin rehearsals in a few days. He said, "Mike Schon will be taking the other male lead." I was relieved, for that meant there would be a friend around to calm my anxieties.

The fictional Sid Davis was a role filled in the original Broadway show by Jackie Gleason. Mike Schon portrayed the other principal character, performed in the original show by the renowned movie star,

Mike Schon and Rollan Melton in *Take Me Along*, 1962.

Walter Pidgeon. Our rehearsals were a delight, as I gratefully absorbed my first formal acting training.

I couldn't have had better direction than I received from the tandem of Semenza and Green. Semenza had directed scores of Reno Little Theater shows following his own exemplary acting career in University of Nevada productions. Sylvan Green had been married earlier to the famed singer, Beatrice Kay, who ran a guest ranch in Reno. He had been a pianist in vaudeville in New York and with touring companies. Green stuck with me, although I was the only principal actor/singer who could not read music. Each spent an inordinate amount of time with me.

My confidence rose, and Semenza's patience began to yield results after six weeks of rehearsal. He hammered to rid me of my monotone, and it worked. He emphasized enunciation. "Everyone, from front to back row and between the aisles, must know precisely what you say and understand the lyrics you sing," Semenza insisted.

Sylvan Green had a live late-night radio show broadcasting from the Riverside Hotel, and he would rasp out directions for us until 10:00 at night and then scoot to the Riverside for his show. "No one sleeps when Sylvan speaks" was his motto. Certainly, those of us who sang for him in *Take Me Along* listened intently to this master showman.

The play was enormously successful, performing to full houses and enthusiastic reviews. Before the run, the thought of a live audience judging me was chilling. I approached the opening performance with dread, as I wallowed in doubt, afraid I wouldn't reach expectations. Yet, it was apparent from the first night that Semenza and Green had superbly prepared us.

I was buoyed by the cast's camaraderie, which mirrored the team spirit that had thrilled me in athletics. Marilyn was involved in the show as well. She designed and sewed the fancy vests that were an integral part of my costuming. I was on-stage in nearly all scenes, and some felt the vests drew more attention than I did.

Being a part of *Take Me Along* elevated my feeling of self-worth, leaving me confident about my participation at the Sierra Nevada Sportswriters meetings, which I continued to attend even though I no longer was covering sports news. Prior to the theater opportunity, I had been scared to utter a peep at these meetings, but now I realized that to maximize whatever newspaper potential I had, I must showcase it verbally as well as in my writing. I began to let people know that I would be pleased to speak to service clubs, at sports banquets, or at civic events. Such invitations came increasingly, and the more I took on, the more confidence I felt.

I was anxious to gain more acting experience. Shortly after my debut at Reno Little Theater, friend Mike Schon founded a fledgling amateur company in Reno. He called the enterprise Broadway West and cast me in the lead of *Tenderloin*, which had had a brief run on Broadway. It was a fun show, with naughty innuendoes galore and several strong singing numbers. It was received cordially by audiences.

Still later, I played the part of the Viennese psychiatrist in the Reno Little Theater production of *The Seven-Year Itch*. Director David Hettich was exasperated by my feeble European accent. When it became clear that I could not talk the European talk, Hettich told me, "Just give 'em a dose of Fallonspeak."

My developing verbal communications skills were to make a big difference in my future. Mike Schon had introduced me to a life-changing experience.

Melton and Dondero Track Mary Rockefeller

Reno, NV On June 1, 1962, Charles Stout announced that Speidel Newspapers had named a new vice president and associate publisher for Reno Newspapers, Inc. Charles G. Murray was from Poughkeepsie, New York, where he had long been the editor of the local Speidel paper. Murray was slender, a shade over six feet tall, with gray thinning hair and a ruddy face. If hallway scuttlebutt was to be believed, he was tough and uncompromising, but he breezed through his first visit to the newsroom, introducing himself to all present and creating an impression of relaxed geniality.

John Sanford accompanied Murray, offering an introduction to each staff member. When they got to me, Sanford said, "Rollan got his start on a rural weekly, studied journalism in Reno, has been our sports editor, and now runs the wire desk."

"That's interesting," Murray said, gripping my hand. "Nice meeting you, Rollan."

That was it. At that moment, for all I knew, Murray could have been another of those transient, mysterious figures who occasionally floated through the newsroom and no doubt spent the better part of each day counting money in the business department. He was anything but! Charles Murray was to have a profound effect on the lives of many at the *Gazette* and *Journal*, and none would be impacted as significantly as me.

Without the union present to caution me about working too many hours and not claiming overtime, I now was free to put in as

"Charles G. Murray was from Poughkeepsie, New York, where he had long been the editor of the local Speidel paper." Charles Murray (l.) with Rollan Melton.

much time as I wished. Overtime pay was infrequent, but I loved my work. I found joy in immersing myself in as many duties as I could take on.

As my second year in the newsroom approached in 1961, I expected a major pay raise. However, John Sanford told me, "You'll now be getting an additional three dollars a week. It was all I could get you this year." I was a slow learner, but I was coming to understand why the union had been formed. I was so discouraged and in debt that I nearly quit to accept an offer to be sports editor of the *Las Vegas Review-Journal*. But Marilyn and I loved Reno, and we decided to hang in a bit longer, hoping for a shot at a junior management job.

Much of my off-duty time in early 1962 was given over to being a stringer for other publications, mainly magazines. The extra income was helping us catch up on bills. My largest non-*Gazette* earnings that year involved my coverage, for London and New York City newspapers, of the divorce residency in Reno of the first Mrs. Nelson Rockefeller.

Mary Rockefeller, wife of the New York governor, had quietly slipped into Reno, where her Nevada attorney, William Woodburn, pledged that she wouldn't be hounded by the press. He was wrong. Mary's decision to divorce Nelson Rockefeller was a political bombshell, for it was likely that he would be a candidate for the Republican nomination for the presidency.

There was no precedent for such a national political figure going through a divorce, and soon I was hearing from tabloids in Manhattan and London that wanted me to do "news legwork" on Mrs. Rockefeller. There was good money involved, and I was excited about the personal challenge of ferreting out information about her six-week residency visit. I teamed up with my photographer friend, Don Dondero.

Mary Rockefeller was residing at the Donner Trail Guest Ranch in Verdi, eight miles west of Reno. Guest ranch owner, Harry Drackert, reacting to the stern edict of attorney Woodburn, had reassured his famous guest that she would enjoy complete privacy. But Drackert hadn't bargained for Dondero's cunning and tenacity in pursuing a story. (The photographer's specialty was shooting "big shots." During his career, he made news pictures of seven men who were American presidents, and he captured countless celebrities on film as they visited Reno.)

Dondero found a source inside Donner Trail Guest Ranch who tipped him each time Mrs. Rockefeller left the compound. He learned that the famous First Lady of New York loved to go horseback riding on the trails around the guest ranch. One day he invited me to ride along as he searched the Verdi countryside for a sighting. Dondero was driving his Volkswagen Bug, and his camera, mounted with a powerful telephoto lens, was in the back seat. I spotted three riders loping towards us—two women and a man.

Dondero blurted, "That's her!" I quickly handed him his camera, and he stopped the car. Simultaneously, Mary Rockefeller saw the camera through the photographer's mud-splattered windshield, and she turned her horse to escape. Dondero's classic picture captured her in flight.

Mary Rockefeller galloped off with the other woman trailing her. Meanwhile, the furious Harry Drackert rode up to Dondero's car. He was packing a holstered gun. Drackert shouted profanities, and we sped away.

Dondero's picture, purchased by Associated Press, appeared in newspapers worldwide, and in *Life* magazine. I phoned-in the details of our encounter to papers in the East and in London, but the whole experience made me feel cheap—an impudent, mercenary intruder into a hounded woman's life. I took no pleasure from this kind of journalism.

Promotions Manager Named
Charles Murray Mentors Him

Reno, NV I had long hoped that I might one day be promoted into management, but there seemed to be little chance of that occurring at the *Gazette*. Sanford and managing editor Joe Jackson were still years from retirement age, and the department's third-ranked executive, Bryn Armstrong, was a fairly young man with a future. However, one afternoon following *Gazette* deadline, Armstrong came over to my desk, and what he said stunned me: "Rollan, I just had a visit with John Sanford, and I told him to go shove it. I've quit. If you want my job, go for it!"

The following day, as I was steeling myself to ask for a shot at Armstrong's job, Sanford walked over to me and said, "Chick Stout and Charlie Murray would like to have a word with you. Now!"

I could barely restrain my joy. "Will you be there with me, John?"

He replied, "No. So far as I know, it's just the three of you."

At last I was going to get a shot at a junior editor's job. As I entered Stout's impressive new office, I was confidently optimistic.

Stout was an imposing figure behind an imposing desk. He began, "Rollie, you may have heard that we have an important vacancy." I smiled and said that I had. He continued. "The Reno Newspapers promotions manager position has been vacant for some time. We need to fill it. We are asking you to leave the newsroom and become our public relations man."

My heart fell. Oh, no, not this .... I had never cared for flacks; now the grinning Stout was asking me to become one. As I struggled to keep my composure, he used one of his favorite words, "opportunity," about five times. Opportunity, hell! He was asking me to leave the news side for a dead-end PR job. Promotion managers come, but mostly go.

"What would I be doing?" I asked.

Stout said, "We want to begin a newspaper-in-the-classroom program, and we want to sponsor a Junior Achievement company for the first time. You would be the students' adviser. You would keep writing too, because we'd want you to put out the next annual edition of 'Nevada Looks Ahead.' Also, we will soon publish a special section commemorating the opening of the sixteen-story building that First National Bank is constructing. You would write it."

Seated alongside me as silent witness, Charles Murray nodded approvingly as Stout clicked off the "opportunities" for the one-man public relations staff. Stout added, "You may want to discuss this opportunity with your wife before giving us your decision."

The more he talked, the more convinced I was that the city editor's job I coveted would never be mine. Goodbye career fulfillment.

"I love the newsroom," I said. "Would I ever have the opportunity to go back to it?"

Stout's reply was measured. "There may be an opportunity some day. We're not certain of what the future may bring."

This gave me no consolation, but I felt that I must accept the offered job. I told him, "I won't need to talk to my wife about this. Marilyn will agree that this is a good opportunity. I will do my best."

"We'll occasionally ask you to sit in on our weekly executive management meetings," Stout said, "so you can let us know about your progress." He smiled. We shook hands.

"When do I start?" I asked.

For the first time, Murray spoke: "Monday. You can move downstairs this weekend. You'll be in an office next to mine."

Stout had made no mention of a salary increase, and I hadn't asked, but as I accepted the promotion "opportunity," the Melton family's bank balance was zero and falling. Nonetheless, the Saturday before I started in promotion, Marilyn led me to the Reno Sears-Roebuck Store, and we bought a vacuum cleaner and the first clothes dryer we ever owned. I would have to dress for the promotion manager part, and I needed something that fit, so we also splurged on a blue serge suit with two pairs of pants. It cost one hundred dollars. We used the time payment plan for all items, and it was a good thing that we did . . . .

The following week, when I asked Mr. Stout if I would get a salary increase with my new job, he hesitated before saying anything. You would have thought I had asked him, "Chick, can you spare ten grand?"

"We had wanted to give you some time to show us what you could do," he said. Then he suggested that eight additional dollars a week would suffice, and I fled from his office before he could change his mind. Marilyn was pregnant with our fifth child. We needed every penny that we could get.

From my first day as promotion manager, Charles Murray became my role model and journalism father figure. I was thankful to report to him rather than to Stout—I carried no "Melton, the striker" baggage with Murray. I learned a great deal from him. My fourteen-month tour in promotion became the equivalent of a doctoral program in the art of putting out a decent newspaper.

One thing I learned from Murray was that micro-managing could be poisonous, the ruination of an employee's creativity. He gave me suggestions and then let me do the work. "You are solely responsible for the 'Nevada Looks Ahead' edition," he told me. "You have three months to hand out story assignments, do much of the writing yourself, and lay out the news pages and send them off to press."

Murray also oversaw my campaign to create a newspaper-in-the-classroom program, in which we provided free copies of both newspapers to thousands of elementary and secondary students in northern Nevada. He directed me to maximize contacts with educators, and he taught me how to get teachers to use our newspapers as teaching devices for geography, math, political science, religion, and the art of telling stories in acceptable English. Like Charles Stout, he wasn't comfortable in the public speaking role, so he also had me fill most of the requests that he and Stout received to speak to community organizations.

My decks were awash with responsibilities, but I was eager to take on more assignments, especially to prove to Chick Stout that he had done the right thing when he decided to re-hire the striker into the *Gazette-Journal* family. I was swamped with work, pressed by deadlines—it was becoming clear that the sun does not rise and set with the news department alone. You can have a superb editorial staff, yet fail miserably if there is too little talent in advertising, business, circulation, mechanical functions, marketing, and in community relations.

Efficient communication and teamwork were essential to a successful operation, and, as Stout had promised, I was periodically invited to sit in on weekly executive sessions. I was barely past thirty-one, and I was a very junior manager with no employees to assign anything to. The *Gazette-Journal* executives, every one of them older and more experienced than me, saw that I was no threat to their career ambitions. Clearly, most of them aspired to a publisher's role, either in Reno or in other cities where Speidel owned newspapers. All I aspired to was to do the best I could in promotion and then return to the news department ASAP.

When I returned to news it likely wouldn't be as city editor, because a bright young prospect, Noel Greenwood, had worked his way into the position. Greenwood had directed news coverage of the two major stories of 1962. One story reported the deaths of Newton Crumley Sr. (an owner and the general manager of Reno's Holiday Hotel) and his passenger, First National Bank of Nevada's president, Edward J. Questa, in the crash of a private plane. The other reported the Golden Hotel fire, which killed five guests and injured many more.

The most entertaining part of my job in promotion was Charlie Murray's daily savage critique of the *Gazette* and the *Journal*. Morning after morning, he would call me in. He would have red-penciled every mistake he could find, and always there were many. Murray was determined to catch and correct all errors of fact, sloppy writing, and generally untimely reporting. He would say tartly, "Now that the *Gazette* has been publishing daily for seven decades, it's time we get today's news into the paper today."

Murray insisted that we give readers nothing less than clarity. "We should never say 'gutted,' unless we mean complete disembowelment," he would say. Regarding "the rot of daily mistakes," he blamed not the reporting staff but "the befuddled creases in our editors' journalism heads." Murray told me day after day, "A decent editor will teach his newsgatherers to load as much detail as possible into each story."

As my bond with Murray strengthened, he began confiding that John Sanford left much to be desired as editor. "If John thinks himself secure in a lifetime job, he may be dead wrong," Murray said. (Sanford was descended from the family that had long owned the *Gazette* before selling it to Speidel Newspapers in 1939.) He was especially distressed about John's insistence that the best editorials were on topics that had nothing to do with Reno, Sparks, and the rest of Nevada. Murray would say, "John is caught up in the Afghanistan syndrome."

Stout left the handling of problems with the editors almost entirely to Murray, who met excuses with stormy rebuttal or at times with deafening silence. His principal strategy was to put the editorial quality burden on the editors. "That's why we hired them," he told me in our private critique sessions: "There is no such thing as an editor incumbent. You've got to win your job and work hard every day to keep it."

Failure to follow first-day stories with subsequent stories made him furious. And: "Goddamn! Just look at how they butchered this headline. No wonder readers lose confidence when we bungle the facts, as we did in this story on page one and that one on page four. Careless reporters and editors are the number one threats to the newspaper."

Murray was a great editor. On and on he harangued, carped, and scolded. In our morning sessions, as he ripped into the quality of our newspapers, he always came back to journalism common sense. Murray believed that nothing eliminates errors so much as good old basic reporting subjected to ruthless editing. He stressed the importance of understanding how events interlock, and he was intolerant of reporters who could be mesmerized by slick-talking news sources—he said that they were fools whom we shouldn't keep.

Murray kept harping on fundamentals. "We do as poor a job on writing obituaries as any newspaper in the country," he once said. "A guy can't die in this town on the weekend—it might not be reported for days, long after the funeral. He would say, "For the life of me, I can't understand how the *Journal* can load up its front page with legitimate local news every day, and yet we can't even get a *major* local story 'out front' in the damned *Gazette*."

By my tenth month in promotion, Murray was requiring me to red-pencil both newspapers. So intent was I on doing well on the assignment that I would arrive at the office around 5:00 in the morning, giving myself extra time to ferret out the writing errors committed by my colleagues in the two newsrooms. Murray would ask me to critique aloud for him. He would typically tell me that I had done all right, but that there were some important things I had missed.

Gazette Names Melton Editor

Reno, NV   In September of 1963, publisher Stout awarded me an annual salary increase. The twenty-dollar raise was the largest I had ever gotten. Still, I couldn't afford a second business suit, and the one we had bought at Sears was getting so shiny I could almost see my reflection in it.

A couple of months later at our usual morning session, Murray told me that there would be no editorial critique that day. "We thought we should tell you in confidence, Rollie, that Chick has decided to ask John Sanford and Joe Jackson to step aside and accept reduced responsibility so that we can bring in a new *Gazette* editorial department leader."

I stiffened. "Bring in?" I said.

Murray said, "Yes. We think we have a very strong candidate within the Speidel company, and we are going to ask him if he's interested in the opening here."

After months of hearing Murray's savage critiques, I had suspected that Sanford might be given a warning or perhaps even placed on probation. Nonetheless, this news stunned me. John Sanford, the man who had hired me fresh out of the military in 1957 and who had persuaded publisher Stout to take me back from the failed strike corps in 1959—my savior, John Sanford, was to be shunted aside. Joe Jackson, whom I admired so much, was in for the same fate.

"Do you have any reaction, Rollie?"

"Can I think about this a bit, Mr. Murray?"

Who could the top editor candidate be? I didn't know any of the other Speidel editors. I thought of my own chances. They were slim. I was only thirty-two, but I believed in what Murray had been drilling into me for the last fourteen months, and I felt I could acquit myself with distinction. Further, if I got the chance, I had a hunch that Sanford and Jackson would be my staunch allies should they choose to remain on the news management team.

Gazette editors, l. to r.: Paul Leonard, John Sanford, Joe Jackson, and Rollan Melton.

I remembered how I had blown my chance at the University of Nevada Alumni Association director's position. Plain and simple, a more aggressive and self-assured self-promoter, Ken Robbins, had convinced campus decision-makers that he was the best candidate. Recalling my earlier failure to say "Hey, I'm your guy!" I told myself that this time I had absolutely nothing to lose and everything to gain. Chick Stout would have called it an opportunity; so did I.

I was waiting for Murray when he arrived at his customary early hour the next morning. He grinned that happy Irish grin and asked, "What's on your mind, Rollie?"

I replied, "I want to succeed John Sanford as editor. I'll do you and the newspaper a great job." I threw modesty away, and he listened intently. I talked for at least fifteen minutes straight, extolling my virtues.

Murray was the most discerning editor I would ever meet, a man who knew all my strengths and weaknesses. He didn't speak for several moments after I finished. Finally, he said, "Thank you Rollie. It's good to learn how you feel about yourself. Let me think over what you've said, and I'll get back to you."

About an hour later, Murray phoned me. "Rollie, would you step down to Chick's office, please?"

I was into the chief executive's office in a flash. The publisher offered me a seat, and I tried to read what was coming. Charles Stout said, "It is Charlie's recommendation, and I agree, that you be offered the opportunity to be the new editor of the *Gazette*. This places upon you much more responsibility than you have ever had, and it could give you more satisfaction than you have ever had as well."

I replied, "Sir, I accept with gratitude. I promise that I won't disappoint you or Mr. Murray or anyone."

Charles Stout smiled and replied exactly as he had that September day in 1959 when I had re-joined the *Gazette* and made essentially the same promises. "We hope so," he said. It was Wednesday, November 20, 1963.

I was vacating my cleaned-out promotion manager's office when Murray walked in. "Rollie," he said, "you and I will be going up to the *Gazette* newsroom in a half hour. I will announce that you are taking over as managing editor and that John Sanford and Joe Jackson will become your assistants, but we've decided to wait until New Year's day before *publicly* announcing this," he said. Management's thinking was clear to me. Before readers were told of the executive change, Stout and Murray intended to make certain that I measured up.

"Are you all set?" said Murray. I assured him that I was. I was euphoric, but I was also anxious about how my mentors, Sanford and Jackson, would take their demotions. On that score, Murray got quickly to the point: "Chick and I talked to John and Joe this morning. We told them that you are taking over immediately as editor, and that if they choose to stay, they will report directly to you. Each seemed relieved, and both say they want to remain on the staff. That may be good or bad. We'll have to see. You can relax—both are happy we've selected you for the job." I owed those bosses so much. I had been strongly influenced by Jackson's work ethic; and beneath Sanford's curmudgeonly veneer was an editor who was devoted to his newspaper, to his community, and to Nevada.

Murray had some advice for me: "Rollie, any community newspaper that fails to maximize local news coverage is at great risk. People can get national and foreign coverage elsewhere. They can only find out what's going on where they live when you tell them. We are weak in local coverage, and you need to fix that." He also told me that there are times when an editor has to have rhino skin and take all the stuff that the naysayers can dish out. "Listen to critics," he said. "Many times, they'll be among your most helpful advisers."

Murray referred to notes he had scribbled in longhand on his pad of yellow paper: "You'll want to take your time in picking a top assistant," he cautioned, "but you definitely will need a good one. If there is no one here, we will have to look outside. You'll do the choosing, Rollie. Choose carefully."

He continued, "Remember what we've talked about before. Don't let anyone say in a story that something is a 'first,' unless you can prove it. If men ever land on the moon, that will be a 'first.' But everything after that would be secondary stuff.

"Teach our people to ask the right questions and to do a lot of listening. There will be errors of fact. When they occur, correct inaccuracies as soon as you learn of them, and don't hide those admissions that you've screwed up."

Despite Murray's admonition to carefully deliberate on whom I picked as my assistant, I had already decided. After the shift ended that day, I took my colleague and fellow striker Walter MacKenzie aside. He was a first-rate reporter on the courthouse beat, and while I hadn't observed his newsdesk work, I supposed he'd be fine as my city editor. MacKenzie was thrilled by my offer, but I was acting from my heart rather than my head.

The news of my promotion was received cordially by the *Gazette* staff, most of whom I had worked with prior to taking the promotion assignment, and I was on an emotional high that first day of my editorship. We got out a decent issue, with Sanford and Jackson deferring to me. On Thursday, we departed from the *Gazette*'s usual non-local approach to page-one news when I directed that some city news be positioned there. I hadn't realized the editor's job would be so easy. My confidence soared. I was certain that there wasn't a challenge that I couldn't rise to.

Kennedy Assassinated
Gazette Doesn't Get It

Reno, NV   My third day as editor was Friday, November 22, 1963. At close to 10:30 that morning, our new clerk, Marilyn O. Newton, was scanning Associated Press wire copy spilling from the machine. Suddenly she screamed. Simultaneously, the AP machine went bonkers, sounding five bells, that era's signal for a major breaking news story. Several of us crowded around to scan the copy coming in bursts from the AP machine: President John F. Kennedy had been shot by a sniper in Dallas.

At first, AP news copy came in fits and bursts as the wire service's reporters struggled to assimilate one of the most shattering stories of the twentieth century. Along with the rest of the nation and world, the *Gazette* staff heard the confirmation of what we most feared. It came with television's Walter Cronkite declaring, "The president is dead."

Our staff was galvanized into a reaction-story mode, drawing up lists of appropriate leaders to hear from, including local, state, and national figures, and especially those in Nevada's congressional delegation. Many of our inside pages had been made up early, and our first edition of the harrowing day reached the streets ahead of our normal deadline.

Not many minutes after we went to press with the first edition, Charlie Murray came into the newsroom looking for me. He said, "Have you got a minute, Rollie?" He took me into my office. The staff had given their all to get out our first edition on the nation's loss, and although Murray seldom praised, I was certain that on this occasion he would have kind words for our performance. I was wrong.

Murray closed my office door and went on the attack, his face reddening: "Rollie, your top headline deep-sixes the most paramount element of the tragedy. The prime news isn't, LYNDON JOHNSON SWORN IN AS NEW PRESIDENT. It is PRESIDENT ASSASSINATED. Who in hell wrote this headline?"

I squirmed and confessed that I had.

"Well, in today's follow-up editions, you may want to rewrite this headline."

With Charlie Murray, "You may want" was not a wish, it was a command. I quickly assured him, "Yes sir, Mr. Murray. We'll do the right thing." We did.

Our young staff responded admirably throughout the day, covering the local angles and patching together the comprehensive coverage the AP dispatched from Dallas, Texas, including news of the arrest of the accused assassin, Lee Harvey Oswald.

Late that night, Joe Jackson and I stood together in the composing room. We were the last of the *Gazette* crew still in the office. Jackson always was calm under pressure, impossible to ruffle, and rarely did he reveal his emotions, but his voice trembled as his sorrow spilled out. "If we are real lucky," he said, "there will never be another American story like this to cover."

Higginbotham: Melton's Appointment An Error

Reno, NV   When I shifted Walt MacKenzie from his news beat to the editing desk, he got a blitz course in headline writing, page layout, and working out efficient copyflow patterns with printers. But practically from the start, I saw that Walt couldn't make the transition from reporter to city editor. A deliberate newsman, noted for his accuracy and breadth of coverage, he was as reliable a beat reporter as we had at that time, but the daily newsdesk requires a hurry-up energy if the paper is to go to press on time. To remove MacKenzie from reporting had been a bad decision. I had to bo back on my promise to promote him to city editor.

Walt accepted my decision with dignity. Warren Lerude, also a Nevada journalism graduate, had left the Associated Press in 1962 to join the *Gazette*, and he was showing promise as a copyeditor and as a director of local coverage. With Charlie Murray's approval, Lerude was named city editor.

The major stories kept coming. Two weeks after the Kennedy assassination, nineteen-year-old Frank Sinatra Jr. was abducted from his motel at Stateline, Nevada, where he was performing at Harrah's Tahoe. While law enforcers hunted frantically for the victim and his captors, the youngster's famous father sweated out the ordeal from his suite at Reno's Mapes Hotel.

Our niftiest Sinatra-kidnapping story came about when Walt MacKenzie dressed himself as a waiter and was admitted, food tray in hand, into the heavily guarded suite. MacKenzie's subsequent story captured the sights and sounds of the crowded suite, and especially the anxieties Sinatra Sr. was suffering. His page-one insider story did not carry a byline, however. We chose not to reveal who had concocted a disguise to gain entry to Sinatra's sanctuary. Young Sinatra ultimately was freed unharmed, following payment of ransom money.

In addition to what I was learning during each news shift, I continued to learn from Charlie Murray. He would wait until just after an issue had gone to press to ask, "Have you got a minute, Rollie?" Then the critique would begin. Murray always talked fundamentals and common sense. At opportune times, I funneled what I was learning back to the staff through Lerude. Our objective was to create an environment of continuing education at the *Gazette*.

The breadth of Murray's knowledge was stunning. If he wasn't picking apart a story, he would be generalizing:

"Eradicate inflamed rhetoric from your people's copy. Reporters and editors need to suspect that it is the accused who's innocent, the cop who's guilty of concocting lies. Your coverage ought to be so accurate, evenly balanced, and timely that it penetrates enough egos to make the local bureaucracy squirm. Any paper that tries to please everybody is going to wind up in the journalism cemetery."

I hoped to earn Murray's approval when I invited him to sit in on my speech at a Lions Club luncheon. My remarks went long, and a sort of dullness set in. I saw guys in the audience nodding off. Afterwards, Murray delivered my grade: "He who makes the shortest speech gets the most applause. Rollie, it doesn't hurt to get a few laughs, either. Humor helps keep people awake."

Murray had exquisite timing. A few months after my promotion to managing editor, he called me to his office and delivered a scorching critique of that day's issue. Finally he eased up to let his stinging commentary sink in. Then he casually added, "By the way, Rollie, I recently ran into your old campus journalism chairman, Al Higginbotham. He let me know right off that he feels we made a major error in judgment by naming you the new *Gazette* editor." I was stunned and angered, but I held my tongue. "Why would Higgy feel that way about you?" Murray asked.

I replied, "Sir, it's a very long story. Some day when you have a spare week, I'd like to share it with you." I silently vowed to work harder than ever to be the best editor I could be, and, in the process, to make Higgy swallow his words.

Murray's criticism often came from oblique angles. He would use someone else as a sad example, when he was actually telling me to shape up. When he became anxious for me to lose weight, he didn't say so outright. "One of your executive colleagues isn't doing himself any favors," he said. "Have you noticed how much heavier (retail advertising manager) Karl Karrasch has become? He is hurting himself in his career, and probably in his health, too."

Murray was proud of our printing staff and wouldn't tolerate any implication that they were beneath the *Gazette*'s and *Journal*'s white-collar help. Once he told me, "Rollie, one of your fellow executives insists on calling printers 'the back shop.' That demeans our excellent typesetters, page makeup people, and machinists. It is more appropriate to address them as composing-room staff." I got the message. Forever afterwards I called my printing colleagues "composing department members."

Charlie Murray was obsessed with his health. In 1964, when he was fifty-seven years old, I first heard him declare, "Every day lived beyond fifty is a real bonus." He said no day was satisfactory unless he took a long, brisk walk. As we drew closer, he confided that he had been diabetic since his late thirties. "I fight each day to keep my blood sugar at a safe level," he said. This helped explain why he was a finicky eater and a steady walker. His periodic discussion of his personal health was his way of urging me to safeguard my own.

Murray Named Publisher
Sends Melton to School

New York, NY In mid-1964, the longtime president of Speidel, Harry Bunker, retired, and the corporate directors named Chick Stout as his successor. An annex was added to the Gazette-Journal Building to house the Speidel corporate staff, which moved from Colorado Springs to Reno. Chick Stout's new office was in the annex. To no Reno executive's surprise, and to the pleasure of most, Charles Murray was appointed as *Gazette-Journal* publisher, succeeding Stout.

The American Press Institute, based on the Columbia University campus in New York City, was the premier continuing education center for daily newspaper executives. No Speidel executive had ever participated in one of API's heralded two-week seminars, and Stout was anxious to get Speidel managers involved. A call came from our new publisher: "Do you have a minute, Rollie?"

I went to Murray's office, expecting another blistering critique. However, to my relief, he was smiling. "Rollie, Speidel wants to get more deeply involved in executive training. Chick wants to send you to the API editors' seminar this summer." As my mind spun, Murray continued. "Chick believes you can use some additional seasoning—you know, Rollie, exposure to the experiences and ideas of others. No SNIer (Speidel Newspapers, Incorporated) has ever gone to the program at Columbia. It's time we got our feet wet."

I wanted to ask, "Why me?" but thought better of it. After all, I was the youngest and newest of the corporation's nine editors. I had much to learn, and to this point, I had never attended a single newspaper workshop.

Murray elaborated. "If you agree to go to API and do as well as I know you can, perhaps we can have you lead training sessions of our own in Reno. For all I know," Murray said, "Chick may even invite you to visit other Speidel news operations. So prepare for a lot of possible new opportunity. Are you interested?"

I again felt the power of unlikely coincidence. Was this all a dream? A blessed accident? Who cared? It was good news, and I was ready to benefit from it, but first I needed to get some suitable clothes. The blue serge suit I had bought when I became the promotion manager was so worn that it could have inspired Henny Youngman's jab, "I like your suit—who shines it for you?" Marilyn hauled me in for a clothing retread. Then, with our fifth child, three-month-old Emelie, in tow, she saw me off to the American Press Institute seminar at Columbia University.

It was a journey of firsts for the rookie editor from Reno: first trip by commercial air; first visit to New York City; first major league baseball game and Broadway show. I also got hopelessly snared in the subway system, attended the 1964 World's Fair, and met the fabled Jack Dempsey, who had many Reno friends.

There were twenty-seven seminar participants from twenty states. Most of us were new editors. I paid close attention to the presentations, took copious notes, and learned much from my fellow students.

I returned to the Reno newsroom truly pumped, but mindful of what famous Kansas editor, William Allen White, had declared in 1917: "There are three things no man can do to the entire satisfaction of anyone else: Make love. Poke the fire. Run a newspaper." I had a long way to go to become a superior editor, and I followed the advice of our API seminar moderator: "Don't rush home and act like a newly anointed expert. Pace yourself."

Goodness, Badness, Weirdness

Reno, NV Dark stories had always been composed in our newsroom, stories that reported catastrophes of nature and human mischief—fires, floods, earthquakes, murders, traffic accidents, thievery, prostitution, governmental hijinks, and man's peculiar tendency to protect woman against every man but himself. Under my editorship, we began trying hard to find examples of faith, hope, and charity in the community. Sports coverage was strengthened, and local news was given priority. We more frequently played Nevada stories on the front page, and we would not shrink from reporting things that might give the reader a laugh. Yet, I was unable to wean John Sanford away from writing editorials about non-Nevada issues. This was my fault. I should have led him, not babied him. When I told Charlie Murray of my frustration, he said, "Keep trying."

Although I wanted to increase the attention given to local news and good news, I understood that it was major stories that kept us running, and major stories are rarely good news. Locally, the Donner Ridge timber fire knocked out electric power in western Nevada for four days, and a sharp earthquake shook Reno in 1966. That year, Stead Air Force Base was fully phased out, and Reno worried about replacing the military presence, with its annual $20 million impact on the local economy.

The Vietnam War was the major continuing story of my editorship. We regularly published stories of young Nevada men killed in combat, and the national war debate spilled into Nevada towns that had lost sons. Speaking at the University of Nevada campus, I was verbally pummeled by students hostile to the "*Gazette* messengers of war." Ironically, Marilyn Melton, wife of the "war news editor," was harassed by older members of her bridge club who were hawks and loathed the *Gazette* for reporting the swelling sentiment to clear out of Vietnam. After national guardsmen killed Kent State University student protesters in 1970, one bridge companion told Marilyn, "Too bad they didn't kill them all." The players charged that her editor husband was "playing up the dissidence to sell more newspapers."

Unexpected events punctuated my work. Once, a bearded young man dressed in kimono and sandals was escorted into my office. He introduced himself as Jesus Christ and demanded an interview. When I tried to make it clear to him that we weren't interested in a Second Coming story, he grew angry and threatened me. I passed a note to a staff member: "Hurry. Call the cops." As police took "Jesus" away, he scowled at me and shouted, "You are Judas!"

We tried for years to capture good pictures of the Reno multi-millionaire eccentric, LaVere Redfield, but he eluded us at the gaming tables, at his lumberyard in west Reno, and during his downtown visits. Exasperated at pursuing photographers, he finally phoned and asked to visit me: "But you must promise not to photograph me if I come in." I assured him that we would not. Redfield was polite and soft-spoken. He gave me the Greta Garbo spiel, "I want to be left alone." We ceased stalking him except when he was in the news. Which was often.

Then there was the story of the naked American Indian, who on successive nights sprinted into Reno casinos, snatched gaming chips, and raced away. Upon his arrest, the *Gazette* police reporter, Dewey Berscheid, wrote of the capture of "Running Bare."

I was sued once while I was the editor. A seventeen-year-old had escaped from the Nevada Mental Institution. All law enforcement units were told, "Subject armed and extremely dangerous," and the cops warned the public to beware. In monitoring our newsroom police radio, I became convinced that the escapee was the equivalent of an adolescent John Dillinger. It was unlawful to identify criminal suspects who were younger than eighteen, but near deadline time, without consulting Charlie Murray, I decided that our story should name the boy and include a head-and-shoulders picture of him. We played the story and picture above the fold on page one.

The juvenile was captured shortly after the *Gazette* press run. On the following day, the family of the youngster hired Reno attorney Peter Echeverria to file a libel suit naming me, the Reno Newspapers, Inc., and numerous "John Does" as defendants. The plaintiff asked $100,000.

The *Gazette-Journal* lawyer, Mead Dixon, took my deposition and that of our news editor, Warren Lerude, who testified accurately that he took no part in deciding to identify the runaway. I took sole responsibility, admitting that we knowingly broke the law in using the name of a minor. I felt queasy while testifying under oath, afraid that Stout and Murray would not want to keep me on as editor.

Dixon maintained that if we went to trial, we would lose to a jury: "You broke the law. This good-looking kid resembles an angelic choirboy. Jurors are hostile to the press; especially now, because of Vietnam." I felt myself balanced on the cusp of unemployment.

I argued that we should fear the precedent of backing down from this kid and his crafty attorney, but Stout and Murray overruled me, telling Dixon to accept Echeverria's offer of an out-of-court settlement. We paid $5,000. Case closed.

My bosses never reprimanded me for my handling of the story. However, publisher Murray did say, "Rollie, if a story like this breaks again, check it with me. If you have a minute." Echeverria's teen-age client was back in police custody a few days later, accused of hitting a highway patrol car during a high-speed chase.

Rollie Has a Minute

Reno, NV Each newspaper day bought learning and challenge. Murray and business manager Clarence K. Jones coached me on how to create a news department budget. Richard Schuster, who succeeded me as promotion manager, was strong on marketing, and he shared both his expertise and his humor with me. He referred to the casual, daily coffee-time bull session of executives as "the hour of charm."

We coached reporters in the unfrocking of news sources who shaded the truth. When laypeople argued that television was the stronger medium of record, I asked them, "If you were accused of driving under the influence, would you prefer the news to be on TV for ten seconds or in a newspaper forever?" (Persons accused of DUI frequently begged us to censor their names from published lists of drunken-driving defendants. No such request was ever granted, including one from a woman whose aged father was charged. I had been the invited soloist at her wedding during our college years, but I had to deny her request. Forever after, she treated me as though I had died.)

Each day, Murray called. "Do you have a minute, Rollie?" His red-penciled news tear sheets were becoming all too familiar. For example, when Lyndon B. Johnson signed the Civil Rights Act into law, we played the story on page one. Murray quickly summoned me. "Rollie, is Johnson right-handed or left-handed?"

I stammered, "Right."

Murray plopped the *Gazette* front page before me. We had mistakenly "flopped" the negative—to my horror, I saw that our picture showed Johnson signing the historic act with his left hand.

Murray pounced: "Congratulations. No doubt we are the only newspaper in America to convert the president into a southpaw."

Murray spent far more time with me than with any other department head. Each private critique of the paper could take as much as an hour, but I knew the excessive time was necessary—I was the youngest and newest on Murray's executive staff, and news was his primary focus.

Once when I left Murray's office after a particularly long session, I found advertising director Al Conton pacing outside, impatient for his time with the boss. Conton huffed, "You're nothing but a brown-nose, Melton."

Competition motivated us. We got the jump on the *Journal* whenever we could, and it was a newspaper sibling rivalry that profited readers. We were encouraged by the fact that Murray was more liberal than Chick Stout on helping us raise staff salaries, and we slowly began to catch up.

The term "glass ceiling" was foreign to us in the mid-1960s, and the *Gazette* had risen to the point where half our staff was female. Reliable Florence Burge was society page editor. During my editorship, she won the national J. C. Penney award for excellence—the first *Gazette* woman to capture a national citation. In Jeanne Toomey, we had a rip-roaring reporter from the old school who had worked the New York newspaper scene as crime reporter. Estelle Saltzman, Pat Rogero Sullivan, and mighty-mite Mimi LaPlante were also able reporters.

I had recruited one of our best women when I was promotion manager. While Patricia Glendon of New York City was in Reno to obtain a divorce, she told me that she intended to remain in Nevada to get her two young sons started in school, and she was looking for work. I encouraged her to visit John Sanford, who signed her on. She became one of our best staffers.

Our male staff members were also competent and competitive. Sanford and Joe Jackson gave the paper depth of experience and indispensable institutional memory. News editor Warren Lerude was aggressive, had the stomach for the fray, and was dependable in the rough-and-tumble news environment. At the Washoe County Courthouse, Walter MacKenzie was a solid journeyman. For the local and state news, the *Gazette* relied on William R. (Bob) Smith, a perceptive political

The 1966 *Gazette* news staff. l. to r.: John Sanford, Warren Lerude, Marilyn Newton, Joe Jackson, Joe Midmore, Rollan Melton, Patricia Glendon, Walt MacKenzie, Chuck Thomas, and Jim Drennan.

columnist, and Edward R. Allison, who had grown up in Carson City and was a strong capitol news bureau writer. Norman Cardoza brought thoughtful straight news and feature coverage. John Lengel, recruited from the Reno Associated Press Bureau, served too briefly. Dewey Berscheid was a strong young reporter before he left to become a university professor.

Joe Midmore had flown combat missions with the Royal Air Force during World War II. He came to Reno for a divorce and applied for a reporting job. I hesitated to hire those hitting town for the "cure," because they so often were staff short-timers. We made an exception with Midmore, an excellent hire who remained with us for years.

Among the special editorial department recruits were two who strengthened us. I convinced Reno Silver Sox baseball club business manager, Robert Nitsche, to apply for a classified department sales job, and then I orchestrated his move to the newsroom to become sports editor. The other promising newcomer was Dean C. Smith, who was a Nevada journalism student and part-time advertising department employee when the 1959 strike occurred. He joined the picket line with the rest of us, but was disgruntled with Guild representative Joe Campo, whom he knew was a danger to newspaper people and property. Smith completed his journalism education and was then re-hired during my editorship. His superb reporting and presence convinced me that he had executive potential.

Seminars Show The Way

Iowa City, IA In mid-1965, Murray told me that president Stout wanted me to present an editorial seminar, critiquing the work of both *Gazette* and *Nevada State Journal* news staff members. I relished the opportunity. It would be a stern test of my ability to teach contemporaries, especially our hot rivals on the *Journal*. I spent several weeks poring over issues of the newspapers, digging out the best and worst examples of reporting, writing, use of photos, and page layout. I studied the background and ability of every employee who was to attend my two-hour critique.

In the workshop, I used techniques I had learned from the American Press Institute lecturers. I also borrowed heavily from my invaluable sessions with Charlie Murray. Experience gained from my live theater and public speaking engagements strengthened my presentation.

I alternately used humor and gentle prodding, and I praised our *Journal* staff competitors more than I did my own staff. In the animated question-and-answer segment, the interaction was excellent.

I made liberal use of a technique that had served me well before—what I called the "praise-criticism sandwich." Meaning "build them up, then beat them up." The recipe was simple; the results were journalistically nutritious.

Stout and Murray observed the meeting. Stout, who seldom praised a colleague, was effusive in his response to my style and the apparent results, and he told me, "Now get ready to take this show on the road to every other Speidel newspaper."

This was to be the first group-wide training program since the Speidel company was born in 1921. It was a grand opportunity for me to get to know the corporation, its history, its people, and its internal politics. Determined to maximize the results, I spent a month preparing for the opening seminar, which was to be held in the newsroom of Speidel's afternoon daily *Gazette* in Chillicothe,

"I spent a month preparing for the opening seminar, which was to be held in the newsroom of Speidel's afternoon daily Gazette *in Chillicothe, Ohio."* (Gazette-Journal *photograph.*)

Ohio in August of 1965. I interviewed the publisher, Robert Schafer, long before my arrival. I asked for biographies of each reporter, photographer, and editor. As part of my preparation, I secured a month's issues of the *Gazette*, and I dissected every local story, headline, and picture, looking for warts and beauty spots. By telephone, in advance of my visit, I interviewed Chillicothe's veteran retiring editor, Boots Oyer, and his young successor, Don Casey.

The first seminar was to be a prototype for those that would follow. We met for two hours each afternoon after the paper was put to bed. At our first meeting, my opening words were, "The *Chillicothe Gazette* is a good newspaper. It can be better. Each of us is here to help make it better." (Thirty-two years later, upon his retirement, Donald Casey wrote me that the "can be better" admonition shaped his professional perspective for the rest of his career.)

The week was a rousing success, and staffers commented on what they termed "Rollie's incredible memory for names and details." There was no magic to it; it was simply the result of painstaking homework.

By the end of 1965, I had given week-long workshops at Speidel newspapers in Poughkeepsie, New York; Salinas, California; Fort Collins, Colorado; and Iowa City, Iowa. I would complete the national circuit the following year.

My week in Iowa City was especially noteworthy, because there I first met the *Press-Citizen's* publisher, E. J. (Jack) Liechty. I ordinarily sought to begin relationships by getting acquainted with new friends and not letting them realize that they were being interviewed. Liechty wasn't buying that. He turned the tables on me, and through our first encounter, a dinner at his home, he kept me talking about my family, my newspaper philosophy, my part in the Reno newspaper strike, and my sports background. He and his wife, Ailene, were curious about whether legalized gambling was a negative influence on Reno community life.

Liechty was a graduate of Drake University at Des Moines, Iowa, where he had been a noted varsity baseball catcher. Lean, baldish, bespectacled, articulate, and friendly, he impressed me as one who, had he not chosen circulation as his concentration, could have been a top editor. He was a charming host, curious about all things, and he had a broad awareness of Speidel history and of the individuals who brought the corporation through its formative years.

"[Jack Liechty] and his wife, Ailene, were curious about whether legalized gambling was a negative influence on Reno community life." The Liechtys in 1969.

In addition to his publisher role, Charlie Murray was editorial director of the Speidel Group. When the Speidel corporate board and publishers met in annual session in Reno in January 1966, he announced the top editorial award for the previous year. He hauled me to the front of the meeting room and announced, "Speidel is honoring Rollie Melton as the group's top editor of 1965." Murray said the citation was being given to me for "turning the *Reno Gazette* into a top prize-winner in Nevada, and for bringing a nationally recognized news training program to our newspapers."

Gazette and *Journal* Get New Publisher
Melton Is Just 35

Reno, NV I began thinking seriously about the future. Where did I want to be when Charlie Murray retired? He was then fifty-nine, with six years to go to normal retirement. That would be in 1971, the year I turned forty. True, the Reno publisher role was coveted by many. There would be much competition for it—perhaps more than any of us anticipated if Speidel went outside the corporation to find a successor. My logical course was the one that had unfailingly served me before. I would do my best, get results, and keep learning.

It is said that it's great to work in the city where your corporate office is, so long as you perform. Otherwise, it can be hell. I would do my best to avoid hell—for my sake, and, I hoped, for Speidel's sake.

In 1966 Chick Stout unexpectedly chose Iowa City's Jack Liechty to join the Speidel corporate staff in Reno, thus lining him up as heir-apparent. Now I realized why the Liechtys had expressed so much interest in Reno.

Later that year, the International Typographical Union elected to strike our newspaper at Sioux Falls, South Dakota. But an hour before the picket line went up, a

United Airlines charter plane—carrying twenty-one Speidel executives, each trained in mechanical processes—landed in Sioux Falls. The shareholder/executives were inside the *Argus-Leader* Building, outfitted in work aprons, when the first picket signs sprang up at daybreak. The strike was crushed by the preparedness that was Chick Stout's hallmark.

Around December, Charlie Murray called and said, "Do you have a minute, Rollie?" I hurried to his office for another critique. But Murray said, "Chick wants to talk to you. The only advice I have, Rollie, is listen to him, then react as you wish. Let's go next door and see Chick and Jack Liechty." I was mystified. What was up? Was I to be asked to leave Reno for a different assignment?

Stout got right to the subject. "As you know, Charlie has diabetes. It is increasingly a challenge for him. So, Charlie has decided to retire as Reno publisher at the end of the year. We want you to be his successor. Now, Rollie, you may wish to talk to Marilyn about this opportunity . . . ." Stunned, I said, "There's no need to talk to Marilyn. I accept."

I couldn't keep a job. With only fourteen months as promotion manager and just three years as editor, I was no longevity prize. Now, effective January 1, 1967, at age thirty-five, I was the publisher of the *Gazette* and *Journal*. I had been hired nine years earlier and had learned much, but I had a long way to go to become a superior leader.

The *Journal's* assistant managing editor was the first visitor to my office on my first day as publisher. I grinned, pleased at how thoughtful he was to come over to congratulate me. But Frank Johnson handed me a one-sentence letter of resignation and then told me bluntly, "I always wanted to be publisher here. But you're younger than me, Rollie, with many years left to be the chief executive. I'm not going to hang around for years for a chance at your job. I'm quitting." A month later, Johnson was named chairman of the Nevada Gaming Commission.

As football coach, army information leader, and editor, I had learned to get results by motivating others to do the work, and it was essential that I implement that method as publisher. Except for Warren Lerude, the new *Gazette* editor, I was the youngest of the front-line executives.

Most department leaders had been at their posts for a number of years—an exception was circulation director Robert S. Lee, who had transferred in to replace a fired manager. *Journal* editor Paul Leonard, a strong writer of opinion, mostly about Nevada subjects, was a person of shining integrity. Business manager Clarence K. Jones had the fast smile of a Rotary Club treasurer. Albert Conton, the advertising director, loved foraging through memories and was a competent trainer of salespeople. Circulation's Bob Lee was a superior manager, who, at the *Iowa City Press-Citizen*, had been the promising protégé of Speidel's new general manager, Jack Liechty. Our mechanical superintendent, Vic Anderson, was without guile and was admired for his generous habit of giving subordinates credit for results he shaped.

As 1966 began, Speidel bought the daily *Fremont Tribune* in rural Nebraska, and Chick Stout sent Reno promotion manager Richard J. Schuster there as publisher. I quickly achieved a gender breakthrough, appointing personable, creative Patricia Rose as Schuster's promotion and personnel successor. She was the Reno newspapers' first female department leader.

I now was reporting to president Stout and his heir-apparent, Liechty, as were the other eight publishers. Stout was a blend of experience, vision, toughness, and intuition. Publishers who felt prepared to answer any question he asked were invariably numbed by his surprise inquiries. He was hard on those who tried to bluff him. Liechty had a grand management style: He was focused and informed, and he impressed those who reported to him by admitting, "I don't know. Please tell me." He loved to use sports analogies: "We need managers who train their backups; let's encourage strong game plans."

It was instructional to see Stout grow impatient with those who tended to talk things to death. I was safe in that regard, for I was no chatterbox. He rarely told anyone that he had done well, and when he did, the accolade was treasured like a bouquet. On the other hand, Liechty would praise people when they had earned it, and his style lifted morale.

Stout's ease with financial data amazed colleagues. We thought of him as a human computer that spit out statistics upon command. Liechty had been a publisher for only four years before coming to Reno's corporate office, but he had mastered all aspects of publishing. He was a superb time-and-motion manager who taught by his good example.

Each made lists of things to do, and Liechty always wrote out an agenda before he led a meeting. Stout memorized the order of topics he wished to discuss. Neither liked small talk, and although Liechty was especially skilled at concealing his impatience, if you saw his fingers tapping the desk, you knew that it was time to get to the point.

When agitated, Chick Stout was scary. He had the unusual habit of smiling just before expressing his displeasure. Mechanical superintendent Anderson used to say, "Be careful when Chick smiles. When he does, you're gonna get whopped."

Charlie Murray was still a vital part of my life. He remained, at Stout's request, the SNI group editorial director, but it was a part-time role. Murray now funneled some group news assignments to me. At the request of Stout, Murray also was writing a history of the Speidel organization. For all his research and writing skills, Murray admitted to me that he was anxious about how Stout would accept his work.

Publisher Goes on the Road

Visalia, CA Not long after I was appointed publisher, Stout told me to finish the group editorial training seminar program I had begun the previous year. So, back I went to the late-night critiques of issues published by Speidel newspapers, from New York to California. In preparing for each visit, I found truth in the axiom, "The teacher learns most." Thus, in my first year as publisher, I also concluded the national project, conducting week-long Speidel newsroom workshops in Visalia, California; Sioux Falls, South Dakota; and Fremont, Nebraska. In every SNI city, many non-news executives sat in on the workshops. I didn't know whether they were there to learn or to size me up. Both, I guessed.

The training program was a dazzling experience for me. I met most of the company's 1,300 employees, had entrée to every SNI executive corridor, and got to know each of the group's eighty executives. I was mastering the power of listening, and I was finding it simple to lift morale. Humor helped as an ice breaker and a way to dissolve suspicion that I might be a spy from the SNI central office.

The myriad rewards included putting my arms around much of the America that I had read about but had never seen. Speidel was like a huge playground where work was both exciting and fun, as I savored the pleasure of developing collegial relationships with executives, with their staffs, and with townspeople in cities across the land.

Speidel Plan Builds Wealth For Executives

Reno, NV I assigned various executives to oversee the Reno operation when I was traveling the Speidel road. Then I'd be home again to catch up on being attentive husband and father. Marilyn was the superb family leader. She was patient with my absorption with work. Though I was now earning considerably more, we were still living on a bare-bones budget, but Marilyn was a marvel at keeping us in the black. Our financial pinch at that point requires an explanation:

Speidel was unique among American newspaper corporations—it was wholly owned by active and retired executives, plus some survivors of deceased executives. Until 1952, Speidel's founder and chairman, John Ben Snow, owned all of the stock in the national company; but in a stunning, unprecedented reorganization that year, he offered to sell ninety-three percent of his shares to company executives. He retained ownership of seven percent, the maximum any executive could hold under the amended bylaws. Snow wanted to make certain that no single person ever gained control of the company.

At midpoint of the century, many media groups existed, and none was publicly held. Hundreds of newspapers were family-owned, and employees owned the *Journal* in Milwaukee, Wisconsin, but Speidel was the only chain whose executives owned all of its papers, numbering eight by 1948.

The optioning of shares to Speidel executives continued for twenty-five years, from 1952 to 1977. The stock value was determined by an annual average earnings formula that was tied to the performance of the entire group, and because we were privately owned, the common stock wasn't subject to the vagaries of the market place. The stock purchase plan was a powerful incentive to bring efficiency to Speidel newspapers, because executives were compensated based on a percentage of profits at their individual newspaper. Management teams termed the compensation and stock-buying privilege, "Owning a piece of the Speidel rock."

Under the leadership of John Ben Snow and the second president of the company, Harry Bunker, the Diamond -S- Loan Corporation was created to make initial loans to new, mostly young, Speidel executives so that they could begin to buy company stock. John Ben Snow tailored the Speidel profit sharing and stock ownership program after the plan that had made him a multimillionaire when he was a corporate executive and board member of the F. W. Woolworth Company. Woolworth's profit and stock plan was called Diamond -W-.

I received an initial $50,000 loan from Diamond -S- Corporation in January 1965, following my first full executive year. Executives and their families lived on a monthly draw—in my case, only $700 a month. Executive bonuses, based on the profit of individual newspapers, were paid each February after an annual audit confirmed the current stock value. Marilyn and I had no family money, so we had to stretch to stay afloat month to month.

But what about bonuses? Didn't they put me and others into financial clover? Hardly. There was always loan interest to be paid to the Diamond -S- Corporation, and we dipped into bonus checks to pay household costs that piled up because of our meager monthly draw.

Charlie Murray had carefully coached me on stock purchases: "Nothing's a sure thing, Rollie, but if I were you, I'd keep building my ownership." Murray himself set a superb example. For years, he and his wife, Nikki, borrowed heavily to buy what later became thousands of Speidel shares.

At first, I had no loan connections with Reno banks, but Stout and Murray did, and they gave me entrée to loan officers at First National Bank of Nevada. The worth of our family's Speidel shares grew markedly in my first year of ownership, so we borrowed enough from the bank to pay off the $50,000 Diamond -S- loan and to take on greater debt to buy more stock.

Stout had pet sayings that both amused and upset Marilyn. He said, "Living on a limited monthly draw is simply forced savings," or, "You can build your estate by buying stock." Marilyn had a reaction, which, fortunately for us, was never expressed to Stout in person: "That estate stuff is fine," she said, "but why can't we have enough to live on while we're still alive?"

A few days after I became publisher, I came home, mellowed Marilyn with a glass of Chardonnay, and meekly said, "There's great news! Chick Stout is giving us an opportunity to go another $100,000 in debt!" Marilyn nearly choked. But we were confident that more borrowing made sense. Annual bonuses and our stock dividends would allow us to pay our loan interest and to reduce some debt, and as values continued their inexorable climb, we could leverage even larger loans to finance more stock purchases.

Learning the Ropes
Rollie Feels As If He's Still On Trial

Reno, NV Charlie Murray became like a father to me, and he often slipped and addressed me as Roger, who was his only child. After I became publisher, I called him "Charlie" for the first time, and he was pleased. But he still was a candid scold, trying to minimize my blunders.

Not long after I succeeded him, Murray asked, "Rollie, who handles your finances at home?"

I told him that I was a slug at bookkeeping and bill paying. "Marilyn does all that."

Murray came down like a hammer on me. "Rollie, if you ever admit that to Chick, you're cooked. He won't let a financial illiterate go an inch above publisher!" His oblique hint that I might rise beyond publisher was not lost on me. My long-ago desire was to be a city editor. I had learned to think bigger.

Hell-bent to live up to Murray's expectations, I intensified my drive to do the right thing for my company, community, and family. As publisher, I was thrust into areas of operations that were mostly new to me, so I was open to being taught by my executives. I was both their leader and their eager student. Some of the things they taught me were that classified advertising volume is a reliable barometer of the local and national economy; that payroll is by far a newspaper's largest expense; that newsprint is the second largest cost; that lax credit and collection procedures can imperil a company; that excessive paper spoilage fritters away profits; and that you can pump brawn and brain into a paper, but if newsprint and ink aren't delivered, you're out of business.

Ordinarily, group executive meetings were held once a week, but I talked to most of my managers individually each day. At first, *Journal* editor Paul Leonard feared that I would spend more time with his *Gazette* counterpart than with him. The veteran editor was pleased to learn otherwise.

Local television competition for news and advertising was stirring aggressively in the Reno-Sparks market, so there was stronger need for us to be more efficient in news gathering and persuasive in ad salesmanship. I likened the keeping of revenue poachers off our turf to gaining superiority in football, where the timid, the procrastinators, and the non-planners are defeated even before the opening kickoff.

Non-news managers expected me to focus mostly on the news side, because that was where I had been reared. Instead, I consciously spent more time with the other departments. It was a way to stress collective achievement and to convince doubters that I didn't play favorites.

As a boy, I had dreaded being the target of my playground tormentors; as chief executive, I pounced hard on the few managers who harassed staff. On playing fields during my boyhood and young manhood, it had bruised my esteem to be chosen last, or worse, totally ignored. In those times, I had disdained so-called student leaders whose cliques excluded others. The remembrance spurred me to be a visible leader who made time to visit everyone.

I roamed each department daily. I came to know all employees and independent contractors. Both day and night press crews regularly had me on their turf, and they were pleased. They were the only employees who were unionized, and a chief executive's presence assured them that their craftsmanship was appreciated.

This in no way suggests that I fancied myself Mr. Wonderful. Quite the contrary. I felt on trial, as if I was still that little boy about to be whacked by his Grandmother Daisy. Some of my foremost helpers were those who saw my shortcomings and told me of them. I could count on the omnipresent Stout to advise me that the rise of production costs should jar me into taking corrective measures.

Some *Gazette-Journal* executives—especially Vic Anderson and Bob Lee—were better time-and-motion managers than was I. I needed to imitate them. Working with our business manager, Clarence Jones, and especially with Gerald C. Bean, the corporate financial leader, convinced me that I still had to master basic finance. What a revolutionary change in the Fallon youngster who had shunned taking any business course!

Ken Ingram, who during my teens was my vaunted teacher and counselor, still alerted me to my failings. He once phoned when I was publisher to explain that he had tried vainly for the last few mornings to find a paper in a newsstand rack at a Reno restaurant. When I reacted with what he felt was indifference, Ingram wouldn't accept my lame alibi. He insisted that I drive across town to meet him and see "the horror your circulation department has created." I did. "What you better do," Ingram said, "is fix this." I did.

I was not well-connected in Reno's business, civic, and social life. Although there were offers to join non-newspaper boards, I turned down everything to avoid the appearance of conflict of interest. Most of my friends had a connection with newspapering, but at a future time, I would regret not expanding my acquaintances outside journalism.

John Sanford Resigns

Reno, NV Charlie Murray was so right when he said personnel problems would be my foremost concern. The most painful episode occurred after the assassination of Reverend Martin Luther King in Memphis, Tennessee on April 4, 1968. The following morning, I told editor Lerude that I presumed opinion writer John Sanford would lament the murder of the renowned black leader, and extol him. Minutes later, Lerude got back to me with shocking news. "John refuses to write anything that praises King."

I immediately went to my old news mentor for an explanation. As always, Sanford was blunt. He said, "I have no respect for Martin Luther King, and I will not write one good word about him."

I replied, "All right, John, I won't quarrel with your right to refuse. No one on this staff is compelled to editorialize on any anything he doesn't believe in. We'll ask someone else to eulogize King."

Sanford growled, "No, I'll write it, but it will be the last thing I ever write for the *Gazette*, because effective this afternoon, I resign."

Rattled, I hurried away to apprise Stout, Liechty, and Murray and to get their advice on how to respond. There long had been ill feelings between Stout and Sanford. In fact, as far as I knew, Sanford was the only one who ever got in Stout's face. That graveled the president. To worsen the relationship, Sanford had once made Stout lose face in front of others. My report to my superiors didn't take more than a half-minute. Stout made his decision in less time than that, not asking the opinion of the three of us. He was emotionless. "John insists on resignation. Accept it."

At that moment in the newsroom, Sanford was composing his final *Gazette* editorial, an eloquent valedictory by a Nevada journalism giant who had poured forty-three years of his life into the Reno *Evening Gazette*. He concluded it with these words:

"Dr. King himself expressed several times that he might become a victim of racial hatred and violence, but he continued his course, unafraid. In the black shadow of the Memphis tragedy, the entire country recognizes that it must work in harmony, and with understanding of human values, to bring about the fair and equal society of all races and classes that Dr. King gave his life to accomplish."

I was stricken. I had never known my savior in the newspaper strike to waver from a decision. He didn't this time, either. He was leaving on principle, a martyr, departing on his own shield. In the late afternoon, I went to his office to say goodbye. But he was gone. John Sanford had cleared out his library and his desk and walked away from his beloved newspaper forever.

Going Public, Getting Hitched

Liechty: "You Are My Choice To Be Vice President"

Reno, NV   Challenges continued without let-up. In my second year as publisher, my special concern was that the six-day afternoon *Gazette* was no longer gaining circulation. Not that long before, it had had many more subscribers than the *Journal*. But our seven-day morning paper was now edging ahead. The consensus was that the *Gazette* was the superior news product, but demographics were changing rapidly. Television newscasts were gobbling up listeners' time. Increased leisure time was a factor. The number of working women was increasing. In cities with competing dailies, advertisers were starting to buy more space on the morning cycle, and a growing number of afternoon dailies were being converted to morning publication. ⎯⎯⎯⎯⎯

Although I had been publisher only briefly, I was speculating on Speidel's possible line of succession. This mind game was occurring at all our newspapers. On June 30, two months after John Sanford quit over the Martin Luther King case, Chick Stout himself reached the mandatory retirement age of sixty-five. However, he remained as chairman of the corporate executive committee, a powerful position.

Jack Liechty was Stout's successor as president. Of course, there was company-wide curiosity about whom Liechty would select to be his backup executive. I didn't believe that I was a contender. I was just a second-year publisher, needing more experience. Liechty was fifty-seven years old, with eight years left to be the president before he reached retirement.

I reached my thirty-seventh birthday in July. Each Speidel publisher was older than me and had more administrative experience. Moreover, Speidel management had never gone outside to hire a top corporate officer, but Liechty might buck that tradition. He had connections in the American Newspaper Publishers Association and the national circulation organization.

In October 1968, Liechty sent me to New York City to attend my second American Press Institute seminar at Columbia University. The two-week session was for publishers, most of whom were new to their position. It was a fascinating, helpful program. Afterwards, I hurried home, an absentee husband and father who was anxious to reunite with his family.

The day I returned to my office, Jack Liechty called and asked me to visit him. He said, "Before the end of the year, we expect to add an eleventh SNI paper. It's going to be good-sized, with many opportunities, but with problems."

Jack paused, and I thought, "Here it comes—Jack is going to ask me to leave Reno to become publisher of our new newspaper."

I had guessed wrong. He talked on. "I'm going to need a strong corporate executive alongside to assist me. You are my choice to be vice president."

⎯⎯⎯⎯⎯

Would a non-fiction writer concoct such a far-fetched story, expecting it to be published? The appointment as Speidel's vice president kept alive my against-all-odds string. Up to this time, the "headlines" in my story included:

The Melton family in 1968. l. to r.: Rollan, Wayne, Emelie, Royle, Kevin, and Marilyn.

Impoverished single mother rears a Great Depression waif; at age ten, he can barely read, write, or add; the drifter boy is a failing student and disciplinary screw-up at eighteen elementary schools, and the petty scrapes he gets into are of his own making; he drops out of school, but then his maternal grandmother intercedes and makes the dropout return to class; football gives him a squirt of esteem serum; then by chance, this hobo adolescent is hired by rural newsmen. They become his true family.

Defying the odds, he wins a full-ride scholarship to the University of Nevada; all the adults on both sides of his family had several marriages, but he weds his college sweetheart, vowing to break the divorce string; two columns that he writes in the campus newspaper, *Sagebrush*, defending a professor in a celebrated academic freedom case, so anger the university president that the student-journalist totters on the ledge of expulsion.

But the former dropout earns both his degree and an army officer commission; a surprise encounter with a senior military officer from Nevada leads to his appointment as information officer of the most decorated U.S. Army division; the military cannot find an experienced person to coach the fort's football team, and, in desperation, selects the former Nevada prep and college player; the rookie coach bumbles through a losing season, but learns what not to do.

Upon his discharge, he becomes sports editor for a newspaper in Reno; but shortly thereafter, he is ensnared in an emotional attempted work stoppage and walks the picket line; he tries to find a non-newspaper job, but companies reject him; however, he becomes one of only two strikers that the newspaper re-hires; he despairs after the accidental death of his infant son; but a friend persuades him to try out for a live stage musical, and he earns the leading role; it is his experience as an actor that diminishes his quaking fear of public speaking.

He is yanked from the newsroom and reluctantly becomes the *Gazette-Journal* promotion leader, but he blossoms under the mentoring of Reno's co-publisher, who is a brilliant editor of the old school; by the age of thirty-two, he is the editor; then, with just nine years in the company, the once jobless striker is named the publisher; two years later, he is appointed vice president of executive-owned Speidel Newspapers, a nationwide group of eleven dailies.

Granted, his work ethic is strong; but he is also the beneficiary of luck, coincidence, and the magic touch of amazing role models who have given him many advantages. He owes them his best efforts and wants never to disappoint them.

Yes, I know. His story line reads as though scripted by the Highest Authority. But this string of events has not been invented by a slap-happy dreamer. All you see here is true. Not by any stretch is this a unique story about one individual, for life confronts everyone with obstacles, some seemingly insurmountable. Challenges rain on the parades of each of us. Yet, if we think positive, we learn to treat them as helpful steps to learning.

By January, 1969, at the age of thirty-seven, I had at last found steady work. I would give my best and trust that when Jack Liechty retired six years later, I would be a contender to succeed him as Speidel president. I turned my publisher's office over to Richard Schuster, who returned to Reno after being our publisher in Nebraska, and I saddled up for corporate adventure.

Liechty thrust me head-first into new challenges. Soon I was wishing I had majored not only in print journalism, but also in accounting, business administration, history, English composition, geography, advertising, public relations, political science, math, philosophy, and even in theology. After all, at times I felt like praying that I would get through my rookie season without going down for the count. I was convinced by now that university curricula ought to require "how to" time-management courses. I was getting much on my plate, with too little time to do everything.

The secretaries in my career gave me crash courses in working efficiently. As Reno's publisher, I had inherited Charlie Murray's secretary, Toshi Hirose. Now at Speidel, I was in the care of one of the best of all time. Jean Brown Roseman had been secretary to Chick Stout when he was publisher and then the SNI president. She became the aide to Jack Liechty, and when I joined the central office, she doubled as my secretary too.

Jean quickly set me straight. "Stop typing letters on your manual, and get to dictating to me," she said. "You can talk as fast as you wish. With my Gregg shorthand, I can keep up with you."

I told her, "Jean, I've typed since I was seventeen, and I can't compose unless I do it with these keys."

Jean shot back, "Rollie, I insist. From now on you will dictate to me."

I grumbled, but dutifully did as told. My attitude adjustment was quick and total. After fits and starts, I was so pleased that I never again wanted to write a letter manually. My desk was cleared by mid-mornings. "See what a breeze it is?" she teased. She was an excellent teacher, and I was open to her suggestions through our years together.

I found myself alongside Liechty enmeshed in dealing with Irving Trust Company, which had the most prestigious business address in New York: One Wall Street. We dealt with Irving in financing, and Liechty had me delving into the heady world of acquisition, studying newspapers that might come up for sale.

I was learning something at every juncture. I functioned in a sort of classroom environment that made me feel that I was back at the university, studying for graduate degrees in everything: corporate tax; group insurance; retirement and health insurance; psychology; statistics; and on and on. It was President Liechty's nature to provide his colleagues with the experiences that might ultimately enable us to become leaders superior to him. That's how smart and selfless he was.

Speidel Acquires Stockton Paper

Stockton, CA   Dead ahead was the purchase of the eleventh SNI newspaper, the *Stockton Record* in California. The owner's widow, Loretta Martin, was confronted with an estate tax bill that ran into the millions. Her only option was to sell the paper. She initially asked fourteen million dollars. However, the brilliant Chick Stout worked up a presentation that convinced her to sell to Speidel for a figure less than twelve million. We were the surprise bid winner, edging out Knight-Ridder, McClatchy Newspapers, and the Newhouse organization. The agreement in principle to purchase the *Stockton Record* was announced in October 1968, and we finalized it in January 1969 as I was joining the company's central office.

The *Record* was an editorially sound newspaper, and it became Speidel's largest paper in terms of paid circulation, which was 65,000. It did present some challenges—they were related to the presence of hard-liner unions and over-staffing in some departments, but its potential was significant.

In an acquisition, Speidel always hoped that it would also fall heir to able managers, as we disliked bringing strangers in to run a city's newspaper. That doesn't set well with townspeople who resent "foreigners." The more we learned about the *Record's* executives, the happier we were.

The best human acquisition of all was the paper's editor, Robert B. Whittington, who had been reared by a single working mother and was an exemplary student with a strong work ethic. He had earned his degree in journalism from the University of California-Berkeley, begun at the *Record* as a sportswriter, and climbed the news ranks to the editorship. He also had been a president of the paper's guild unit, and union members respected his professionalism and even-handed style.

Speidel paid a chunk for the *Record*, so it was imperative that we have the best leader on hand to protect our investment. Liechty, Stout, and I agreed that Whittington was the perfect choice to become Stockton's publisher. (He had filled the role on an interim basis while the owner worked towards a sale.)

"The best human acquisition of all was the paper's editor, Robert B. Whittington." Whittington and his wife, Marie, in Stockton, California.

Our choice got a rousing, positive reaction at the *Record* and throughout the community. Upon formal announcement of the sale, Whittington also declared that the *Record* would add a Sunday edition as it went to a seven-day week. Readers and advertisers were overjoyed.

Stockton was a perfect new Speidel city for another reason: My mother, Rusty Marrs, had lived there for many years. I was reunited with her on my visits, which were frequent in the months following the sale.

We needed to maximize our goodwill in the community, so I accepted an invitation to be keynote speaker at the annual luncheon meeting of the Stockton Chamber of Commerce. Several hundred attended to get a look at Rollie Melton and Speidel. In their eyes, would Melton wear a white hat or a black one?

The person who introduced me revealed that my mother had lived in Stockton for a number of years. I began my speech by telling the audience about an extended long-distance call I had received after the *Record* acquisition was announced. The caller had laid down the law to me, saying, "Now that you own my newspaper, don't go off half-cocked and screw it up." After patiently listening for several minutes to what Speidel should and shouldn't do, I had answered: "Yes, I agree completely, and we do give you our pledge that we won't screw it up. That's the honest truth, Mother."

Two-Time Pulitzer Winner Hired

Visalia, CA The lack of a strong contingent of second-tier managers had benefited me in my personal climb up the corporate ladder. There had been few competitors for the opportunities presented to me. That worked to my advantage, but not necessarily to the company's. We needed to prepare many younger people to contend for future openings. It is good insurance to have a bunch of young monkeys mixed in with the older inhabitants of the zoo.

Without a plan of succession, management is at risk. As an army football coach, I had gone too thin on reserve player depth and also on securing a cadre of reliable assistant coaches. Because of that, we lost many games, and it was my fault. I would work with president Jack Liechty to avoid that situation in our newspaper future.

Preparing young men and women to take our jobs some day was high on Liechty's agenda. I aggressively joined him in that mission. In this regard, my journalism classmate and football teammate, Ron Einstoss, was among the persons we most wanted to hire. After he graduated in journalism from Nevada, using contacts arranged by A. L. Higginbotham, Einstoss

"[My] journalism classmate and football teammate, Ron Einstoss, was among the persons we most wanted to hire."

was hired by the Speidel-owned newspaper at Visalia, California. He was a sensational reporter, and in 1961 he was recruited away by the giant *Los Angeles Times*.

By the time I joined corporate in 1969, Ron was in his eighth year of covering major news at the Los Angeles Hall of Justice. He was a superlative journalist who had participated in the *Times'* investigative team efforts that won two Pulitzer Prizes: the first for coverage of the Watts riot, and the second for exposing corruption in city government. In 1968, after the mortal wounding of presidential candidate Robert F. Kennedy, police arrested Sirhan Sirhan, and while the suspect was questioned for hours, Ron Einstoss was the only reporter present. He scooped the rest of the journalism world.

Visalia Times-Delta publisher John Brackett, a Nevada native and 1938 journalism graduate at the Reno campus, called me and said, "I've got a feeling Ron Einstoss may be getting sick of living in the San Fernando Valley and commuting by freeway up to seventy miles a day. I'd better make a run at him and try getting him back to Visalia. It would be great to work him into management." I doubted we could lure Einstoss away from the prestigious L. A. *Times* where he was the fair-haired favorite of everyone, including publisher Otis Chandler, but I said, "Sure, Johnny, go for it!"

At first, Einstoss said he wasn't interested. Brackett kept at him. "Come be our editor, Ron. I'm not going to be *Times-Delta* publisher forever. We'll see what happens after I hang it up." Brackett persisted. Two years later, Ron Einstoss, at age forty-one, returned to Visalia as managing editor. We had acquired one of the best journalists in the nation. Besides, he was one of my closest friends. No way could I forget the big Nevada football lineman who gave a comical sneer to center Melton and yelled, "Being center is easy. All you got to do is lift the ball six inches."

Charlie Murray seemed down in the dumps as I neared the end of my first year as vice president. I worried, and when I asked him whether I was sensing accurately, he said, "Yes, Rollie. Remember that history of Speidel that Chick Stout asked me to research and write?" Of course I did, because Murray had me read it before it was seen by anyone else. Murray went on, "Well, I handed it to Chick. He took it home, and the next morning he braced me with that smile. I knew trouble was coming. He said that except for one thing, he thought I'd done a good job. But Chick came down hard because I had described his leadership style as 'autocratic.' He wanted that word taken out. I argued that like it or not, 'autocratic' accurately described his style, and I told him I wouldn't edit it out. Rollie, I don't think my book will be published."

At the end of 1969, Murray retired from his part-time role as Speidel group editorial director, and the torch was passed to me. He was correct in his prediction. Although his manuscript was meritorious, it was never published.

Speidel Makes Melton Its President

Reno, NV During Chick Stout's four-and-a-half-year administration, he had led a modernization program of SNI buildings and mechanical functions, including presses, so we were in excellent condition in that regard during the Liechty presidency. The Iowan directed me to research as many potential acquisition prospects as I could get to. He encouraged me to accept invitations to critique California dailies in annual summer conferences at Stanford University, and I did for four consecutive years, with excellent reaction for Speidel.

Liechty took Marilyn and me with him to April meetings of the American Newspapers Publishers Association, where he and I attended private breakfasts with leaders of newspaper chains. "Get to know as many as you can," Liechty said. He followed his own amiable example, introducing me to every attendee.

Liechty was in excellent physical condition, being a regular walker and a straight-shooter on the golf course. He was a social conservative who drank little, paced himself carefully, and let the rest of us draw strength from his personal life and executive example. He was the most laid-back of any corporate leader I worked with, and he also was an incredible delegator, the epitome of the leader who gets results through others, then fades quietly, causing people to overlook the truth: that it was Jack Liechty who put in motion the elements that got things accomplished. He never expected personal credit, but he deserved it.

In the spring of the second year of my vice presidency, Liechty and Stout called me in and said it was time I met John Ben Snow. I flew to his home city, Colorado Springs, Colorado. I had butterflies, realizing that if I failed to get on well with the founder of Speidel Newspapers, I might as well fold my executive tent and call it a career.

Snow had been a rugged outdoorsman and horseman much of his life. His career with Woolworth was studded with successes. He had been associated with them for thirty years, spending much of that time developing the corporation's stores in England. After returning to the United States, intending to retire, he instead renewed an old friendship with newspaperman Merritt Speidel, who needed financial help with his little string of newspapers.

Snow was fascinated by newspapers as potentially lucrative investments, so, with Speidel's assistance, he began buying properties around the country. He didn't like the public light and had no desire to be involved in day-to-day newspaper operations, so he named the emerging group of dailies after Speidel. As the latter neared retirement, Snow had his closest friend and business associate, Harry Bunker, running the group. Bunker was a dream administrator with whom people loved to work.

By the time I met John Ben Snow, he was eighty-seven and bent with age, but there remained in him a twinkle and a kind of playful pixie streak, and he put me at ease. We were together about an hour. When I returned to the Reno office, Jack Liechty asked how the visit had gone. I said I thought all right, and Liechty said, "That's what I'm hearing."

Increasingly, Liechty and his wife traveled home to Iowa City, sometimes for a couple of weeks or more. The absences opened up more opportunities to me, for I was acting president when he was away. As my second vice presidential year was winding down, before leaving on his Christmas vacation to Iowa, President Liechty called me in and said, "I suppose most SNIers believe I'll stay on for another four years and retire when I reach sixty-five. But that's not going to happen. When the publishers come in here next month for our annual meeting, I am going to tell them that I will take early retirement at the end of 1971." At this point, I was hanging on each Liechty word. He continued, "I will then explain that a year from now I intend to ask the Speidel board of directors to elect Rollie Melton as my successor." Liechty shook my hand and congratulated me.

During all of 1971, he kept a low profile, but he was always there when I needed him as I functioned as president-designate. It was a great transition, orchestrated by a great, thoughtful leader. In his remarks to publishers in January 1972, Liechty had generous comments about me, asking that everyone continue the support they had been giving me. I was forty, and said to be the youngest

"[Jack Liechty] encouraged me to accept invitations to critique California dailies in annual summer conferences at Stanford University...." Rollan Melton critiquing news stories at Stanford c. 1970.

president of an American newspaper group at that time.

Liechty's valedictory dwelled largely on Speidel history and how fortunate we were to be executives/owners of the company. He acknowledged that in the last few years, many newspaper chains had gone public. "but," he said, "I can never see the day when the Speidel Group will be publicly held."

A month after I succeeded Jack Liechty, our closely held world would be turned topsy-turvy. We would have to go public in my rookie year as president.

SEC Spanks Speidel
Company Forced To Go Public

Reno, NV Before leaving Reno for his beloved Midwest, Jack Liechty dropped a little joke on us: "The difference between a rich Iowa farmer and a poor one is that the latter washes his own Mercedes." Thanks to the wisdom of our Speidel forebears (and Chick Stout and Liechty and a bunch of hard-working employees), company shareholders could now afford something friskier than their tired post-war jalopies and still have enough left over for wash-jobs. Their personal worth had risen with Speidel net income.

The growing family of prospering shareholders included me. With my Uncle Wilbur I had once ridden the rails from Boise to Portland and back. In my youth I drifted from family to family, living in five states before reluctantly settling in a rural Nevada town. In my sophomore year in high school, for an assembly skit, Don Ferguson and I, our faces smeared with coal dust, wore coveralls, hung knapsacks on our shoulders, and danced the jig. Fellow students dubbed us the "Hobo Kids."

———

Four weeks after Liechty's retirement, Speidel was rocked by bad news. Fifteen years earlier, the company's independent accounting and legal firms, both based in Cedar Rapids, Iowa, had asked the Securities and Exchange Commission whether SNI reporting practices to shareholders were adequate. The SEC affirmed its comfort with Speidel procedures, because there were so few owners/stockholders.

In the following years, the company had bought newspapers in South Dakota, Nebraska, and California, markedly increasing the number of stockholder executives and family-member owners. Concurrently, values of the private shares kept climbing. In early January 1972, our advisers in Iowa said Speidel should return to the SEC to learn whether our reporting still complied with securities regulations. The answer, brought back to us by senior accountant partner Donald Schmidt and attorney Donald C. Meyer, was a bombshell. The SEC told them, "Speidel has grown to 205 shareholders. Your client is a quasi-public company right now, and it has to be subject to much more thorough reporting accountability to its owners. We can't force anyone to become a public company, but for Speidel's own sake and safety, you should look hard at this situation."

Schmidt and Meyer came to Reno with their own recommendation: "Speidel must be realistic. Like it or not, you are confronted with going the public route."

Earlier, I had asked Robert Whittington to leave his position as publisher in Stockton to become my vice president. He and I hurriedly summoned retired presidents Stout and Liechty, who sat with me on the powerful executive committee, which could make decisions in behalf of the corporation on virtually everything except selling the company. We told them of the Schmidt-Meyer

Three Speidel presidents in 1974. l. to r.: Jack Liechty (1968-1971), Rollan Melton (1972-1977), and Chick Stout (1968-1971).

conclusion: That we had no substantive option other than going public.

We had another concern—one foreseen by Stout and Liechty, but not acted upon when each was president. Because we were private, our 205 shareholders had no real liquidity. We knew the ages of individual owners, and we kept tabs on their health. Studying actuarial tables, we didn't need genius IQs to realize that in twenty or fewer years many would die, leaving their heirs with substantial death taxes to pay. A stock buy-back agreement existed between the private corporation and its shareholders/owners. We were confronted with a Catch-22. We would be damned if we went public and damned if we didn't.

Many retired executives were in the same age range. If they died in close order, the need to buy back their stock over a compressed period of time would create enormous financial pressure on Speidel. Huge outlays on buy-backs would markedly dilute our cash flow, inhibiting our ability to buy more newspaper properties, to continue modernizing plants and equipment, and to move forward on what Whittington and I knew was the urgent need to provide higher salaries and better benefits for our employees.

The executive committee, chaired by Stout and with Whittington concurring, reluctantly recommended to the full board that Speidel Newspapers surrender its independence and go public. The board members were

Stout, Liechty, Whittington, William H. Leopard (our publisher at Sioux Falls), and myself. Speidel had no other alternative: our own success had thrashed our desire to remain private. The golden goose had laid too many golden eggs. It was time to turn around and become the best little public company that we could be.

We could not delay, but our actions must be well planned. Only a precise script and recruitment of certain specialists would assure a successful transition. At the same time, day-to-day operating results had to continue to improve, as was the company tradition. Whittington and I emphasized to corporate staff and executives of Speidel units across the country that all of us had to coordinate, communicate, and execute more efficiently than ever.

To win, a team needs commitment, an abundance of trained players with individual skills, and the will to harmoniously meld into a team. We did have in place certain specialists, but we would need more. This enlarging of corporate staff would cost a substantial amount, but fortunately, the fiscally conservative Liechty and Stout accepted that. We had to hire heavy hitters if we were to have credibility with Wall Street and earn the confidence of stock underwriters, lawyers, and an expanding menagerie of others. As an inducement to come aboard, we promised stock options and year-end bonuses for those who performed up to expectations.

We recruited two exceptional accountants, Larry Gasho and David Licko, from the firm in Iowa that handled Speidel's accounting. They would team up with our senior accountant, John Koll, in the Reno office. It was essential that we have savvy in-house legal counsel, and Don Meyer was champing to join the Speidel team. We were delighted, because this bright Iowa Law School graduate had prior experience with publicly owned companies as clients.

Sue Steff Stout was recruited from our Iowa City newspaper to be corporate director of public relations and marketing, a new position. This was another milestone in creating gender balance—she was our first female corporate department chief. Business-wise, we needed a new generation of computer-driven office equipment, and to manage it, we were fortunate to sign a home-grown Reno talent, Daniel Stockwell. Payroll costs zoomed, but the cost of doing little or nothing would have been beyond calculation.

In New York, we interviewed firms to head up our underwriting syndicate, finally selecting Kidder, Peabody & Co. from three finalists. Kidder management schooled us in preparing formal pitches to be made to influential financial advisors in major cities around the country. Our "due-diligence" travel squad drew individual scripts, then rehearsed them with each other. Don Meyer spoke the language of the "Street" persuasively, and he was an indispensable, constructive critic of each presenter's remarks. At rehearsals, we jabbed at each other with questions that we anticipated we would get from our live audiences.

The long process of preparing to go public was arduous, but we hung together. Whittington's thick mane was jet black when he came aboard for the corporate ride, but as 1972 perked on, silver was creeping in. Licko was becoming an excellent speaker, and his accountant sidekick, Gasho, brought credibility to our financial presentation. I was smoking up to three packs of Marlboros a day. Clinton Howard, the excellent Speidel corporate director of benefits, said he could hear me coughing a half-block away. I would live to regret this lousy habit.

We were the newest of the media groups going public, and we were the smallest in net income. We struck out on the road show, opening in San Francisco, moving on to Los Angeles, and thence to Chicago, Boston, New York, Philadelphia, and finishing up in Dallas. Our pattern was a set one: I led off with an overview; Whittington followed with concise insight into operations of our eleven newspapers in eight states; Licko and Gash took turns on the financial side; each of us replied to questions in our specific areas of expertise; and we bailed each other out when we were stumped, which was seldom. Whittington was by far the most expert on all aspects of operations. We would have a follow-up self-critique after making each presentation, striving for steady improvement in the cities to follow.

Our average earnings per share were such that chief underwriter Kidder, Peabody recommended that we split the closely held Speidel stock fifteen shares for one before the initial stock offering to reduce the opening share price to an attractive level. Early in the going-public campaign, which took ten months, Kidder predicted that our opening public price would approach thirty-five dollars a share, but the market petered out as the year progressed. The Richard Nixon administration was asking for voluntary wage and price restraints, and that cooled investors' ardor.

After the official due-diligence session on Wall Street with financial gurus and stock portfolio managers, we steeled ourselves for Speidel's public debut. It was decided to open on the over-the-counter market. The initial offering went at just eighteen dollars a share (a dollar lower for Speidel employees), and first-day trading was brisk.

In an instant, our veteran insider shareholders had gained liquidity; but now all of us were subject to the vagaries of the open market. We had better prepare to live with the intangibles that affect public stocks.

Our Speidel travel squad was back in the Reno home office on November 18, 1972, the day we went public. All through the opening session, we monitored the SNI price, which held well. After the afternoon close of the New York Stock Exchange, Bob Whittington mopped his brow and said, "Rollie, get used to this. Our lives are never going to be the same."

That evening, a bunch of us convened at Reno's elegant Vario's Restaurant for a celebratory dinner. Don Meyer, seated next to my wife, alluded to our fifteen-for-one stock split, and said, "Marilyn, how does it feel to be a millionaire?"

Stunned, she said, "I don't know. I didn't know I was one."

Mary Jane Webert, the longest-serving business employee in our office, put things in perspective a few weeks later, when the euphoria induced by the early prices was dampened by a blip in the Speidel stock. "There's an old saying: 'What goes up, always comes down.'"

Nixon's Phase I, II and III of wage-price restraints drove markets lower, and SNI prices declined steadily until we bottomed at slightly better than eight dollars a share. Oldtimers' spirits sagged, and at that point there were a lot more doubters about our decision to go public than there were cheerers. But Melton, Whittington, and team were convinced that we had done the right thing. We had known it wouldn't be easy, but somebody had to do it.

Don Meyer kept schooling us with his wisdom: "Let's never surprise The Street. It will be curtains if we do." He also advised us that we should never tell a securities analyst anything that we didn't want the whole world to know."

Nobody ever told us that going public would be simple or that life following the transition would be easier. One thing it did was expose us to the possibility of a takeover.

Travel Squads Learn and Inform

Reno, NV Five years earlier, I had become the first Speidel executive to attend an American Press Institute (API) seminar. Now we routinely sent a swarm of SNIers to that premier place of higher newspaper learning. I also returned a third time for a workshop for chief executives of newspaper groups. While there, I was invited to join the API board, and I served on it for eight years. We needed more visibility in the industry, so we were encouraging our executives to become involved in state, regional, and national associations, to polish their speaking skills, and to work themselves into visible roles.

We were nourishing a higher profile because we were public, and that was a factor in SNIers increasingly being asked to sit on professional boards. On the editorial side, our top emerging "outside" players included editors Ron Einstoss of Visalia and Warren Lerude of Reno. The latter won applause for his lecturing at API and for his championing nationwide of newspaper shield laws. Einstoss testified to Congress in behalf of press freedom.

Historically, Speidel had wisely promoted from within, but Bob Whittington and I realized there was a wealth of talent at other companies, and we decided to make a concerted run at it. While at Stockton, Bob had recruited a former *Santa Cruz Sentinel* officer, Robert Uecker, to be his controller. When Whittington left for Reno, Uecker succeeded him as publisher.

Lerude and I first met Jim Hushaw, a young editor from Southern California, at the Stanford Editors Conference, and Lerude hired him to succeed retiring Paul Leonard as editor of the *Nevada State Journal*. Another University of Nevada school of journalism product, N. Walter Ryals, was recruited for Reno executive roles and later was the publisher at Santa Fe, New Mexico. I also had tried hard to sign on the University of Nevada's journalism department chairman, LaRue Gilleland, for a top editor's position, but we couldn't bring it together. He was the high-quality type we needed.

The Vietnam War still held American journalism in its thrall. Richard Nixon sicced his vice president, Spiro Agnew, on us to blunt growing press skepticism about the necessity for America's participation in that gruesome war in Southeast Asia.

Speidel's first-ever exposure on national television was an outgrowth of the national debate about Vietnam. ABC-TV's Frank Reynolds interviewed me in Reno, and I focused on the need to "protect our most precious freedom—an unfettered press." The day after the segment aired, my mother called from Stockton, exclaiming, "Son, all of a sudden you came popping into my living room! It was nice to see you there."

Despite all the distractions, the top company priority remained to publish the finest newspapers we could. This was accomplished best through nurturing pluralism. I would have none of micro-managing, an ugly practice that diminishes creativity and undermines morale. Our credo was, "Let your people do their work."

On the corporate side, our "to-do" agenda kept growing. Whittington led operations the old-fashioned way: he mowed down projects. His focus amazed me. He'd carry on long phone conversations while simultaneously tending to mail, scribbling reminders onto his "to do" list, and quaffing cup after cup of coffee.(He was also the master of an old reporter's trick—sitting across my desk and reading materials upside down.)

Each April, our "travel squad" appeared at the Lee Dirks Newspaper Forum, held so that financial managers could hear formal presentations by the corporate teams of the (then) twelve publicly traded print media companies. Dirks would give each company fifty minutes, so there was time to state our case. But we adhered to the advice of our lawyer, Don Meyer. The gospel according to him was "Don't tout Speidel stock. Use straight talk to persuade analysts."

Speidel always drew well at Dirks programs. There was curiosity about SNI's pre-tax profit margin, which was edging close to 35 percent, the highest in the public print sector. Attendees always mined us for information about Speidel's acquisition prospects.

We talked about our cost controls, the quality of Speidel newspaper markets, our executives, and myriad other topics. The nation's most-followed investor, Warren Buffet, was a perennial attendee, and he owned Speidel stock. He amused me with his understated asides following Speidel presentations. Focused, sincere, and interesting, he came off as a simple old boy from Omaha. He was from Omaha all right, but he wasn't old, and he was far from simple.

Speidel presentations always drew lots of questions, and, as we had done in our cross-country dog and pony show while going public, each of us reacted to specific questions in his area of strength. In the hustle-bustle, give-and-take question and answer segments, we were careful not to upstage each other. It was a discipline I had learned from Edwin Semenza, my storied Reno Little Theater director.

The Dirks Forum and other speaking venues indeed were theater. It was exhilarating to perform before live

"ABC-TV's Frank Reynolds interviewed me in Reno, and I focused on the need to 'protect our most precious freedom—an unfettered press.'"

audiences, as in my younger days on Reno stages, except that now I wasn't delivering lines that a playwright had composed years before. We were our own playwrights, so to speak.

Newspaper Groups Seek Marriage

Reno, NV The exploration of potential acquisitions for Speidel fell to Meyer, Whittington, and me. Trips into markets took a lot of time, as we sought to ingratiate ourselves with owners. We were traveling salesmen, trying to peddle our wares, but without sleight of hand and snake oil. We worked diligently at growing, because size gives the bottom line more heft. It also comes in handy if a friendly or a hostile force wants to take you on. Most of the other newspaper groups were hustling just as hard; some harder.

We were not talking of only acquiring single properties; we were among the groups hankering to "get married" to other groups. The romancing of Speidel had commenced immediately after we went public and our profit margin became known, but rather than be swallowed up, we hoped to draw other properties into the Speidel family.

Contacts with the John P. Scripps chain, based in San Diego, California, were cordial, but unproductive. We had serious visits with the top officers of publicly held Lee Enterprises, an attractive group of dailies based in Davenport, Iowa, but we were at loggerheads on the vital questions, "Who is to be the surviving corporation? Who will be the chief executive of the merged company? What will the composition of a merged board of directors be?" We finally suspended the dialogue with Lee. Discussions with the private Duane Hagadone Corporation, based in Idaho, went kaput for the same reason.

Our focus on non-public groups included the eight John P. McGoff community newspapers in Michigan, and McGoff invited me to do a presentation for his editors. The session at Traverse City, Michigan went extremely well, but our negotiations didn't. Again, it was a case of colliding egos. Few CEOs want to surrender their power positions, and who can blame them? But we kept at it.

Don Meyer learned that sister dailies in Minnesota were to be sold out of an estate. I went to St. Cloud, ninety miles north of Minneapolis-St. Paul, for a look, and I was impressed with the potential for our approach to journalism to succeed in that wholesome market.

The heir to the papers was the deceased owner's widow, and she escorted me on a tour of the Times building. It was a real dump, not fit to ask people to work in. I promised her that if we were chosen as the buyer, we would move swiftly to build a new building. The companion property was a small daily at nearby Little Falls, which was historic because the Lone Eagle, Charles Lindbergh, was born there.

Whittington, Meyer, and our numbers pushers took a look at the papers, and our offer of eight million dollars was accepted in 1974. It was Speidel's first acquisition since 1969, when Stockton was bought.

I had learned to cope with rejection in my childhood and as a striking sportswriter who couldn't find another job, so disappointment was a familiar companion; but it was never a breeze. We worked diligently to acquire the fine *Mail-Tribune* at Medford, Oregon, and became close with the widow owner and with her attorney. But other newspaper groups were intensely competitive on acquisitions, too, and at Medford, we were outsmarted by the Dow Jones Company. The owner of the *Wall Street Journal* charitably "loaned" one of its promising young executives to the owner to "help run" her property.

The widow owner ultimately sold to Dow Jones, and her lawyer soothed us with a refrain we were sick of hearing: "You are great, Speidel, and you were a close second in the bidding." There are no close seconds. Only losers. Dow Jones appointed a new publisher in Medford—its loaned executive.

The more I heard owners plead, "It's not the money that counts to us, it's the quality of the potential acquirer," the more I knew it was the money. The "I want to marry you" waltz among groups purred on without letup, and just as in other industries, tried and true acquisition techniques included stroking egos, providing freebie junkets, and lathering a target with soft soap.

I had become a member of the board of directors of the American Newspaper Publishers Association, and I was closely associated with some of the big boys and girls of newspaperdom. The camaraderie was pleasant, and it frequently led to merger mating dialogue.

My friend Kay Graham of the *Washington Post* was a charmer, not very aggressive as an acquirer, but she expressed possible interest in a marriage to Speidel, because her late husband, Philip, had owned the *Sioux Falls Argus-Leader* before Speidel bought it.

The beat went on. Helen Copley loved to dance, and she thought me a competent two-stepper with rhythm. But when I broached the possibility of Speidel acquiring her Copley Group (San Diego, Springfield, Illinois) she two-stepped right out of my life.

Times-Mirror board chairman Otis Chandler had Marilyn and me to his Los Angeles mansion. He lamented our hiring away his best investigative reporter, Ron Einstoss. "Rollie," he said, "you can make me feel a lot better if Speidel and the Times-Mirror Corporation put a deal together." Chandler and I had a couple of things in common: at Stanford University, he had been a track and field teammate of my Fallon High School teammate, Charles Renfro; and Chandler's (then) wife was named Marilyn.

Interaction with the paramount players among publicly owned newspaper groups was vital for an additional reason. If Speidel ever had to cut and run from a hostile force, we wanted to know ahead of time who to make a run for. Only a fool is careless about who he takes up with, in love or in newspaper ownership. Thus, I kept up friendships with leaders of other groups, and I listened to their overtures. Most were oblique pitches. They came from the chief executives of Knight-Ridder, then based in Miami, Florida; Allen H. Neuharth, president of the Gannett Company, then based at Rochester, New York; and the Tribune Company, owner of the *Chicago Tribune* and other metropolitan giants. Neuharth had been instrumental in getting me the ANPA board directorship.

Fortunately, the "little boy" always remained in me. The more I knew, the more I wanted to know. The greater the rewards from personal linkage, the more convinced I became that the hackneyed cliché is right on: *It is not what you know, but whom you know.*

The spice of the reporter's life is curiosity. My *Fallon Standard* mentors had first implanted that in me years before; and now, increasingly, it was a welcome ally for the boy reporter turned newspaper leader. Yet, it was urgent that I live by the adage, "It's the position, not the man." Remembering that was a surefire way to avoid the taint of overconfidence.

I was scooting around the country on missions. Once, while en route to visit our paper, the *Poughkeepsie Journal*, I did an overnight in New York City at the same time that Warren Lerude was there. He suggested we bunk together to save costs. The following morning, he harpooned me about what he alleged was my snoring. "Here I'm in a city of eight million people," he groused, "and I get stuck overnight in the same room with you." I looked at him closely. His eyes were red. For lack of sleep, I guessed.

Whether I was home or away, Bob Whittington skillfully oversaw our operations, managing with wisdom and sensitivity, while tuning me in on should-know events. This selfless executive's talents included making colleagues believe they were drum majors in the newspaper parade. His example taught others to empower subordinates.

Speidel had business interruption insurance, but our best protection was a program held every January in Reno to train executives in production fundamentals. Chick Stout had hatched the plan amid the Reno strike, and it had rescued the company then and again in 1966 in Sioux Falls when printers walked out. Jack Liechty zealously continued the plan, as did my administration.

The Speidel program was a gem in the industry, studied carefully by counterparts from around the nation. The cross-training was beneficial in many ways. An editor was a composing-room page-makeup man for two weeks; a classified ad manager would learn to run a press. When participants went home, they felt a deeper kinship with fellow employees.

A new Speidel corporate vice president, Robert Wingard, coordinated the mechanical training, while the foremost in-house trainer was Donn Wheeler, the *Gazette-Journal* mechanical superintendent. The "insurance" program spared us grief on occasion at the *Stockton Record*, where unions frequently probed to see if we had the guts to fight. We did.

We made no attempt to train executives in secret. Clearly, revealing our preparedness was a subtle way of making organized labor think hard before giving us an ultimatum. At one juncture, Wheeler and his Reno composing, press, and mailroom lieutenants counted more than fifty Speidel manager/shareholders they had trained—over half of our group's executives.

President Meets President
Meltons Visit White House

Washington, D.C. Despite our jammed "to do" agenda, I never lost my love of writing for the public print. But now, there was too little time to compose. I did make an exception in 1975, when the ANPA board was invited to the White House for an "intimate visit and lunch" with President Gerald Ford. From the time I arose on that memorable day, I kept copious notes.

After America's main man, President Ford, spoke to us, he invited questions or comments. I waited my turn, then stood and told him, "Mr. President, a long-ago friend of yours lives in Reno. Phyllis Crudgington

Phillips sends you her kindest regards." The president blushed, for he instantly remembered Ms. Phillips, whom he had dated for several years when they were students together at the University of Michigan. Ford reacted, "Well, tell Phyllis I said 'hello,' but don't tell my wife that I said this."

Back in my room, I hurriedly wrote a long "White House Diary" feature on my portable typewriter. It was neat to be a real newspaperman again, racing against the deadline clock. I phoned the story to Bob Nitsche, who was by then in editorial management in Reno. The minute-by-minute account of my visit with Ford appeared the following morning in the *Nevada State Journal*, and the text included my dialogue with the President about his former girlfriend.

I sent a copy of the diary to Ford, believing that it would never get closer to him than some young mail clerk. He did see it. Three weeks later, Marilyn called me, bursting with excitement. "We just got an invitation from Gerald Ford to join him at the White House for the state visit of Emperor Hirohito." Marilyn showed off the big, gorgeous invitation around town until it was dog-eared, then shopped for a suitable outfit and bought a fake diamond ring at Macy's.

When we got to Washington, I hailed a ratty, beat-up Yellow Cab at the Madison Hotel. We tooled over to the White House and waited in line amidst a row of shiny limousines bearing other Ford guests. I tried to soothe Marilyn, saying "It's the Speidel way. A taxi is a lot cheaper." I thought she was going to croak.

The Hirohito dinner was glittering stuff for two kids from Nevada, and following the meal, the toasts, the speechifying, and a mini-concert by Van Cliburn, the president led a few of us to the small vestibule inside the front door of the White House. Marilyn and I sat at a small table with Ginger Rogers, whom we had seen entertain at John Ascuaga's Nugget but had never met. Ginger agreed to dance with me, and she politely asked me not to swing her around. I suspected that many a guy who fancied himself to be another Fred Astaire had "swung her around."

I asked Ginger, "Do you mind if I show you my Fallon two-step?"

She said, "What's that?"

I replied, "Miss Rogers, you know about Reno and Sparks. They're just outside Fallon. My hometown's famous for its high-steppin' two-steppers." Her eyes glazed, so I dropped the subject.

John Ben Snow Dies

Rival Buys His Shares, Threatens Speidel

New York, NY The Speidel founder and financial angel, John Ben Snow, died in 1973 at age eighty-nine, leaving an estate estimated at thirty-five million dollars. The probate was tricky, the more so because his residency was in both Colorado and New York, but by 1974 it was ready to be closed. A total of 393,900 shares of Speidel stock was in the estate, held by the executor, Irving Trust Company, in New York. The Irving told us that the stock was available for sale, with a price of close to nine dollars a share.

Speidel's lawyer, Don Meyer, urged us to buy the Snow stock and retire it to our treasury. He was jittery about having 6.8 percent of Speidel's outstanding shares dangling around. Whittington, Meyer, and I took the recommendation to our executive committee, chaired by Chick Stout, but Stout balked at the price. "With the market in the doldrums and driving values down, we should wait and hope that we can pick it up at lower cost. It won't hurt to delay," Stout persisted.

We had no appetite to debate Chick Stout, who could get testy when someone disagreed with him, so we said all right. But Meyer fretted, again warning, "We had better keep on top of this."

In the midst of the 1974 whirl of business, I received a call from an acquaintance, Gordon Strong, the publisher of the *Oakland Tribune*. "Hi, Rollie! Just checking in to let you know that I'll be visiting Reno later this week. I wonder if it's convenient to drop in and say howdy?" Being with the gregarious, folksy Strong was always pleasant, and I checked my calendar and said, "Great! Let's do it." We set a time.

Bob Whittington and Don Meyer were off on a road trip the day that Strong came in to say "Howdy," so I was holding down the Speidel fort alone. Secretary Jean Brown buzzed me: "Your newspaper guests are here." I didn't know my friend would have someone with him. Not that it mattered. I stepped out to meet him, and Strong introduced me to his companion. "Rollie, shake hands with my associate, John Tory."

We cruised through the usual "How was your trip?" and "Sure envy your weather here in Reno." Then Strong got down to business. "Let us explain why we are here. Our corporation, Thomson Newspapers, based up in Toronto, just bought all the John Ben Snow estate shares through the Irving Trust."

I stared at him, my mind racing. "Yeah," I thought. "Thomson Publishing . . . some of the most ding-a-ling, rag-tag newspapers in the lower forty-eight . . . cash-register journalism . . . an outfit that will never be accused of having bright editorial products . . . ."

Now John Tory spoke. "Mr. Melton, I am the legal counsel for the Thomson Group in North America, which, as you know, publishes high-quality dailies—forty-eight papers in the United States; thirty-two in Canada."

I had never learned how to play poker, but I nonetheless tried to cover up my anxiety. I was saying to myself, "What a lousy time not to have Whittington and Meyer with me." I fixed each visitor with a sober stare. I remained silent.

Tory plunged ahead with the remarks he had carefully rehearsed. "So, Mr. Melton, our new major position in Speidel stock should entitle us to representation on your corporate board. We would think one, maybe two directors. After all, we now are your largest single shareholder." He smiled. "Of course, Mr. Melton, we have been carefully watching Speidel's sterling performance since you went public in 1972. We admire your company and your management team and your markets so much that we are prepared to buy the remaining 92.2 percent of your shares. If that is attractive, we can talk about price."

Tory let his message sizzle on my burner. I looked at Gordon Strong, who had set me up, and then I turned back to Tory. I wanted to fling these guys out, but the brawls of my younger years were no longer appropriate. This was like a scary movie, with me huddling in the front row and the bad guys plotting up there on the silver screen. If only I still had my World War II BB gun, I would shoot them. But I stood and shook their hands and said, "I will tell my guys we have a new shareholder. We'll be in touch with you."

Tory's parting message was, "Mr. Melton, we'll be pleased if you do that." I got them out the door where they could chortle about the pain left in their wake. Then I turned to my secretary and said, "Jean, get Bob and Don on the phone. Fast!"

Baby-faced Don Meyer was slender and seemingly fragile, and those who didn't know him well might have misread him as someone who had been easy pickings for schoolyard bullies. When he joined Speidel in 1972 as our corporate lawyer, he instantly became popular with the staff. He kept Adeline Hageman, his administrative assistant, in stitches with his wit, and she was in awe of his ability to digest statistics and make meaning of them. Veteran staff members sought his counsel on matters ranging from how to cope with pesky door-to-door salesmen to personal estate planning.

Meyer was a major factor in Speidel's strong performance. He was a super-bright corporate comer with versatile skills and great instincts in business and law, all topped by modesty. So, did it figure that Whittington and I made him the lead horse in steering Thomson Newspapers away from the Speidel stable? You guessed right.

Meyer was a quick read on company matters, especially when opportunity or danger came knocking. He had bemoaned Chick Stout's judgment in overruling us on purchasing 393,900 shares of Speidel stock from John Ben Snow's estate. Now, Thomson Newspapers had craftily slipped in, without the courtesy of telling us what it was up to, and grabbed the Speidel stock block at a bargain price. We had blown it. Now we must fight back with all our might.

Thomson was a formidable match in any setting. That year of 1974, it owned eighty newspapers in North America. In the American publishing family, non-public Thomson was known to have high pre-tax profit margins—higher even than Speidel, whose 30 percent-plus figure was tops among the thirteen publicly traded newspaper groups. But Thomson was, at best, publishing papers that from an editorial standpoint were run-of-the-mill. American news people perceived Thomson's products as advertising shoppers, with a tiny portion of news dubbed in. The company was a cash cow.

Thomson's chairman was Kenneth Thomson, son of Lord Thomson, the famous press baron in England, but there was said to be no official linkage of the North American and England groups. In fact, the father was honorary chair of his son's empire, and Kenneth was co-chairman of his father's gaggle of papers in Britain.

Kenneth's executive vice president was wily administrative veteran St. Clair McCabe. The corporation had as its lawyer John Tory, who was experienced in acquisitions and all matters legal. So, on the face of it, Speidel was outweighed; and, to date, it had been out-maneuvered.

Bob Whittington and Don Meyer and I figured that Thomson's secrecy in snatching the Snow stock amounted to an unfriendly campaign, but Thomson protested otherwise. We felt that Strong's setting me up with the subterfuge of merely dropping in to say "Howdy," and Tory's direct pitch to have up to two Thomson people on the Speidel board, revealed the corporation's true intent.

At that time, America's daily newspaper leaders were mainly a nationwide family that might pick on non-newspaper people in their communities, but who were generally hospitable to newspaper counterparts. In no instance up until then had one group of dailies made an overt run on another. Thomson's snatching of the outstanding shares of Speidel was followed closely by owners and publishers of dailies across the nation. Many were wondering whether this event signaled the start of a trend.

Thomson was much larger than Speidel, which boasted of its "newspapers for the home" persona, but it was soon jolted by Speidel's brilliantly conceived game plan and boot-camp toughness. It was chiefly Don Meyer, the Speidel sultan of mirth, who took the lead against Thomson. Meyer had never met a contact sport he liked, but when it came to cunning mind games, survival instinct, and shifting to the offensive, he was the best. Bob Whittington was a gentle man who had a large streak of toughness under his hide, and I brought to the fray a love of competition and survival instincts that tracked to my Depression-era boyhood. Given those combined strengths, and the rub-off experience of former presidents Jack Liechty and Chick Stout, we carried a can-win, must-win attitude.

Behind Meyer's soft-spoken, choir-boy persona was a brawler with alley-cat, get-in-your-face mentality and resolve. We loosed this legal junkyard dog on our adversary, and Meyer waded in gleefully, publicly labeling Thomson a foreign giant picking on a poor, small American newspaper chain—the powerful Brits versus the good-intentioned Yanks.

We worked the phones with our press contacts, focusing on the theme of the beleaguered little company being harassed by the Goliath from abroad. In our spiel to the media, we avoided mentioning that Thomson was centered in Canada, that friendly nation to our immediate north. Always, the Thomson group was portrayed as something sinisterly foreign from across the Atlantic. Two of the most-read and credible newspapers, the *New York Times* and the *Wall Street Journal*, were now hot for the continuing story.

The Speidel troika was making it sound like a World War III newspaper battle, but this time with the reeling, innocent Yanks being picked on by Britain, the huge Axis-like power. The *Wall Street Journal*'s opening paragraph on its November 12, 1974, story was, "Is a major foreign newspaper group about to move in on a small, but highly profitable chain of U.S. newspapers? Speidel isn't taking any chances."

Don Meyer kept pulling Thomson's chain. Customarily, our annual meeting of stockholders was in April, but we shifted it to November, four months ahead of schedule. Meyer announced to wire services that Speidel's shareholders would be asked to prevent any "alien" from owning or controlling the company or voting more than 10 percent of any class of its outstanding shares. Shareholders would also be asked to vote that no one representing an "alien" company, affiliate, or associate serve as a director of Speidel. Meyer admitted to us that what we were asking was probably illegal, but in any event, now it was Thomson being jammed into defensive reaction.

St. Clair McCabe, managing director of the "alien" company's Canadian arm, told the *Wall Street Journal* that he was "extremely surprised by the lengths to which Speidel has gone to prevent foreigners or a foreign concern from gaining a meaningful interest in that company." McCabe protested, "We bought our shares in Speidel strictly as an investment, with no thought of a takeover. We're a newspaper company, there was a large block of Speidel shares around, and we purchased them. It's as simple as that."

The Speidel offensive kept gaining yardage. It was the small U.S. outfit of working stiffs at such obscure places as Chillicothe, Ohio, hounded by "aliens" who were tied to such publishing giants as the *Sunday Times* of London. What Melton, Meyer, and Whittington didn't mention to the financial press was that the American arm of Thomson also published in small, lesser-known communities—for instance Canton and Marion, also in Ohio.

As to McCabe protesting his company's decent intentions, Speidel noted that ten of Thomson's forty-eight newspapers in the U.S. "were acquired in the last four years. Accordingly, there isn't any assurance that the expressed 'investment' intention wouldn't change in the future." We also emphasized to the media that "foreign companies and individuals have been particularly active in such takeover attempts in recent months." We neglected to mention that no such takeover attempts involved newspaper companies. We timed the flurry of Speidel feints, jabs and pokes in Thomson's eyes to arrive six days before Speidel shareholders were to vote on protection amendments against "aliens."

On November 18, the two-year anniversary of Speidel's public debut, and in an overwhelming response, Speidel shareholders approved amendments to the SNI certificate of incorporation, "reducing the threat of a takeover and creating an unprecedented limitation on foreign ownership." The vote results were a stunning affirmation of Speidel's position and of our corporate leadership in the campaign. Just one percent of shareholders voted against the amendment.

Bob Whittington and I didn't have a spare Medal of Honor to hang on the chest of our smooth, street-fighting, anti-takeover commando, but Don Meyer had earned one. His work was not yet finished, however. Ahead of us lay a struggle with the most successful newspaper acquirer of all, the Gannett Company, led by the colorful World War II combat infantryman, Allen H. Neuharth. The Gannett president and chief executive was a man who knew what he wanted and almost always got it. Al Neuharth was known for his propensity for taking no prisoners.

Locals Win Pulitzer
Gazette-Journal Deep in Talent

Reno, NV When type-setting equipment was born, Mark Twain remarked, "Those machines can do everything except drink, smoke and go on strike." But no technology lasts forever, and a revolutionary development in the newspaper industry began as the 1970s arrived. In 1974 Speidel cast aside the beloved old Linotypes of my printing boyhood. They were mechanical dinosaurs, and they were put to permanent rest. In their place, SNI introduced dazzling electronic gadgetry that spat out words at phenomenal speeds. Newspaper photo composition sounded the death knell of hot metal.

In the period 1974-1977, Speidel advanced in other ways. On the executive front, irrepressible Ron Einstoss, who put other people's interest ahead of his own, was appointed publisher at Visalia. In 1976, just a year later, as Richard Schuster retired, we brought in Einstoss to be publisher of Speidel's crown jewel and top moneymaker, the *Reno Gazette-Journal*.

J. C. Hickman, who earlier was Visalia editor, was our new group editorial director. He cautioned against focusing on the winning of prizes, reminding SNIers that, "It's what you do each day, and not how big a splash you make on a certain single story or in a running series." Then along came a thrilling citation any newspaper would bust its buttons to get. The Reno editorial-writing team of Norman Cardoza, Foster Church, and Warren Lerude scaled the Mount Everest of journalism, winning the paper's first Pulitzer Prize. The public service award was for their scathing unfrocking of Nevada whoremaster Joe Conforte and his perpetual influence-peddling.

For the third time, including his *Los Angeles Times* honors, publisher Einstoss had a big, committed hand in winning the most coveted prize in journalism. Whittington was five years older than me, so it seemed a given that someday "Stoss" would become my new Speidel corporate co-captain. I had known him since we were undergraduates, had admired his sparkling career, and had observed that he never swerved from top quality and career growth.

One of a corporate leader's most vital obligations is to produce managers who are meritorious enough to one day become the leaders. Among the future top managers during this period of the 1970s were Warren Lerude and Dean C. Smith, both with the *Gazette-Journal.* Some Lerude detractors thought of the competitive, high-speed Reno executive editor as the Godzilla of Nevada journalism. However, what many others cherished about him was his love of getting today's news into print *today*.

Lerude drove hard for breadth of coverage and for quality editing, page makeup, and solid graphics to complement the total package. His mouth was always flapping, "Give me more news hole." That's what news disciples should demand of bosses, but often don't. Lerude was still in his thirties, a brassy champion of press freedoms.

Dean Smith had grown up as a Reno street kid, and he burned to excel. He had been a highly competitive prep and university athlete, worked as a common laborer, a bartender, advertising rookie, and surveyor, and he had been a 1959 striker against the *Gazette-Journal*. Smith was a University of Nevada journalism graduate and a crack reporter. He had sprinted past veterans to become the newspaper's advertising leader. Although he was the youngest such manager among his Speidel peers, he already ranked among the best in classified and retail advertising.

I identified strongly with how people handled hardships, especially when they were

"[Dean Smith] had sprinted past veterans to become the newspaper's advertising leader." Rollan Melton with Dean Smith in 1965. (Photograph by Dondero.)

young. I was fascinated by their life stories, which often provided a road map of how far they might go, given their own commitment and the type of wonderful breaks that I myself had received.

At this point, I had clearly escaped the grip of poverty as I maneuvered up the ranks. I had earned $77,000 in my final vice-presidency year and was closing in on the $100,000-a-year level early in my presidency, but I was determined to keep my success in perspective—many of the people responsible for my rising good fortune were just as hard-working as me, but they had not been as blessed as I with good timing, good luck, and influential mentors. I was grateful and I tried never to be smug.

Marilyn Takes On A Project

Reno, NV Always I kept thinking "What do I do if I lose my job? Suppose I'm sick—who's to take care of Marilyn and the children? Am I getting people ready to take over SNI in case that seemingly harmless light ahead is an onrushing train?"

In our nationwide company, I was accustomed to seeing marriages go belly-up because a Speidel person was consumed by a time-devouring job. Observing that, and coming from a dysfunctional family myself, reinforced my resolve to work at the best marriage we could have; but I was on the road much of the time, especially in 1972 when we went public and I flew close to a hundred thousand miles.

Not long before Marilyn and I observed our twenty-fifth wedding anniversary, we bought a new home on Mount Rose Street. By then Marilyn was carving out enough time to paint portraits and landscapes. As the years sped along, her blooming artistry made the home a remarkable showplace.

I got a kick out of a delicious irony: the home was the one where University of Nevada president Minard Stout had lived when I took him on in 1953, beating him up in two columns for his illegal firing of a professor in a famous academic freedom case. He had wanted then to wring my young neck or throw me out of school; but he was fired, and now I owned his house.

Marilyn's foremost mission was raising our four children and me. She would say, "I'm working on Rollan, who is my chief project, and I'll keep working on it till I square him away."

Screwing up on the hard stuff could occasionally be excused. My tendency was to botch the simple things. Trying to rent a car in Columbus, Ohio, I was turned down because I had let my Nevada driver's license expire. I showed up at my dressy high school reunion without socks—Fallon frowned on such tacky dress.

When a third-level Reno bank officer refused to loan me an additional $100,000 to buy stock, I was so ticked that I refused to do an end-run and plead my case with First National Bank's president, Arthur M. Smith Jr. I might have swayed Art, because I could have statistically proven I would handle additional debt, pay the interest, and still reduce the principal. But what did I do? I pouted. I did nothing. I flat blew it. Given the many stock splits that followed, the $100,000 loan I failed to obtain because I was so dense would be worth approximately $7 million by the year 2000.

William F. Harrah, the long, lean, and, some said, disenchanted hotel-casino chairman, couldn't stand overweight people. He never once spoke to me until seeing me across a crowded room at a Reno party. (That was the year I walked everywhere and put just eight miles on my Volkswagen bug. I was trimmer than in many years, tanned, rested, and wearing a spiffy new sports outfit.) Harrah rushed to me, actually smiled—maybe the first and last grin he ever gave a media guy—and he pumped my hand and said, "You look great! Keep it up!" He did a quick about-face and hurried off. The next time I saw him, I had regained most of the lost weight. He never spoke to me again.

Reno insurance executive Nello Gonfiantini Jr. once wired me, "I'm happy to see a fat man making good." Years later, the two of us were in a diet class together. Future publisher Walter Ryals told me, "If you keep getting your name spread around, Fallon might become as notorious as my hometown of Marked Tree, Arkansas."

I lost things—my wallet in an Ohio restaurant and my voice, which was rendered silent by laryngitis a few hours before I delivered my presidential message to the annual meeting of Speidel shareholders at Iowa City in 1976. I had to whisper into the microphone. My SNI brothers and sisters said it was my all-time most eloquent speech. "Not a soul heard a word you said, Rollie."

Humorless Joe Conforte was often unintentionally a good laugh. After Reno's capture of the Pulitzer Prize hit the news wires, the king of Nevada cat-houses phoned Warren Lerude from Rome and croaked, "You guys could have never done it without me!"

After my White House Diary story was published in 1975, Ron Einstoss called a friend who was an aide at the White House and reminded him, "President Ford was a football center at the University of Michigan. The president of my company played center, too." Einstoss put in his request. A few days later, I received a framed picture of Ford, which the president had signed, "To Rollan Melton, from one center to another."

Personnel Problems Prove Pesky

Reno, NV As Speidel president, and in earlier leadership roles, my hardest moments arose from personnel problems. I'd just as soon do hard labor or go into solitary confinement as deal with them, but as the corporation's leader, I felt that I should be the one to do the heavy disciplining. We now numbered close to one hundred executives, and the vast majority were women and men of trust who didn't use people or discard them. But there were other cases in the Melton years that proved that some people do the dumbest things.

A longtime controller, formerly a member of the Central Office staff and serving at his second SNI newspaper, often told colleagues he was getting rich off his pig farm in Iowa. The truth was that he was robbing us blind at a Speidel city in the Midwest. Our auditors should have caught his misdeeds, but didn't. He hadn't taken a vacation for a few years—how's that for a big fat clue? He finally took off a few days, and our publisher there was alerted to accounting discrepancies by a puzzled staff member.

We rushed lawyer Don Meyer and accountants out there, and their investigation confirmed wrongdoing. One of our corporate staff members urged that we not press charges, but I overruled him. If someone rifles your wallet or purse and is let off, you set a dangerous precedent that says to others, "Nothing bad will happen to me if I steal. If others get off, so will I." The Midwest controller was convicted and did prison time, but not much. A lenient court sprung him just before Christmas. Would you believe what a church in his community did? It hired him as business manager.

I believed all positive and negative episodes should be learning experiences for the company. After the Midwest defalcation, our corporate financial staffers and independent accountants swung us into the practice of surprise internal and external audits at all our newspapers and at corporate headquarters.

Our corporate sensors were routinely up to sniff out all kinds of trouble. The secretary at a Speidel paper in the Midwest said our publisher there was making unwanted sexual advances. I immediately flew in, documented his guilt, and put him on probation on the spot. He resigned the following week.

The Speidel policy under Melton and Whittington was that every driving-under-the-influence charge was to be published. We learned that an executive had ordered the pre-publication deletion of such a charge against one of his subordinate managers. We put both on probation. The episode reminded me of how Visalia's Johnny Brackett handled "Don't use my name in a DUI listing" requests. He would whip a yellowed news clipping out of his wallet, and say, "Look what I did to my own relative. I can't leave your name out, either."

The strangest case of malfeasance involved the veteran publisher who made us too much money. His profit margin was so high it rivaled a Thomson newspaper. He was warned several times, "So what if your newsprint costs do sharply increase? Don't run a shopper. Loosen the news hole and fill it up with what's happening." And, "You *must* raise employee salaries! You are running a sweat shop, and we are wide open for unionization!" Alas, this publisher was a creature of habit and did not change. After he failed the final warning, I retired him early.

Newspaper Business Can Be Health Hazard

Reno, NV I had been chugging in overdrive for years. I had tried unsuccessfully to quit smoking, and I wasn't doing a bit of exercise. My days didn't have to be as long as I made them—I was going to bed too late, arising too early, and I would catch myself slipping into sleep when conversations got dull. Talk about lighting one's own fuse!

In 1975, at about 6:00 one morning, I was at home when an agonizing pain crept around my midriff. I didn't know what it was; I couldn't shake it off. Marilyn bundled me into the car, and on the short drive to the hospital, she had to stop three times while I threw up in the street. Every tiny bump in the road felt like I was humping along in an unstable wagon crossing the Rockies.

Hospital attendants dinked around interminably, trying to figure out what had hit me. They concluded it was a kidney stone, and they gave me a pain-killing shot, the first time in my life I enjoyed having a needle stuck in me. At last, I had a personal health story to bore people with. Afterwards, I found a woman who gone through a tough childbirth and later a kidney stone attack. I felt vindicated when she said the stone hurt her a lot worse than giving birth.

I didn't want my dying words to be, "If only I had spent less time at the office." At Marilyn's insistence, I pulled back, took some time off, resumed walking, then eased back into the Speidel saddle.

In early January 1976, publisher Einstoss climbed the stairs to my office in the SNI annex. He was so out of breath that I asked if anything was wrong. "I'm not sure. The last few days I've been puffing at the least exertion." The big guy hadn't been in Reno long enough to line up a doctor, so I sent him to Noah Smernoff, a gifted general practitioner and close friend. Blood tests were taken and Smernoff summoned him immediately. "Ron," he said, "something's not right. I am referring you to oncologists." Further testing was done, and Ron Einstoss got the horrible news. He was suffering acute leukemia. The doctors gave him eighteen months to live. Doctor Smernoff later told me, "The minute I looked at Ron's test, I knew he was a dead man."

Ron Einstoss, my cherished friend, came to me immediately after the results were in and reported the prognosis. He said, "I'm fighting this with all I've got. I'll keep working as long as possible." He did.

Gannett Comes Calling

Long Beach, CA Midway through 1976, I was scheduled to do an editorial critique for California daily editors in a conference aboard the majestic ship *Queen Mary*, which was berthed at Long Beach. Gannett's Al Neuharth phoned a week before, said he had seen notice of my appearance. He and his boss, the corporation's chairman, Paul Miller, would be attending, and they'd be "mighty pleased to visit, providing you've got the time, Rollie." I said that would be fine. Bob Whittington, Don Meyer, Jack Liechty, and Chick Stout were apprised of the forthcoming visit, and we accurately predicted what the Gannett leaders would talk about.

In advance of our meeting, I reviewed what we knew about Neuharth and Miller. The latter had a long career with Associated Press and was the AP's bureau chief in Washington, D.C., before joining Gannett. Neuharth had grown up poor, one of two sons of a widowed mother in South Dakota. He was a boy newspaper wunderkind, then a rising editorial star for the Detroit News prior to joining Gannett. He swiftly rose to the presidency.

When we met, Neuharth was wearing his trademark colors, black and white. A short man, with flecks of gray in his wavy hair, he was the epitome of charm. Miller was rangy and folksy, making me think that here was a Gannett version of Jack Liechty. After the opening exchange of pleasantries, Neuharth began, as we had guessed he would, talking about the Speidel block of shares held by Thomson. "We just wish we could have gotten those shares instead of Thomson—and with your prior consent, of course, Rollie."

Neuharth got right to the point. "We've had some casual talks with the folks you know at Thomson," he said. "We've made it clear to them that we wanted to talk to you before much was said. We would never do anything with respect to that stock without your full approval."

Neuharth continued, "As you know, Gannett owns the *Newburg Evening News* in New York, across the river from your *Poughkeepsie Journal*." I nodded. "Now, if you approve, we're thinking of buying the Speidel shares Thomson picked up as an investment. If Speidel and Gannett were ever to 'get hitched,' one option for us would be to give Thomson both cash and our Newburg paper. That would eliminate any Justice Department questions."

Gannett was way ahead of Speidel on acquisition acumen and success. They already owned fifty-three newspapers in seventeen states, compared to our thirteen properties in nine states. We'd been monitoring Gannett's growth for some time, as we did other publicly traded and private companies.

In the last few years, Gannett had acquired the Pacific Newspaper Group, owned by the famous Hawaiian investor, Chin Ho, in a deal that included the big, prosperous *Honolulu Star-Bulletin.* A short time before our meeting with Neuharth, Gannett and privately owned Federated Newspapers had done a tax-free merger by exchanging stock, with Gannett winding up as the surviving corporation and owner of Federation's eight dailies, many in the Northwest.

"To summarize a bit," Paul Miller said, "we know that you folks have a premier company and a grand future. We see so many similarities in your markets and ours—all college towns, all in non-competing environments, all growing at healthy rates, all prosperous.... At least, the last time I looked, most of Gannett's were still in the black." Snicker, laugh, slap thighs.

I answered with all that I could then say. "Speidel is happy just as we are. We've held the Thomsons at bay, the times are good and getting better, and we love our independence. I will brief our guys on this visit."

Reflecting on how Thomson had bushwhacked me, I was grateful that Gannett had done its talking above the table. We would be seeing their people a lot, I reckoned. As things turned out, I was much more right than I then realized.

Speidel Prospers, Competes For Acquisitions

Reno, NV Much more was on our minds than the merger overtures of Gannett and other companies—we were trying to do the right thing for Speidel employees and shareholders. Never out of my thoughts were some ideas that I had for changes which would result in significant advances in employee benefits. As president, I had been a somewhat calculating conformist, biding my time until Chick Stout retired as chair of the executive committee. When that occurred, I wanted to dramatically enlarge the scope of our company profit-sharing plan.

Since 1952, only executives had been permitted to "own a piece of the Speidel rock." The company had performed spectacularly in that arrangement, but I knew that opening up profit-sharing opportunities to our other employees would reward and empower them in an unprecedented manner. With the added motivation that profit-sharing brings, we would become a juggernaut, generating even greater profits and rising to new heights of quality in our work.

My dream scheme would have a domino effect: If we considered all our people managers in their own right, and sharply jacked up their monetary rewards, they, too, would have "a piece of the Speidel rock." Making each one a shareholder would lead to greater profits, which would yield more resources to dedicate to growth and improvement, all of which would translate to "better and bigger."

Since 1964, SNI had routinely sent its young managers to API seminars. Now, we also were holding internal managerial workshops, with Speidel executives from around the nation visiting Speidel cities. All my life, I had seen women held back—my mother's case was imbedded in my memory—and now, at last, we were giving females a crack at management. Bob Whittington's work with colleagues of color and mixed ethnic backgrounds was a factor in his drive to diversify our employee force.... That, and his innate sense of fair play, and his awareness of how much we would enrich ourselves, professionally and culturally, by kick-starting the diversity movement.

We were prospering, with increases in revenues and net income, quarter after quarter. Since going public, our annual net profit increases had run about fifteen percent, an average satisfactory to Wall Street. We always maintained that we wouldn't let The Street whack us with undue pressure to reach greater profit levels, but no manner how you sliced it, pressure was there.

Don Meyer did most of the dealing with the analysts who came to Reno. They were lured by a desire to see us in our home environment and by the "Biggest Little City's" reputation for making visitors feel welcome, particularly financial people waltzing in with unlimited expense accounts.

The analysts invariably serenaded us with the same old lyrics: "We know what you've done lately. We want words on what you'll do tomorrow." Pressures were even greater because of our margins—in 1974, gross profit ran thirty-five percent, the highest among publicly owned newspaper chains. Analysts asked, "How are you going to do better when you're already at the top?" Then they'd say, "Acquirers of new properties usually show the greatest growth of net income. Since 1966, Speidel has bought only two papers. We are quite aware of your internal success. But tell us, what is Speidel doing about external growth?"

These were hardball questions asked by people whose conclusions markedly affected how Speidel would be judged on The Street. The bottom line was the worth of SNI shares. The value per share was eighteen dollars the day we first traded publicly. Four years later, on the last trading day of 1976, our closing price was thirty dollars. As good as that was, what if The Street hadn't panicked because of the Nixon administration's voluntary wage and price controls? What if Speidel had acquired several properties that were large enough to beef up the company's bottom line?

We were striving to respond to the expectations of employees, shareholders, and The Street. Vice-president Whittington was doing a superb job of overseeing individual property and group-wide performance, but the heat was on to grow externally.

Meyer and I traveled extensively looking for newspapers to acquire. We were driven by the urgency of our task, but our acquisition beat was immense, encompassing all fifty states. We were also constrained by the thinness of Speidel's acquisition cadre—two of us to do the work of what should have been four or five staff. Then there were the costs of constant time and travel involved in the acquisition race (we were flying commercially to prospects' doors, while the newspaper Big Boys were cruising in company jets, maximizing use of the clock and cutting down on their fatigue); the better linkage that bigger, more established groups had with prospective sellers; and our competitors' superior acquisition track records (success begets success). Finally, there was the brand name factor—if the *New York Times* comes calling in any American newspaper market, and little Speidel pokes its lesser-known nose in the same tent, who's going to get the most attention?

By no stretch did those challenges strip away our confidence. We worked consistently to overcome each problem, and our forecasts of likely earnings gave us confidence that we could move salary and benefit levels higher. Whittington and I were hard-liners against any corporate move that might cause fear among subordinates. Worker bees never function up to potential when they are stung by hotshot higher-ups.

With the full retirement in 1976 of Chick Stout, after his distinguished twenty-nine-year SNI tour, we brought to the board the first outside director in the fifty-five-year history of the company. The move suited me, because it is always profitable to be examined by objective eyes. We had gone public, and with Stout gone, it was time. Selected as his successor was B.L. "Bill" Barnes, dean of the School of Business at the University of Iowa. He had been recommended by retired Speidel president Jack Liechty.

Nineteen seventy-six also marked the first away-from-Reno annual meeting of public shareholders. It was held in Iowa City, where the first Speidel newspaper had been acquired in 1921. Laryngitis rendered me mute at this meeting, but to our good fortune, Liechty was in full throat. He introduced the whole room of shareholder attendees—every individual—without referring to a note.

Liechty's memorable recitation that day was a down-home reminder of how neighborly and sensitive about people Speidel remained. It represented the sort of genuine interest and friendliness that long had been our hallmark. We were proud of it, and we intended to maintain that quality, no matter how large we grew.

No matter how pushed we were, it was in-company morale that we needed to sustain. We urged anew that each Speidel newspaper's executive staff members do things to affirm their appreciation of their employees. Like saying thanks.

I continued to talk up the importance of publishers visiting daily through their plants, strengthening camaraderie with the people who did the work. In my athletic youth, I had first observed how coach Edwin "Tip" Whitehead, of Sparks, Nevada, befriended opposing players in post-game visits, even if his team had been defeated by them. That lesson stuck with me as a reminder that civility to the enemy is a good idea.

Our pursuit of potential acquisitions continued, and we made forays into the Southwest, including to Midland, Texas. We had learned from an Associated Press writer that the Jimmy Allison family there was considering the sale of its newspaper. I had met Allison at publishers' conventions. He was a real good guy, unspoiled by his celebrity. Allison was widely respected in Texas, and before he took over his parents' newspaper, he had been a key insider in the congressional campaigns of George Bush.

Discussions of a possible sale of Allison's *Reporter-Telegram* to Speidel went nowhere. Yet, we maintained our friendship. One never knew. Circumstances constantly change, and you don't want a prospective seller to change his mind about you if his or her opinion is already good.

Family-owned companies are often compelled to sell for a variety of reasons, and Don Meyer had impressed on Whittington and me that if we paid top dollar and also had a cordial relationship with prospective sellers, we had a better chance of doing a deal. We were not unique. We were doing what worked for other companies.

The fact was, however, that John Ben Snow's acquisition conservatism had drastically diminished Speidel's opportunity to grow in the 1970s. By 1948, with its purchase of the *Visalia Times-Delta*, SNI had grown to eight newspapers, but in the following fifteen years, the corporation acquired not a single property.

Other acquirers had paid relatively modest sums for their acquisitions from the 1920s through the 1950s, especially in the Great Depression years of the 1930s, when so many owners were forced to sell because of the mean economic times. I dislike revisionism, which seems to me to be the harpooning of forebears by grandstand coaches who weren't present when the games were played. Yet, the fact is that Gannett, Hearst, Ridder, Knight, Scripps, Media General, Cox, and the Multimedia groups had been gaining heft back then, while Speidel stood inert.

Snow's back-to-back-to-back presidents, Merritt Speidel, Harry Bunker, and Chick Stout, were from the conservative mold of the founder, but who could blame them for not arguing with John Ben Snow? He had little truck with subordinates who told him to happily assume heavier debt. Not that his presidents didn't try. Stout once told me that numerous SNI offers to other papers were indeed made from the 1920s through the 1950s. "But we probably sharpened our pencils too much," he admitted.

While Speidel stood idle, other groups gained the size that made them formidable profit-makers and prolific acquirers. An ancillary bonus of growth was that girth means superior defense in the event that someone unfriendly comes rapping on your door. With that in mind, when Gannett and other suitors came calling, we politely listened. We learned.

We didn't belabor past fumbles. We did not speak ill of the key Speidel men who had done their best. What we did do was let history tell us where we should go and suggest how we could get there. There were roads yet to be traveled, and we would do our best to travel them safely. Not a member of the Melton corporate team believed that our ride would be easy. We were right.

Reno publisher Ron Einstoss was fighting acute leukemia, but the great journalist toiled on as though his illness was just a nuisance. Even through his many blood transfusions, he refused to back off, and his prodigious outpouring of work faltered only with his periodic hospitalizations. He knew, as Grantland Rice put it, that one Great Scorer would eventually come to call his name. His was an ordered mind. He had Don Meyer counsel him on his estate plan, getting things ready. Preparing for his medical absences, he had various members of his Reno executive team oversee operations when he was being treated. Advertising director Dean Smith was most frequently his choice.

Speidel And Gannett Get Hitched

Reno, NV Our plan to expand by acquiring newspapers from families who were faced with huge estate taxes wasn't working; but although we weren't growing, we remained a highly profitable company. Gannett's Al Neuharth came calling again, as though saying, "I'm here to comfort the already-comfortable." He was a cordial chap, and when we reaffirmed how much we valued our independence, he said, "I'd feel the same. It is not good to move too quickly on the big things."

Neuharth checked in once in awhile, but not often enough to be consigned to our pest list. Other groups, lusting to be our masters, made passes, giving us a sense of what the pioneers must have felt when Indians circled their wagons.

Neuharth again came tapping on our door. "Here's an interesting map," he said. It had color-coded pins stuck in Gannett and Speidel cities. "Look here, if we ever got married, we would be by far the largest group in the country," he said. His math was good. He counted seventy-three total pins. We added up sixty for Gannett, thirteen for Speidel, and got the same total.

We were pragmatic, realizing more and more that while our independence was cherished, defending it indefinitely from friendly parties could eventually result in our takeover by a powerful hostile force. Don Meyer had come to idolize our company in his brief time with us. Though he wasn't happy at the prospect of crawling into bed with the opposition, he agreed that it would not hurt to hear a proposal from Gannett. So, in November 1976, an exploratory visit occurred in San Francisco. Present were Speidel's top management and Gannett's Neuharth and his chief financial officer, Jack Purcell.

Speidel did not wish to become Journalism Jonah, swallowed by the Gannett whale. "Never would happen," Gannett assured us.

Speidel favored a tax-free stock exchange, so that its early owners/shareholders, who had a very low cost basis per share, wouldn't get massacred by capital gains taxes, then running 35 percent. "No problem," Gannett said.

We grew sharp with each other on a serious issue: the stock exchange ratio. When Speidel argued for as high a figure as we could worm out of Gannett, Neuharth went into a snit. He and his colleague angrily marched from the room. We recessed.

Neuharth, the superb negotiator/actor, came back in, and the two sides agreed that there was no deal and that we should call the whole thing off. Neuharth made a renewed pitch for a lower figure, saying that, "At the ratio sought by Speidel, Gannett, the surviving corporation, would be left with dilution of earnings for two, possibly three years, and The Street will kick hell out of us." We said too bad. Each party adjourned and went home.

In the following days, Speidel directors and management decided that we would not find a better deal with any other newspaper group. Gannett and SNI were a good fit for several reasons: Many of our newspapers were of comparable size; each company was hot for local autonomy; the deal would sit well with our shareholders, for they would have more liquidity, higher dividends, greater size; and the combined company, through its sheer size and combined executive talent, would be a Goliath without warlike tendencies. A merger would make the combined company America's largest, and the deal, to be valued at $180 million, would be the largest in American newspaper history up to that time.

I called Allen Neuharth and told him that we agreed to a merger and to the exchange ratio proposed by Gannett: eight Gannett shares for every ten Speidel shares. We could have held out for something higher, but if dilution did occur, Speidel's shareholders would take it in the shorts along with

Gannett's. Giving either side a chance to sharpshoot the deal wasn't to our liking.

The merger in principle, if leaked prematurely, would leave the good ship Gannett-Speidel in great pain. Both parties kept the deal quiet. On December 6, 1976, we told the public the news. Speidel and Gannett had agreed to wed. Allen Neuharth predicted that this would be a newspaper marriage made in heaven—not an original declaration, but one that seemed appropriate.

It was nice that this wasn't a shotgun deal. We were hoping for an extended honeymoon and that we'd all be around to see how it turned out, but time was running out for my dearest newspaper friend. Ron Einstoss, sick as he was, put together his thoughts on page one of the *Reno Evening Gazette*. "The merger is good news for our readers and advertisers," he said. He was a colleague who was never wrong. He told me, "I want to hang in here long enough to see if I'm right."

What did Speidel's merger with mammoth Gannett mean to our readers? In a twinkling, Speidel's thirteen dailies would for the first time bring their readers news coverage provided by the eighteen-person Gannett News Service in Washington, D.C. Heretofore, we had relied solely on our wire services, but often it took minor miracles to jar Associated Press and United Press International loose to ferret out news from the House and Senate members representing the nine states in which Speidel published. Our advertisers profited, too. Now they had access to the marketing and research facilities of Gannett, and of Louis Harris and Associates, which Gannett also owned.

Seventy-three newspapers under one corporate roof was too cumbersome to manage efficiently. So, as a condition of the merger agreement, Gannett chair Allen Neuharth created the first true regionalized newspaper mosaic among American groups. Our Reno office became the new Gannett West division headquarters. I was kicked upstairs to be chairman of the expanded western turf—eighteen newspapers, including the six Gannett properties in five Far West states. Bob Whittington went from vice president of Speidel to president of the new division. As part of the deal, all Speidel headquarters personnel remained in place. In an important element of the merger, Whittington, retired SNI president Jack Liechty, and I all became members of the enlarged Gannett corporate board of directors. Whittington and I remained in Reno.

On May 10, 1977, five months after the merger agreement in principle, Speidel's annual meeting of shareholders was held in Reno. There was only one prime topic on the agenda, and it was the most vital in the fifty-six-year life of SNI. With Whittington, Liechty, and Al Neuharth beside me on the dais, I ticked off the merger advantages that would accrue to Speidel's owners: A favorable stock exchange ratio; substantially increased dividends; Gannett management's excellent credibility with The Street; and the major following of institutions in Gannett stock. I called for the vote. Shareholders approved the merger almost unanimously.

Gannett moved quickly. That afternoon, a Gannett jet whisked Whittington, Liechty, and me (and our wives) to Rochester, New York, where the following morning, Gannett shareholders also endorsed the merger. So, we were hitched. There was none of that strut of the conquerors stuff that too often bedevils mergers. In fact, the cagey Neuharth talked as though God had tapped Gannett with His golden wand, linking Neuharth's company with "the best little newspaper outfit in the whole darned land."

Mergers often are stabs to the morale of employees of acquired companies. This was painfully true in the wave of bank "downsizings" following mergers that were done routinely two decades after the SNI and Gannett partnership was struck. Whittington and I led the expedition to soothe the jangled nerves of our longtime colleagues nationwide and in the Reno central office. But we were realistic. There were economies of scale at play here—meaning, why keep two employees when one can efficiently do the same job? But for the time being, all our people were unscathed.

Although our *Argus-Leader* newspaper in South Dakota was geographically located in the newly formed Gannett Central Division, it was our Gannett West responsibility. We had a zoo of an operation situation there, and so the publisher was ordered to take early retirement. The paper needed a strong new chief executive. In June, a month after the merger, Whittington announced that Reno advertising manager Dean Smith would be the new publisher. It was a perfect choice. Smith always was good at taming uneasy creatures (employees) who suffered for lack of sensitive leadership.

Ron Einstoss Dead At 47

Reno, NV Three weeks after the merger came news we had dreaded. I was in Washington, D.C., when Warren Lerude called. Marilyn and our two youngest children, Kevin and Emelie, were with me. Ron Einstoss was dead. Leukemia had taken his life.

The incredible Reno publisher had shared in the winning of three Pulitzer Prizes in his Los Angeles and Reno positions. What they say about the good dying young must be true—my colleague and pal was only forty-seven.

I came home to eulogize Einstoss, and I said: "Ron was neither architect nor builder of physical things. He wrote no books or songs. He never claimed to be a poet. While he was famous with the many who knew him personally, he did not reach for public acclaim. When attention was lavished on him, he changed the subject. Given more time, he would have become a national figure. That would have pleased him. Ron always did favor broad arenas in which to serve."

An Einstoss-schooled editor, Robert Ritter, wrote of his former boss: "Ron could yell; my God, the man could yell. But when he laughed, the earth shook. Ron Einstoss didn't die. As long as there is a free press, he never will."

Einstoss was so profound that in all my later years, as I groped for an answer, I'd have conversations with my absent friend. I would ask, "What would you do?" Ron would tell me, and, as usual, he would be right.

Time marches on. The characters hiking across the stage inevitably change. Participants in life's real show are forgotten. In 1999, a young editor was transferred to Reno from Visalia, California, where my dear lost buddy had been editor, then publisher. I asked the newcomer if he had heard the name Ron Einstoss. "No, I never did," he said. "What did he do?"

I answered, "Well, it's a long, sweet story. Someday I'll tell it to you."

We appointed Warren Lerude to succeed Ron Einstoss as Reno publisher.

Gannett VP
G-J Columnist

Executives Reassure Employees

We were in a post-merger burst of activity. Our corporate lawyer, Don Meyer, turned all Speidel acquisition files over to Gannett, but he continued to gather additional intelligence about newspapers that might one day be candidates to occupy a Gannett tent. We got acquainted with our new teammates at newspapers that were now in the Gannett West division. Whittington and I made visits to all of them: State capital cities of Salem, Oregon; Olympia, Washington; and Boise, Idaho. There were others: Bellingham, Washington; Santa Fe, New Mexico; and San Bernardino, California.

Wherever we visited, we helped calm jitters. We were learning to say "us," meaning the merged companies, instead of "we," meaning Speidel. Workshops were held, bringing together people from both sides.

It was thrilling to us to see that Gannett had so many females in managerial slots. That set a standard former Speidelers were anxious to emulate. Many people of ethnic background were employed at our newspapers in Santa Fe and San Bernardino. All of "our" people, meaning those at former Speidel newspapers, were growing because of the rub-off of peer knowledge.

There was that outside newspaper world, too. Travel unfailingly provided new adventure and learning. In New York's Waldorf Hotel, a woman rudely bumped me as she sprinted off the elevator. I said, "She looks familiar. Who is she?" My companion said, "That's Amy Vanderbilt, the etiquette expert."

You could celebrity-watch all day, any day in the Waldorf lobby, as I found out on one of my first visits as a Gannett person. I spotted the great old broadcaster, Lowell Thomas, prowling unrecognized among the potted palms. I introduced myself and had an immensely enjoyable visit.

Al Neuharth had maneuvered me into being the chairman of the national convention of the American Newspaper Publishers Association in San Francisco. I opened the convention of hundreds of publishers from the U.S. and Canada by introducing the city's mayor, George Moscone, who delivered a delightful "Baghdad by the Bay" welcome. In the blur of activity, I scarcely had a chance to visit with him one-on-one. Perhaps later, I felt. But there would be no later. Not long after that, Moscone was assassinated at City Hall.

Rollan Melton as a member of the Gannett Board of Directors (1977-1997).

Bush Visits, Marilyn Irons

One interesting experience occurred after Neuharth began involving me in on-site acquisitions for the merged company. My friend Jimmy Allison, owner of the paper at Midland, Texas, was perilously ill with leukemia in a Houston hospital. It was terribly awkward for me to look in on a special acquaintance who was so sick, and to engage him in an exchange about the future of his newspaper. I could see that he was in the last stages of his terminal illness, but he immediately put me at ease. We chit-chatted, and Allison said, "I'm thinking a lot about the options my family and I have with our newspaper. I want to make a decision while I'm still around. If I decide Gannett ought to be a part of that decision, I'll tell you, and you can come visit again."

Allison laid there, hair mussed, pajamas flapping every which way, and he kept joking and urging me to stay longer. He said, "Remember the last time we were together, I told you of my involvement with the political campaigns of George Bush?"

I nodded, remembering that this was the Bush who had served Texas in the U.S. House of Representatives, was later a U.S. ambassador, and still later, chairman of the Republican National Committee.

"Well, hang around, Rollie," Allison said. "George promised he'd come by this evening for a visit. I want you two to meet." I hung around.

Minutes later, George Bush strolled into the room, unaccompanied. He warmly greeted his buddy. He vigorously shook my hand and said, "Oh, you're likely a friend of my friend, Senator Paul Laxalt from Carson City." Bush seemed to know everything about Laxalt, the former Nevada governor, except his waist measurement and hat size.

Bush plunked down on the edge of his friend's bed, and they went earnestly at their chattering for a good fifteen minutes. It was a visit filled with names of Texas leaders I'd never heard of, but it was fascinating, because here were two special buddies, yammering away, and all three of us realizing that before long, only two of us would remain.

Bush paused long enough to say, "I'm going out for dinner when I leave here. Please join me, Rollie."

Now we were on a first-name basis. "Love to, Mr. Bush," I said.

It was time for us to leave. George Bush, perched on Allison's bed, pumped his dying friend's hand for several seconds, and tears were coming from the eyes of both men. Bush's voice choked. It was time to say the last goodbye.

In the hall outside our friend's room, Bush and I chatted, and his voice was miraculously clear and his eyes dry. He quickly dropped the subject of Jimmy Allison. "Let's go eat. I have a favorite steakhouse nearby," he said.

We dined, and Bush spent an hour grilling me on Nevada politics: Who had the big bucks? Who brought real influence? Which Democrats would likely file against his Republican cohorts? What were the chief concerns of Nevadans? I fumbled for answers, but not to worry. Bush already knew more about Nevada's political scene than anyone except Senator Laxalt.

Six weeks later, I saw Bush again at Jimmy Allison's freshly dug grave. Bush, a pallbearer, was somber and verging on tears. Of course, he would get over it. Most of us have to.

The next time I saw Bush, he was the sitting American vice president. It was at the Melton home in Reno at a quiet little gathering, attended by the secret service, sniffing police dogs, the FBI, Marilyn and me, one hundred or so diners, and the man who one day would be the president of the United States.

In the late morning of the day George Bush dropped in at our house to visit, I phoned Marilyn from the office and said, "What's doing?"

She replied, "Oh, nothing, really. Just standing here talking to the secret service while I fold underwear."

Executive Burn-Out

In early 1978, Al Neuharth asked me to seek a directorship on the Associated Press board. "It's rare that anyone gets elected on his first try," he said, "but I'd like you to get better known nationally among newspapers." He entered my name as a Gannett representative.

The entire AP membership could vote, so I sent a flood of tailor-made letters, badly overworking our secretaries, Jean Brown Roseman and Joan Dunphy. Neuharth was correct. First-timers don't usually make the cut. I didn't, finishing sixth in a ten-man race; but I was just one body away from winning an eight-year term on the board. Dan Ridder, a high muck-a-muck with the Knight-Ridder group, was a few votes ahead of me.

I was relieved to have it over. I explained to Marilyn, "After watching Dan Ridder try to dance last night, I wonder how a lead-foot like that edged me out. It would never have happened if only I had done a better Fallon two-step."

Neuharth wanted to bring me permanently to Gannett corporate headquarters in Rochester. We visited, and he said, "I like your management style, Rollie. I'll need someone to succeed me as president when I retire or am kicked out, whichever occurs first. You could be a contender. I emphasize the word *could*."

I liked the way Neuharth said that. No right-minded leader should ever promise anyone anything, as dumb Rollie Melton had done back in 1964 when he talked to Walter MacKenzie, speaking with the heart rather than the head. Nonetheless, Neuharth eventually told me that the position of senior vice president was mine if I wanted it. I told him that I would discuss the opportunity with Marilyn, because, if accepted, this would be our first newspaper-related move.

All of our children were still in school; Marilyn's parents were in Reno, and aging; my mother and father were in the West and in fragile health; but Marilyn said, "Where you go, I go. You're not getting rid of me." I phoned Neuharth and told him it was a go. It was the end of April of 1978, and Gannett announced that I was to be the corporation's senior vice president for administration and planning.

Though I had said nothing to anyone, including Marilyn, I was pretty tired—I had been on a fast track for thirteen years. I was forty-six, and maybe it was time to ease up . . . but ambition ruled. I seized the opportunity to become Gannett's senior vice president.

I was pleased by another, related development. When I was promoted, Bob Whittington moved up to be the top leader of Gannett West. He was the most versatile newspaperman with whom I had ever worked.

Before I lit out for the East, Whittington did me an honor that has thrilled me ever since. In the twilight of his Speidel leadership years, Chick Stout had created the Speidel Newspaper Charitable Foundation, fueled by his own major gift and gifts from other SNI executives. SNCF had made small, important local grants during its brief history. Now the foundation was to be dissolved, because, in its stead, our communities would benefit from grants made by the giant Gannett Foundation. Whittington was aware of how I yearned to see minorities in our newspaper ranks, so he took the core assets of the dissolving Speidel Foundation and gifted them to the American Press Institute, stipulating that income from what he called the Rollan Melton Fellowship would underwrite the API seminar participation of journalism educators who were of color and/or were ethnic minorities.

Going into our merger, I had held high hopes that small Speidel could persuade giant Gannett to do many things the SNI way. My longtime colleagues hoped I could convince the merged corporation that the little acquired outfit had ideas worth implementing. But realistically, could a lightweight boxer teach Muhammad Ali how to be a heavyweight fighter? Could a Triple-A club win in the big leagues? I was but one voice amid a batch of corporate officers, many of whom I had yet to meet.

Just prior to my transferring east that spring, Marilyn and our youngest children, Kevin and Emelie, left on a six-week school tour of Europe. I had talked to Marilyn earlier about whether to sell our Reno home and buy in Rochester. "We'd be better off waiting until we see how things work out in your new position," Marilyn said. So off they went, and away I flew.

My adrenaline had been pumping through the five-month merger process. Before that, I had taken Speidel public in my rookie season, my toughest year; and in the ensuing five years, I had poured my strength into trying to become a first-rate chief executive. I was not good about taking vacations. I spent so little time with our children that it was almost like they were growing up with Marilyn as their sole parent, but my longtime colleagues were counting on me, and I must keep pushing. I hadn't realized I had driven myself near to exhaustion.

I had learned to do a number of things well, but pacing myself wasn't one of them. Al Neuharth installed me in an attractive office at a Rochester high-rise. I dug in. He had given me much to administer, including labor relations, employee benefits, and the Gannett air corps—three jets and one propeller-driven plane.

I was determined to prove to Neuharth that he had made a superlative choice. Later, having the advantage of viewing myself through the rear-view mirror of my memory, I saw what had happened to me. The more I had to do, the more additional work I glommed onto. I was working hard, but not very smart. Gannett talent was all around me. In retrospect, I should have used it better.

Working out of the eastern office, three thousand miles from home, I finally realized how much I had been relying on Bob Whittington, Don Meyer, J. C. Hickman, Bob Wingard, and other Speidel headquarters talent. The absence of Whittington was the toughest void in my new administrative life. I rated him a superstar. Now I understood how good he had made me look.

I pitched Gannett on adopting the Speidel bonus plan for executives, but the corporation had its own mature version and didn't want to change. I also hoped to get involved in Gannett's acquisition thrust, but this was the turf of two of the keenest newspaper acquisition experts of all times, Neuharth and Douglas McCorkindale, who was the corporate secretary and legal counsel.

They didn't need me—I had had only modest results out of years of trying to buy properties. Gannett had grown to sixty newspapers, while Speidel had joined its new parent corporation with but thirteen.

Throughout my executive life, I was addicted to taking detailed notes during meetings. Confucius must have had guys like me in mind when he said, "The faintest ink is better than the best memory." But after I had joined several of my new Gannett colleagues on a corporate operating committee visit to our Northeast properties, Neuharth told me, "If I were you, I would avoid making so many notes. It makes some of the others on the committee nervous."

I had been the Main Man for so long that the transition to subordinate vice president, reporting to the man on high, would take some getting used to. The more deeply I rooted into work, the more I realized two other things: As a kid, I could easily pick up and move at the flick of my mother's whim. Now I was a creature of habit, roiled even by moving to a new home across town, let alone across the nation. Additionally, I had devoted myself for years to trying to rise to Speidel president. Now I wondered, "Is it worth busting myself like that again, and perhaps falling short?"

I was flying to a Gannett city at least once a week, to a meeting here and a meeting there. I used my own company Falcon jet, and while Marilyn and the kids were still away in Europe, I flew to Reno every Friday afternoon, returning east on Sundays. In retrospect, I wouldn't push myself like that again.

Fatigue had never troubled me before, but now I felt like a human tire with all its air let out. I was staying in a midtown apartment adjacent to the Gannett quarters, so I would lumber over to my office around 5:00 in the morning and work late into the night. If I had been Rip Van Winkle, I would have put myself down for a very long sleep. I was also smoking too much and imbibing too much Scotch and water. My stamina diminished; my weight increased.

Finally, my head cleared enough for me to get my predicament in focus. I was in trouble physically and emotionally. This wasn't Gannett's doing. I alone had pushed myself beyond the limit. Gannett was a speeding streamliner, with Neuharth leaning on the throttle. I thought of myself as nothing more than a passenger that the other players could easily do without. As to the welfare of my SNI colleagues, they were faring all right: Don Meyer was leaving the company to pursue other opportunities. Speidel's excellent benefits director, Clinton Howard, was taking an early retirement. All others seemed set.

I called Marilyn in Europe, telling her that I was on the ropes. I thought that I'd better look into dropping out of executive life. Her advice: "Think this over with care. We should talk more about it."

There was no change in me in the following days. I was creeping along on fumes rather than on a full tank. Finally, I called her again and said, "I've had it. I'm telling Al Neuharth tomorrow that it would be a mistake for me to continue in Rochester."

Rollie Returns
Royle Energizes Reception

Reno, NV I felt that I was a drag on Gannett corporate, and I told Neuharth so. He offered to modify my responsibilities, lightening the load if I wished. I said I felt it best to leave administrative life. If he was agreeable, I wanted to return to Reno and resume what I had been trained early to do, but had not been able to do during the last sixteen years: write for the public print. "If Reno agrees," I said, "I'm going to give the *Gazette-Journal* something it needs very much—a column about Nevada."

Neuharth said, "Reno will agree. I'll take care of that. Your present salary and all benefits will continue until you return to work. About doing a column: that's what I want to do someday." An agreement was reached to begin my column in the *Gazette-Journal* on October 8, 1978.

The touring band of Meltons returned home to their temporarily jobless head of the household. Marilyn admitted that she was shocked and deeply concerned when I hung up my executive spurs. "Let's hope you truly do intend to make writing your permanent focus," she said. "One of the things we have to work out is the future education of Kevin and Emelie. While you're at it, Rollan, you can keep supporting me, too."

I had come home to reinvent my life, happy that I would continue to be what I was born to be—a newspaperman. Nonetheless, I questioned myself:

Should I have driven for the merger? Yes. If you sit on your hands too long, you get your whole backside blown off. Mom-and-pop outfits were an increasingly rare species. We joined a newspaper supermarket just in time.

Was I a fool to believe that our little outfit could force-feed ideas into a titan? You got that right.

Did I leave my colleagues in the lurch? God, I prayed not.

Did falling from senior vice president to obscure columnist bug me? I'd be a liar to tell you no. In the months following my decision, those who used to call, to write, to ask help, steered clear of me. I became a nonentity, much like the widow who loses identity and recognition when she loses her spouse.

Did I err in having collected as my close friends mostly those who were in the newspaper industry? Absolutely! One of the dumbest things I ever did. When I left executive life, many such friends drifted off. That's natural, I suppose, when you no longer work together every day. Now I had to build a cadre of new acquaintances. I did. Non-newspaper people were there in big numbers. It was about time I learned that single focus can make Rollie a dull boy.

When I was a cocksure young professional, I was told, "Don't forget, it's the position they bow to, not the man." Now I knew how accurate was that caution. In the aftermath of my leaving corporate life, colleagues nationwide wondered whether I had fallen from the Gannett tower or was pushed, but did they mourn their departed newspaper brother? No. For a year or so, I had the feeling that they thought I had died. Someone once observed that life is for the living. I wasn't dead, but I had the luxury of observing my graveside service and overhearing tender thoughts: "Rollie's gone. Let's do lunch."

I was amused at the comments I heard: "You're pouting, Rollie—is it because people no longer pay attention to you? Buck up, old friend, you're not traveling steerage in the Purgatory Express. What do you want to be when you grow up—a writer or something? You're forty-seven—much too young to act like an orphan."

While I was taking my hiatus, my father died in Boise. Marilyn and I went there, and I did his eulogy, one of scores I would do in the decades to follow. The turnout was small for this non-public man. My dad had been sober for so long that many friends weren't aware that he'd ever been anything but dry. I set the facts straight. "Once he was a troubled guy who wrecked those around him," I said. "Then he crash-landed to the pits and confessed to himself, 'There's a better way. I'll find it.' He did."

The transition from the rarefied corporate air to newsroom typewriter hadn't put me out of the corporate mainstream entirely. My Gannett directorship continued to give me a window on the newspaper world, and this would be so for eighteen additional years. In the countdown before I turned columnist, Gannett directors met in Reno. Marilyn and the children were still traveling, so I invited my fellow directors to our home for an outdoor reception. My wife coached me from afar. "Get this caterer... Arrange for parking... Invite so-and-so... Be certain you fix the sprinklers so they don't wash guests away."

The guests came, famous dudes—Bill Rogers, secretary of state and attorney general under Nixon; Jim Webb, whom President Kennedy selected as the key man to put an American on the moon; many others. All of them were enjoying a lovely time when the sprinklers fired off. People ran every which way, pursued by spray. Most people didn't think it funny, except Neuharth, with his bizarre humor. He said, "It's time you go back to writing and give up your unusual approach to yard work." Our eldest son, Royle, offered famous last words. "I thought I had the sprinklers all taken care of, Dad."

The Rollan Melton Column Debuts
Zingers Abound

Reno, NV   Not working drove me nuts. After two months of rest and relaxation, I was ready to scream. I ached to lean into my typewriter and see if I could make anything appear on blank paper, but I had not a clue as to what to say or who to say it about.

In just two weeks my column would debut, and I was not sure that I was ready. I hadn't written a column since I was a sports editor, nineteen years earlier, and most of my former information sources were no longer around. Besides, I wouldn't be writing about sports—my beat now was general interest.

I knew that the only way I'd burn the carbon out of my writing engine was to show myself and my readers that I could still string words together in sensible fashion. For nearly two decades, just about all I had written were interoffice memos, profiles of acquisition candidates, and messages to shareholders and to securities analysts and critics of chain newspapers. Writing for the public print was a very different matter.

I would try to fill my friends in on what was happening in their world, doing it with a homey, gabbing-over-the-back-fence style. The tricky part: There are tens of thousands of friends out there, each unique, each with special needs and a fixed notion of how a column should be written. How would I meet their expectations?

My feature was to be called "The Rollan Melton Column." I wasn't egotistical enough to name it that—my new bosses, who formerly had worked for me, had dreamed it up.

Given free rein and the latitude to develop a style that fit me, I had decided that I would write about Nevadans or visitors or those who used to live in the Silver State. In other words, I would write about almost everyone, so long as the Nevada angle was present.

Readers want news about those they regard as the most important souls on earth: themselves. For years, I had urged my colleagues to report on the deeds of locals—the heroes, the hoity-toity, the have-nots, the want-to-be's, and the role models who hang in there to build rather than tear down. Now it was my turn to do what I'd long been preaching.

My first column appeared on Sunday, October 8, 1978. It was an "item" feature—a collection of unrelated topics strung together. One item quoted the Reno bartender-turned-entrepreneur, Bruno Benna, as saying, "A true conservationist is the guy who already owns his own house at Lake Tahoe."

I was to do four columns a week. In the beginning, my news cupboard was so bare that I went begging people to give me items, but the more stuff I cobbled together, the more the contributors came out of the woodwork with their ideas, affirmations, dissents, comical one-liners, advice, consent, tidbits, ticklers, and stories of happiness, tears, and of people great and small.

Zingers aimed at me were in good supply and frequently came from rural Nevadans. Yerington's octogenarian curmudgeon, Walter Cox, wrote, "Melton, I like your column. Each one is better than the next."

From Gardnerville came a literary knife. A woman wrote, "I can't stand what you say or how you say it. My first husband was a scoundrel, and you, Melton, are the spitting image of him."

Banker Ernie Martinelli claimed "Melton's undershorts won the Greater Reno balloon races," and hefty Ben Akert alleged that "Rollie has willed his four chins for medical research."

All of a sudden, the trickle of people's contributions to the column turned into a torrent. Over the years, readers have said, "It must be so hard to fill up those columns," but the fact was that after awhile, I could barely keep up with all the mailed, phoned, and hand-delivered material. Out of necessity, my writing got leaner—lean writing is also a courtesy to readers, who can detect literary flab from 20,000 leagues away.

I would also vary the column format: Items columns, strung together a la Herb Caen or Walter Winchell, but without Winchell's people-cutting hatchet, dominated, but I would also write single-subject columns. Some of these were about issues, but most featured lesser-known citizens who, in their own way, had made a positive difference. Readers don't give a hoot about editors' logos or the governor's pesky cold—they want to read something new, or what they already know or suspect.

While my secretaries, Mickey Wessel and later Sandi Sei, were trying to bring order to my desk and to my work life, I was settling in for a long run. Marilyn had suspected that while I was an executive, I might be blowing smoke when I said that I dreamed of one day writing again. On the anniversary of my first column year, she said it was good of me to stay that long to prove myself.

Like the mighty Truckee, my river of words rolled on. Millions of them. Thousands of columns. Tens of thousands of persons written about—gorgeous people, half-wits, true-blues. I listened to their stories, identified with their humor, empathized with their grief, celebrated their successes, commiserated with them in their failures, applauded their courage, tenacity, and dreams.

I bragged about my readers' kids, and I invited youngsters to let me give them some ink. In 1983, I reported that Rebecca Goodwin, a second-grader at Dayton, Nevada, had written to Ronald Reagan at the White House: "If I was president, I would tell the truth, I would not steal, I would not make the prices go higher. I would let our country have a big party. Then I would go pick someone else to be president."

In Carson City, twelve-year-old Lesley Remington detected an error on a Model Dairy milk carton, a misspelling not called to the company's attention in all the years of its use. "You may want to check your spelling of 'pasteurized,' she wrote co-owner Tom Bahan. The dairy gave her five hundred dollars and a trip to Disneyland.

There were descriptions of Nevadans at work, at play, and at their quotable best. Reno's cheerful optometrist, George Hamilton, had a desktop that "looked like a dumpster." Former Reno mayor Bruno Menicucci "looked like a beach ball with arms." Sage observer Gary Bullis said, "A fool and his money are soon accepted in the highest social circles." Reno centenarian Emma Margrave told me on her 101st birthday: "Life continues to be of great interest to me, so long as I can keep my tongue wagging." A local politician stood out because he had his hands in his own pockets only.

U.S. Senator Chic Hecht, Republican from Nevada, chattered away on the problem that so worried him: nuclear "suppositories." Activist Clark Santini was "the mouth that roared." Fellow columnist Cory Farley "slept better at night, because Ronald Reagan was sleeping."

There was the sign in a Winnemucca, Nevada, library: "I have been reading so much about smoking, drinking, overeating, and sex, that I have decided to give up reading." Old-time printer and cracker-barrel philosopher, Bert Crampton, of Fallon, said, "What this country needs is a new child labor law to keep kids from working their parents to death."

I interviewed the visiting old heavyweight champion, Jack Dempsey, who said, "Fighting was what I did best. It let me flex my manhood." When Catholic priest, Robert Bowling, complained about golf balls landing in his yard, which was adjacent to the Reno Municipal Course, the former Reno-Sparks Chamber of Commerce president, Jud Allen, told him, "Monsignor, that's what you get for living in a neighborhood of hookers."

The hulking former professional football lineman, Peter Lazetich, said he would cheerfully "eat everything on the menu, except 'Thank you for dining with us.'" Newspaper photographer Marilyn Newton, when asked why she was married and divorced three times, replied, "Slow learner."

With every living and dead person, there are stories. The rehabilitated former Nevada first lady, Jackie Laxalt, candidly told how she was able to stay sober over the years—one day at a time. There were profiles of Dr. Mary Fulstone of Mason Valley and Dr. Noah Smernoff of Reno, and their long journeys of healing.

When I interviewed Harold Smith Sr., namesake of the famous Harolds Club Casino, he yelled at me during our interview and then burst into tears, saying, "My daddy, Pappy Smith, was a fantastic man. They've put up this portrait bust of him. Last week, I went up to it and put my hands on his bronzed face, and I said, 'I love you, daddy.'"

Gloria Cortesi Garaventa, who had lost her son in an accident, told me, "For most, time diminishes the hurt; but not for a mother. When a mother loses a child, she cries forever." The storied Nevada coach, Jake Lawlor, in a reflective moment said, "I've won many games. But my proudest times are when my players march across that commencement stage and get their degrees."

I tried, but not always successfully, to keep my disgust at certain types of behavior out of print. When a Reno mayor's former wife posed nude from the waist up for *Playboy* magazine, I wrote, "She is like crabgrass or the seven-year mumps. She refuses to go away."

Telling of Judy and Robert Seale's last day together, before Judy died in an airplane crash the following morning: "On Sunday, they went riding on their beautiful horses along big Washoe Lake. It was a gorgeous day, one to savor as Nevadans, and as husband and wife. What mattered so much was being together. Living for such precious moments. Until tomorrow came."

Describing an autumn day: "Radio play-by-play broadcaster, Jim Stone, and color commentator, Don Manoukian, chanting the football language at Mackay Stadium. A new season of colliding young men, battling each other over one hundred yards of turf. Hail to our sturdy men, loyal and true; march, march on down the field, old Silver and Blue."

Stories, stories, stories. A delightful in-depth interview at my office with stately Mabs Martin, the coach of young models, a week before she and a student were lured by a man to his Stateline, Lake Tahoe, home and murdered. Reno's Jack Streeter, Nevada's most decorated World War II soldier, described his battle ordeal in the D-Day invasion. The column was published fifteen years before the movie, "Saving Private Ryan." Yet, Streeter told his story, and the movie's, with the most telling three words: "Death was everywhere."

A quotation, dropped into a philosophical piece: "God is too big to fit inside one religion." An observation from Hawthorne, Nevada, publisher Jack McCloskey: "Rollie, you're getting to be a geriatric hippie."

A comment from a politician: "I first knew Paul Laxalt long ago, when he still thought Henry Cabot Lodge was a motel in Yerington." A first-time news disclosure, twenty-seven years after Reno's catastrophic Golden Hotel fire in 1962, that the hotel elevator operator, George Cease, had quietly rescued some fifteen guests that terrible day.

The rabbi from Reno, Abraham Feinberg, alighted from his cab at a downtown library. He was eighty-six years old, and his young taxi driver handed him a free pass to the Mustang Ranch whore house. The Rabbi grinned and said, "You flatter me."

On June 26, 1982, I suffered a heart attack at home. When I regained consciousness, my cardiologist, Stanley I. Thompson, told me, "On a coronary Richter scale, you got about a six-point hit. With some luck, you'll make it through." I was hospitalized ten days and resumed writing in eight weeks.

In 1984, I had my closest call, cancer of the lymph nodes. A very humbling experience. Six months of chemotherapy treatment, followed by thirty radiation treatments. My white cell count dropped perilously low, leaving me defenseless against infections, and I was hospitalized in isolation for twenty-eight days. Then my medications were at last adjusted, and the white cells zoomed to normal. Good thing, too. Visitors to my room had to scrub up and wear masks, but the doctors put me at risk. They'd drop in, unmasked and unscrubbed, shake my hand, cough on me at times, and then depart to the safety of the outside world.

I was so determined to use work as part of my good medicine that, except for the isolation of four weeks, I worked every day, keeping the column going. I was afraid that if I dropped out, no one would miss me.

In later years I underwent two cataract surgeries and suffered a collapsed lung, but, thankfully, I never got a single hangnail. Throughout my run of poor health, I stayed positive. Author Norman Cousins, after his heart attack, wrote a book about the power of positive thinking and of imaging, so that a recovering patient could see himself recovering. Buoyant Cousins's advice was medical magic for me—at least four friends sent me copies of the book.

After my recoveries from various health scares, whenever someone told me that they were opposed to medical research with animals, I told them, "Try not to get sick. But if you do, thank God that such research has given all of us new chances."

I had gone against all odds again, and I had kept pushing as family man and as newspaperman.

Restored health fueled my serenity, putting me in the mood to tell my readers: "Now on another anniversary of our statehood, here is a toast to Nevada's rugged beauty, to its great citizens, the old-timers and newcomers. If we treat Nevada right, she will prosper us even more." And this: "It is nighttime in rural Wellington, where Nevadans live off the bounty of the generous land, where there is a vast supply of elbow and running room, where the air is sweet and clear, and stars peek through the cloud fluff." Plus my Thanksgiving Day column of 1990: "Thanksgiving is when we dine in the sanctity of our homes, surrounded by the most important people we shall ever know. Thanksgiving is our own personal holiday and it is not commercial and it is not for sale."

Customarily, I wouldn't have written about comedian Bob Hope, for he was a non-Nevadan, but after all, he was speaking in Reno. Thus, he was column fodder when he said, "I haven't had a facelift in years, but I do have my entire body sandblasted annually. By the way, your university coach-athletic director, Chris Ault, looks like a young Mickey Rooney. I wonder if they'll let me adopt him?"

Nevada Lieutenant Governor Robert Cashell was frequently quoted (or misquoted), and after going to a fat farm, he told me, "I was so damned hungry I almost ate a bar of soap." Comedienne Phyllis Diller had some advice when Cashell and his wife, Nancy, encountered her in a hotel in Washington, D.C. "Get a nose job, Mr. Cashell. Lose sixty pounds. Then maybe you'll look halfway good."

For years I had been pooping along on my Underwood manual, hacking out words and trying to jam fresh typewriter ribbons into the flaky, overworked machine, while all around me were reporter kids, plunking away on computers. So, what was I doing burdening my tired, patient secretary, Mickey Wessel, by having her input my hard copy into her computer?

I resisted getting in step with those who were using current technology. Then along came a new young Lifestyle section editor, Catherine Mayhew, who refused to accept my excuse that "I've always done it this way." The exasperated redhead, her temper ablaze, her resolve unswerving, put it to me bluntly: "Look, I don't care if you're a director of Gannett or whatever you are. You're going to learn to use a computer, like it or not." I nearly roared to my feet, saluting her. She reminded me of Allen Neuharth. Neither cared much whether they took prisoners.

Column writing is the ultimate adventure in newspapering, for it entails constantly being a reporter. One must ask short, tailored questions; listen intently, which is an art form; write for the readers instead of the newspaper contest judges; get things right, but swiftly correct the stuff you screw up on; and develop an army of news sources, the lifeblood of those who write for the masses.

All that is required in being a newspaper columnist is research, ideas, subjects to write up, a Rolodex, a dictionary, our newspaper library, a phone with a fat directory alongside, energy, and, in my twentieth-century and Third Millennium case, a trustworthy, constant companion—the computer. The Pulitzer Prize biographer, David McCullough, feels that real success is finding your life's work in the work you love. You shouldn't worry about making a living, about popularity or fame. He said that what you do should count more than what you own.

I seldom let poetry steal its way into my column, but when a self-professed Vietnam War veteran shared with me a poem that he claimed to have written while in deadly jungle combat, my interest was piqued. He was so convincing in his account of how he scratched out his verses amongst the terrors of combat and the horror of his dying buddies that I picked up and printed his poem in its entirety. My phone began ringing as soon as the paper reached my readers. I was too experienced and should have been too wise to fall for a liar's story, but I had. He had lifted the work of another, changed a couple of words, and faked me out of my embarrassed socks.

Which leads me to these poetic closures:

Bert Crampton, the golden oldie penman from Fallon wrote,

> *A writer of smut, to an editor wrote,*
> *Please publish my filthy enclosure.*
> *You don't have to pay me one dime for the stuff,*
> *I just need indecent exposure.*

And, with apologies to Ogden Nash, this verse frequently quoted by my friend, photographer Don Dondero:

> *I love a finished columnist,*
> *I really, really do.*
> *I don't mean one who's polished,*
> *I do mean one who's through.*

USA Today Is Launched
Melton Is There

Reno, NV I spent twenty years (1977-1997) on the Gannett board of directors. Talk about a memorable ride! Here's this long-ago school dropout studying the world of business from a front-row perch. There were many newspaper industry headlines in that period, with Gannett creating more than a few of them. Marilyn and I got to associate with some of the most talented, fascinating people anyone could possibly know.

At home in Reno, I was a three-times-a-week columnist at the *Gazette-Journal*, as good a job as there was in print journalism, but my other life as a Gannett director—a life not generally known to my Nevada friends—it was the one I most enjoyed. It was the crème de la crème of newspapering.

During my directorship the board met 122 times. I missed three meetings, one after my heart attack and two when I was hospitalized and in isolation after treatment for lymphoma. In my 119 sessions, and in a like number of corporate committee meetings, the time spent with board colleagues and Gannett corporate staff seemed like a bonus that went far beyond the usual rewards of a career in the newspaper business. Memories are made of this:

It is 1982, and Marilyn and I are the guests of chairman Allen Neuharth at his Cocoa Beach, Florida home near the space center at Cape Kennedy. Neuharth and I relax at poolside. He casually asks, "Rollie, is there any way you can see that Gannett could publish a general interest newspaper, distributed coast-to-coast?"

He hunches his shoulders, turns his palms skyward, as though asking Someone for guidance. I give him my earthly reaction: "Al, I can't see it. You'd have to have a ton of print sites, and even if you could transmit pages to them, it would be impossible to distribute nationwide. A sprinkling of news racks perhaps, but not home delivery."

Neuharth nods approvingly, as though saying, "Right on Rollie. You're no more anxious to waste money than I am." I am pleased that this most flamboyant twentieth-century newspaperman should ask advice from a guy who as a kid had trouble getting the weekly *Fallon Standard* from house to house. That subject exhausted, we move to other topics.

The Gannett board met six times a year, moving the meeting places from city to city, but always going at least once each to New York City and Washington, D.C. At the meeting following my sage pronouncement on the cockamamie idea of a national paper, Neuharth revealed that for a year he had closeted four young Gannett whiz kids, including Paul Kessinger, who had been on our Speidel corporate staff. They had been tucked away at his Florida diggings, and he had had them brainstorming what now seemed to me worth pursuing, since he was clearly behind it.

On the face of it, the idea sounded nutty, but Neuharth was as much a risk-taker as he was a painstaking, analytical, and awesome visionary. He had more guts than an army of brass monkeys, and he was a daredevil flier, but he also was a planning perfectionist.

Directors were unanimous. "Keep looking at it." Neuharth was happy. The preliminaries went all right. He knew they would, for he had prepped in advance some of the directors he was closest to. Next meeting, he came with figures, preparing us with the worst-case scenario. Neuharth looked grim, yet he had a bit of a smile as he said, "Our venture, if you approve it, will cost a ton of bucks. The potential return is there, we believe, but we'll be in the red for maybe up to five years." Directors pumped him with questions, and, as always, he fielded each with quick answers, reinforced with financia numbers. All of us voted to proceed. *USA Today* was born.

Gannett Executives Are A Diverse Lot

Reno, NV   Al Neuharth was an ego-driven leader who, in his maturity, still sparked with the cocksure wunderkind spirit he had had as a South Dakota boy. When Gannett directors were out of earshot, he could and did drive people like a trail-boss, whip in hand. Or he might be textbook kind to his people.

When I joined the board as a condition of the 1977 Speidel merger, I saw that the board members were a collection of diverse thinkers who brought to the boardroom varying disciplines and pride in the company. The initial cadre included Gannett chairman Paul Miller, who came from the news side to ultimately be an Associated Press news leader in AP's most important bureau, Washington, D.C. He had hand picked Neuharth, knowing that in a few years there had to be a passing of the torch. It was no contest. Neuharth already had a lock on the throne.

Another key director whom I instantly admired was James E. Webb, who was federal budget director in the Kennedy administration. However, he became most famous after the Russians fired Sputnik. President Kennedy quickly got us into the space race, and he chose Webb, a superb organizer, to direct the National Space and Aeronautics Administration (NASA). Kennedy told Webb that his mission was to get an American on the moon first; to beat the Russians up there.

William Rogers was another admirable director. He had been President Richard Nixon's attorney general, then secretary of state. I observed this charming man with the easy smile and wondered how he had dealt with Nixon. Never in my many visits with Rogers was he comfortable talking about the disgraced president. With Rogers, it was a highly classified subject.

Another director I was close to in my early board years was retired Associated Press president Wes Gallagher. He sported John L. Lewis eyebrows that were thick enough to comb. He was a gruff, contrarian director who was cautious in reacting to management's and directors' visits about costly expansion, equipment, or acquisitions. For instance, Gallagher was at first wary of Neuharth's national newspaper scheme. He was the crusty living legend of the Associated Press, having earned the label from his war correspondent years (1941-1945) and thence during his rise through the AP ranks to its presidency.

Others on the first board on which I served: My Speidel colleagues, Robert Whittington and Jack Liechty; John E. Heselden, senior vice president of Gannett staff and services; J. Warren McClure, Louis A. Weil Jr., and Robert B. Miller, whose newspaper groups merged with Gannett prior to Speidel's partnership. Many on that board were chairman Paul Miller's choices.

After Neuharth succeeded Miller as chair, he was the architect of a dynamic new breed of directors. He felt that the governing board should be representative of the racial and gender composition of Gannett and of America. As aging directors retired from the board, Neuharth moved his hand-picked directors into place. Some were African-Americans, such as Carl T. Rowan, the enormously talented, nationally syndicated columnist and television and radio commentator; Dolores D. Wharton, chairwoman of the Fund for Corporate Initiatives, who also was a trustee of the Kellogg Charitable Foundation; and Andrew F. Brimmer, who was a member of the Federal Reserve Board under Lyndon Johnson and was also a director of many other brand name corporations. The brilliant lawyer and investor, T. K. Stuart Ho, an Asian-American, was from Hawaii, and he had international business and social linkage.

Four of the directors had come up through the news ranks: Rowan; John Curley, who ultimately succeeded Neuharth as Gannett chair; Neuharth; and me. Gender balance was provided by Wharton and three others: Josephine P. Louis, a businesswoman from Chicago; Meredith A. Brokaw, author and New York City businesswoman, and the wife of NBC-TV anchor, Tom Brokaw; and Rosalynn Carter, author, businesswoman, and America's former first lady.

Other directors included Drew Lewis, the retired chairman of the Union Pacific Railroad, who was one of the nation's foremost transportation industry leaders. Two directors who had principal roles in media groups that had merged into Gannett were Peter B. Clark, an intellectual who formerly was president of the Detroit News Corporation, and brilliant Chicago lawyer Thomas A. Reynolds Jr., who earlier was a trustee of Combined Communications, a mixed media group (newspapers, television, outdoor advertising) that had joined Gannett two years after the Speidel merger. Julian Goodman was a retired president of the NBC network and a power in the broadcasting industry; and Douglas McCorkindale, Gannett's vice chair, was a chief financial officer and principal lawyer.

We were a convivial gang. None was to the manor born. Each was well-educated. Each was a solid family person. Each had special leadership expertise in business and civic endeavors. Marilyn and I were close to all directors, but Rosalynn Carter, Meredith Brokaw, and Carl Rowan were extra special pals.

Rosalynn Carter was extremely cordial, and there was a down-home goodness about her. She fussed over how her children were doing and told us that she had long since given up trying to slow down President Carter. Rowan had great humor, was an outstanding writer and author, and networked smoothly in top business, political, and government corridors of the nation.

We once had Rosalynn Carter as our house guest in Reno, along with several Secret Service and FBI operatives. We had invited her to speak to the Nevada Women's Fund, and she was a big hit, as she was in every setting in which we saw her.

Meredith Brokaw also joined us in Reno, again to support the Women's Fund and its president, Fritsi Ericson. Brokaw was the epitome of positive, and just one time did I hear her poke another. It happened in Reno when she met His Honor, Mayor Peter Sferrazza, who was a bit of a social bumbler, never on time, and a disjointed public speaker. Marilyn and I took Brokaw to Reno-Tahoe International Airport to see her off. We exchanged hugs, and she got off a parting comment: "I had a wonderful time with everyone. But tell me, where in the world did you find your mayor?"

While Neuharth was chair, we were a globetrotting gang. In winter, board meetings were in Hawaii or St. Thomas, where we owned newspapers. Doing international business, especially after the *USA Today* launch, led us to meetings and tours in Switzerland, Hong Kong, Singapore, Italy, France, and China. All my Gannett corporate trips were educational and sheer fun. As for Marilyn and the other spouses, each had her black belt in shopping, and, collectively, all were endlessly creative in contributing to the prosperity of credit card institutions.

After Neuharth's retirement, his protégé, John Curley, moved into the chairmanship, bringing a bedrock foundation of financial prudence. He perpetuated the practices that had made Gannett a premier company. He demanded excellence, and he had a sixth sense about doing the right thing.

Like so many Gannettoids, as I called them, Curley, though he was understated, had a rich vein of humor. He got a roar of laughter at his first meeting with Wall Street analysts after becoming chairman. Curley said, "I want to advise you that more than a million dollars has suddenly gone into Gannett's bottom line." He paused as his audience awaited an explanation. Curley said, "Al Neuharth has just retired."

The flamboyant Neuharth's spend-spend tempo notwithstanding, he had been a great leader—after all, it had been he who had picked John Curley as his successor. That was among his all-time best decisions—Neuharth had laid the foundation on which Gannett continued to build. Marilyn Melton aptly described his remarkable tour as the Gannett leader: "Al was a tightrope walker and a daredevil who carried the company. His successors are keeping great care of the store. But let's remember, it was Al who built the store."

Sonny's Five "W"s

Fallon Made Him What He Is

Reno, NV My corporate tour with Gannett concluded in 1997 as I reached sixty-five, the retirement age for directors who had been corporate officers. It had been an incredible journey, with wonderful fellow passengers along the route. You might say that it was in its way the culmination of an against-all-odds trip, from ragamuffin little kid to director on the governing board of one of the premier media corporations of all time. But always, Home Means Nevada for me, Marilyn, and our family.

As to my columnist role, in the words of a *Detroit News* investigative reporter, "I get paid by Gannett, but I work for my readers." In Reno, that beat goes on for me, as I draw closer to beginning my forty-fourth year with the *Gazette-Journal* or its parent corporations. Every material thing I have in my life derives from my newspaper career. Then there is that special "Pooh" in my life, bringing enduring love.

I may appear immodest in reciting what I have done well, but I do think that I merit some applause. After all, I had the good sense not to marry the first girl I dated . . . and I hope you agree it was better that I worked instead of trying to win the lottery. Along the way, I met some who felt that the nicest thing was to be important; but, truly, the most important thing is to be nice. I'm glad I never tried to earn my bread writing poetry. I've always loved getting paid, and I haven't missed a paycheck in 2,704 weeks.

Gosh, I'm glad that I didn't hang out on the journalism sideline. I am so lucky that my Fallon fairy godmothers and godfathers tapped me with their wands and said, "Rollan, the greatest issue of the time is what you do with your life. We're counting on you." Fallon made me what I am.

One of my close Gannett director friends, Walter Fallon (no pun), was the retired chairman of Kodak. Not long after we first met, I told Mr. Fallon that I was reared in Fallon, Nevada, went to high school there, and had my first newspaper job there. He said, "You know, once as I flew over Nevada, I looked at my aviator's map and saw a small dot that said Fallon next to it. Is there really a town called Fallon?"

"Indeed there is," I said. "It's a community that changed my life and gave me the strength to do something with it. Someday I'll tell you the story."

Melton Tells All
His Story Ends For Now

Reno, NV As we say in the newsroom, this is "30" or "closer," our way of signing off on a story. Just think of me here as the central figure in a play. After the final curtain, I return to center stage and visit with you and share what in the newsroom we call the five W's of the story: Who, What, Where, Why, When. At times, there is a sixth W. As in "Wow! I didn't know *that* about him!"

WHO?

From the time I was born, everyone called me Sonny. Until my mother enrolled me in the first grade, I didn't realize that I was Rollan Melton. I was named after my father.

WHAT?

I was a kid from a dysfunctional family. Back then, such folks were called screwed up. Most of my relatives didn't go far in school. Some could barely scratch out a living. Though they couldn't afford to lose, some of my people gambled. Most were heavy drinkers and smokers, and they got old before their time because they treated their bodies as if they had spare ones in their trunks.

My relatives feared the police, though I never knew a one who was guilty of anything except being drunk in public. All were divorced and remarried, some several times. They were uneducated and unskilled, but they were incurably optimistic about finding the gold that they believed was just over the next hill.

We Meltons were rootless people, with so few stabilizing ties that it would have been accurate to say that we were Okies of the Far West—migratory souls, trying to break out of our dreary lives.

Both sides of my family were re-inventions of their ancestors, swimming upstream and falling farther and farther back. They were a happy crowd most of the time, and they didn't feel that they were inmates of the places they had sentenced themselves to, but they were bitter about "the higher-ups," putting the blame on others for their own shortcomings.

My relatives were animated storytellers, inventive pranksters, and joke masters who shredded their puns so crazily that we had to laugh at them and with them. All of us danced, and back in the 1930s there would be jigs alongside Mother's or Grandmother's range stove, with a pot of Great Depression stew simmering, its contents generously ladled out to fill hungry stomachs.

My people loved black humor, the better to describe their lives. Such fun they were! I grew up with their music, with grandfather Clair plunking on his old banjo, and us little ones blowing tunes through our tissue-encased pocket combs.

While they had scant schooling, my mother, father, sister, Aunt Neta, and grandmother Daisy were charming, prolific writers. Each was gifted at turning phrases; all wrote vividly descriptive letters to each other telling the "headlines" of their personal lives. Chronicles of their happiness and pain, their frustration at being jobless and hopeless, and the cheery litany of things gone right: "Found a job; met someone nice; shook actor Jimmy Stewart's hand—Sonny, I swear, I'm never going to wash that hand again."

Good God, I loved them so, and how I wish I had told them more often than I did how dear, important, gifted, courageous, and noble they were. Given a new chance, I would commit everything they told me, or I overheard, to memory and to paper. Alas, as I was growing up, I gave scant notice to their life stories. As I look today at their photos, their happy faces belie what they were going through—the photos mask their worry and their fatigue. I wish I had sat with them and really listened and made notes in journals. Now all of them are gone, and I am the sole survivor, the one person left who remembers their sadness, their nomadic paths; the only one who can recall and savor their merriment and love and their wish that my sister and I be happy.

WHERE?

I have lived in many towns in many states. Mostly, my people rented or they bunked with relatives. A handful bought modest homes, but very few would ever own their places outright. I lived in many interesting places, from tumble-down shanties to a converted chicken coop to married student housing that my wife dolled up with her designer touch and a once-upon-a-time Army barracks that was crudely made over into apartments that were so tiny we almost had to let the air out for all of us to fit.

After achieving some success in the newspaper business, for years we lived in a big, stunning home that glowed with Marilyn Melton's creative genius. Somehow we found enough cash to pay for upgrades and to keep our bankers at bay. It embarrassed me when people called that home a mansion, because the label reeked of elitism. Now we are living in a tidy condominium in which Marilyn can paint and I can tinker with writing. We invite the curious in to see how we live.

My boyhood hangouts varied, from a wide-spot-in-the road mountain town in Idaho to Fallon, which was then so small that it was said we had to share the town drunk with Yerington. And then my adult newspaper beats: From weekly newspapers—fragrant with the aroma of ink, paper, and industrious sweat, sweetened by the presence of those trying either to get something into print or to keep it out—to primitive and (later) dandy plants that had newspaper logos tacked up out front; and finally to the states in which Speidel Newspapers and the Gannett Company put out advertising and news, most of it fit to print. The adventurous news and administrative beat extended nationwide, taking me from Okie of the Far West to worker bee around the U.S.A., and for the last twenty-one years, to the office where my columns have been hatched. Yes, I

Marilyn and Rollan Melton in 1998.

still like to see my by-line. Sonny's stories, Rollie's columns. Whatever. I am very critical of my work, and I am vain enough to believe that my best writing is in my future, not my past.

WHY?

I have written this memoir for many reasons. Marilyn encouraged me, believing that my life made a good story: twists, hairpin curves, smooth sailing, close calls, luck, God-given mentors, heroes, villains, characters who doubled as my relatives, employers who felt I was worthy, a cast of thousands of co-workers who made me look good, and friends and readers. I want this memoir to affirm that no man and no woman, regardless of talent, fails or succeeds alone.

I want also here to tell the potential executives who escaped before I could sign them up that I regret not enlisting them. The most striking example is former University of Nevada journalism department leader, LaRue Gilleland, a big-league talent. It hurt bad that I didn't get him aboard.

To the question, "Why write it?" I answer why not? To attempt an accurate and revealing memoir of one's life is to take on a daunting task, to be sure. Some of the stuff in here I would rather not have re-visited. But what the heck—it happened; it is true. If my story fails to interest, perhaps it will help some readers see what works or doesn't in life.

So, I have given you *Sonny's Story*, and I have introduced most of the cast that brought this non-fiction work to the stage. Minor players, some with non-speaking parts, are heard briefly, if at all. The major cast members, often doing miracles for me, appear in my life without prior notice, as if a master director set them in my path to do me good. Were their entrances into *Sonny's Story* a confluence of chance events, or were they pure, simple, fantastic luck? I am uncertain.

Consider some of them and imagine what might have come of me had they not been a part of my life:

My grandmother. **Daisy** had to put up with me because I was her grandson. She reminded me over and over, "Sonny, you don't amount to nothin', and you'll keep failing. You don't get it in school. You deliberately wet the bed to make me wash your damned sheets and hang them and have to make your bed every day. You won't cut it, Sonny. Wait and see."

I hated my grandmother, wanted her dead, out of my life, because she said I took but never gave. She would also say that I was so fat that I was busting out of my bib-overalls, but then she'd force-feed me more homemade sweets. What my father said of her must be true: she was Warlord.

When Father let me drop out of school, Warlord pounced, as if on cue from the director. She said, "Sonny's going back to school. Right now! I'll take him." As it turned out, Grandmother Daisy did love me, and she was to be not simply loved by me in return, but sainted. She saved me.

My mother. **Rusty** feared I would get hurt in football, but how would she know if that ever happened? In my eight years as a player, she never saw me in a game. Her absences had something to do with slaving in restaurants to hack out a living.

Mother never wanted me to be a gypsy, a hobo kid, the boy who tooled in and out of eighteen grammar schools. I didn't want to be Nomad Sonny, either. I was the young stranger, failing at school, taunted, told by the other kids, "You're a dummy, and that's so, 'cause we seen the red marks on your report card." At last, Rusty got me to Fallon. For the first time, I remained tethered to the same school. At last I was developing friendships, and my aptitude for football led some kids to tell me, "Good game!"

When I was seven or eight, Rusty took me to the doctor, and he told her, "There's nothing wrong with Sonny that I can see. I don't know why he's wetting the bed." In Fallon, when I reached fourteen and knew I'd stay there, I quit wetting the bed. Rusty had used no medicine and she hadn't punished me. What she did do was provide my first stable home-and-school environment. I was getting a whiff of self-esteem, and it was rare perfume.

When the Marines came to get me when I was seventeen, Rusty said, "You're not taking my boy," and she drove them off our arthritic stairs. The war came to Korea two years later and lasted into 1953. But for Rusty, I no doubt would have been there when our Marines were slaughtered. I wasn't. Accident? Coincidence? No, it was my commonsense mother, tougher than a leatherneck drill sergeant. She was my guardian angel.

Claude H. Smith. My boss at the weekly *Fallon Standard*. When I was sixteen and still in my first apprentice printer season, he pulled me aside, the acrid smoke from his Camel smoke his glasses and the ceiling, and he told me, "We're not satisfied with your work. If you don't start doing better, we'll have to let you go." I did better. I was saved because Mr. Smith put it on the line. What in the world would I have done had he not put me on notice and I had not then taken him seriously?

Alfred Leslie Higginbotham. The journalism professor set a terrible example by using subterfuge and duplicity to make a fool of me.

Minard Stout, the campus president. Had he succeeded in kicking me off the campus, by hook or crook, what would have become of me? I've thought of that many times. My answer never changes: I don't know.

Leon Etchemendy. Our amazing chance encounter at the Army post in Kansas delivered to me my first administrative job. My mistakes were costly to the military, but I learned so much, and the knowledge remained with me, to be used in many ways. Was it pure coincidence to come upon Major Etchemendy fifteen hundred miles from home? Perhaps. But had he not known my name from Nevada high school sports and been one of my coach's best friends, then what?

Charles H. Stout, publisher/president. No risk-taker was he. Yet, he took a chance and let me back in off the picket line. Why? See next item.

Charlie Murray, my editor/publisher/mentor/hero/savior. I believe he kept telling Stout, "Sure, Rollie's got a lot to learn, but he tries hard. Let's hang in with him and see how he does." Murray once told me, "Rollie, you never had a childhood. Now you're a good man."

John Brackett, outstanding editor and publisher of the *Times-Delta* at Visalia, California. After I was named the *Reno Gazette* editor, I learned that Chick Stout had first offered him the job. Although he had strong Reno ties, the devoted father chose not to move his young family. As I climbed the executive ranks, Johnny teased, "Don't forget, Sonny. You owe it all to me!"

Higginbotham re-visited. He did me a fantastic favor when he told Charlie Murray, "You've made a bad error in picking Rollan Melton to be the *Gazette* editor." I had learned to tolerate my negative role models, learning from them about what not to do and responding with the hardest work when they implied that I was an alley cat, not worth having around. But mark me well here—Al Higginbotham was also a great man who at the end of his colorful life did a noble thing. After the longtime sufferer of multiple sclerosis died in 1967, it was discovered that his last will and testament directed that his body go to medical research to help solve the terrible MS problem.

Jack Liechty. Providence must have sent him to me. I have worked with brilliant people, and their lessons have greatly influenced me, but Liechty was the smartest leader. Not a bit of micro-manager in him. He let you do your own work. When SNI's Colorado publisher, Robert S. Lee, once asked Liechty how he should cope with a tricky problem, Liechty said, "You are the publisher. You fix it."

Dorothy and Bill Royle. The parents of Marilyn Melton wanted to brain me when I eloped with their nineteen-year-old daughter. Maybe the reason they didn't was that she needed a provider. More likely it was because I tried to prove that though our backgrounds were vastly different, she had married the right one.

Marilyn Melton. Someone Up There broke the mold when He or She invented this child/woman. She was given an immense talent for rearing children, mostly by herself, and she is an expert at planting thoughts that ultimately blossom into superior ideas for which others get the credit. The superb artist and home designer continues to work on her project, Rollan Melton, with the right dabs of praise and criticism.

WHEN?

One story, with countless sub-stories folded within, a story running from 1931 to now, 1999. I am trying to get ready for the tomorrows, to see how they turn out.

HOW?

I never believed that I would find gold just over the next hill, but I have long known that I was blessed by good timing, good luck, and a desire to succeed which always is in overdrive.

I won't try to fool you: I turned in the longest shifts and toiled beyond what the average bloke does because I didn't have more than run-of-the-mill brains. Much learning was missed en route to high school because of circumstances I could not manage, and I took the easier courses at the University of Nevada, afraid then that if I studied deeper subjects, I would fail and lose face as I had in grammar school. So what to do? There was but one option: outwork others. I became more knowledgeable than some, and I attracted management's attention . . . and I focused on my mistakes, tried not to repeat them, and used such lessons to expand my opportunities.

How and what would I have done had I not accidentally stumbled into journalism? I honestly don't know. But if it had been something I loved and was suited for, I believe I would have done it well.

If I had it to do over, I would never have treated my body like I had a spare one in the trunk. I tried to quit smoking four times, twice going nineteen days before giving up. I quit cold turkey on December 3, 1980, after a chest x-ray frightened me terribly. Fortunately, it was a non-malignant cyst. At one time, especially in my administrative years, I was drinking too much. Recognizing that I was headed down a path that had led many of my kinsmen to unhappiness and pain, I gave up the hard liquor and have since only sipped on wine or non-alcoholic drinks.

After leaving corporate for the life of a columnist, I plunged with fervor into community volunteerism. There have been many great associations. I limit these remarks to three of them.

I was founding director in 1989 of the Washoe County At-Risk Task Force (WAR). Always, I identify with kids dropping out of school. I know from my own life that dropping out can bring one despair—it hammers a youngster's potential. I am proud that I've had a part in helping young people avoid that fate.

I was enriched by my six years (1993-1998) as a trustee and secretary of the Reno-based National Judicial College. It is the premier continuing education institution for American and international jurists, and after being a close part of it, I know why.

My foremost charitable role has been as a director and trustee of the John Ben Snow Foundation and Memorial Trust. Chick Stout selected me as his successor trustee, and for two decades, I have directed grants to a wide variety of non-profit causes, especially in Northern Nevada. My association with such John Ben Snow principals as foundation president, Allen R. Malcolm; the late Vernon F. Snow; his son, Jonathan Snow; Joseph Mitchell, the institutions' brilliant attorney, and others is a paramount thrill of my volunteer life.

Regrets? There are some significant ones.

I should have concentrated more fully on a liberal education. That I did not goes back to my habit of trying to take the easy academic way out.

I often feel trapped when I use the "item" format in my column. People badger me to plug their upcoming events, when what I really want is to write more issue pieces and compose more single-subject profiles, especially about the have-nots, many of whom are desperate to escape the elements that warp their potential. When I have spoken in a louder, brassier column voice, I've made an important difference. Yet, I chug along, a sort of human community bulletin board. I argue within myself about the other side: people want to know about people and what they're doing. Besides, I rationalize, I can leave it to the opinion writers to play hardball with the readers.

I wish I had been more attentive to my mother. She never owned a brand-new car or her own home, and she wouldn't fly. We tried to buy her whatever she wished, but she declared, "No, I can't bother fixing my own house. I'll let my landlord do mine. Getting me a new car is a waste. Forget it." This from the remarkable woman who, after my high school graduation, bought a small ad in the *Fallon Standard*. After nearly fifty years, I still treasure what she wrote: "Thank you, Fallon, for all you've done for my son, Rollan Melton."

About the Melton children: I was too busy trying to be a hot-shot newspaperman, and I didn't give my sufficient attention to them. It seems like their childhoods vanished—all of a sudden they had grown up, and I had missed out on their vital formative years. They needed me, and I didn't fully put out for them. This was my most major error and my keenest regret. That this guilt is shared by so many who drive to reach the top is no excuse for my having done it. I am sorry.

The fact is that I am tremendously proud of each of my children. Royle is a lawyer at the National Council of Juvenile and Family Court Judges. By the time you read this, his first child will have been born. Wayne is a veteran reporter/feature writer at the *Gazette-Journal*, and among the five professional writers in our immediate family. Kevin is a jolly fellow, reminding me of my reporter friend Bill Eaton's quip, "It takes a heap of heapin' to make a heap a heap." Big Kev is a role-model father of two and a veteran dealer at the Sands Regency Hotel-Casino. Our daughter, Emelie Williams, who was a gold medal playwright at Santa Clara University, is a public affairs writer with Saint Mary's Regional Medical Center. She is the mother of two of our cutest little granddaughters.

That's about it for now. There won't be another Sonny's memoir—not in this lifetime, at least. If I am reincarnated, I'd rather not be recycled—being a columnist again would suit me fine. Meanwhile, the readers are my court of last resort. When they applaud me, I am appreciative. When they scorn me, I've usually got it coming.

How fortunate has been Rollan Melton, alias Sonny, who never has felt fully dressed without a smile and has never been completely happy without someone for whom to write. How fortunate to have the privilege to provide a forum for all voices, to follow the precepts of those who two centuries ago said, "Here, Americans, is your opportunity to do grand things. Here, Americans, are your freedoms. Uphold them with all your might."

Journalism—what a noble path I took by chance. It has given me the opportunity to be with people I admire; to help tell my countrymen what's happening; to heed what a wise man is alleged to have said: "You have two ears and one mouth. Use them in the same ratio. Devour five newspapers a day. Never play poker with a man named Doc. If your mother gives you her age, check it out."

Newspaper people are the most fascinating critters. While others work, play, or sleep, the journalism guys and girls work for you. We cast aside our quill pens long ago and have since progressed through all sorts of writing and printing technology. We transmit news and advertising (an unsung guardian of freedom, by the way) in continuously evolving ways. Many great journalists who were my friends have left us, but while they were here, they did their best to tell you Who, What, Why, Where, and When. That will never change.

Editors and writers and people with cameras are joined every day by colleagues who never get a byline, never go out where news happens, never take a public bow (or have to face a reader/critic). They are the unsung, invisible aristocracy of our profession: the printers, ad proof runners, business office denizens; the guys with protective headgear who run the presses; the people who manufacture a product, print it, tear it down, and then rebuild it, 365 days a year. They are the circulators—talk about unsung heroes who make their appointed rounds! They are the guys who muck around my desk, wondering what my manuscript is all about.

Believe this: The greatest issue with all of us is how we spend our lives. I have spent mine just where I belong, enjoying the journalist's front-row seat, watching you and the world around you, trying to tell you what's going on and why, and who's doing what to whom. It has been satisfying and rewarding.

Bless each of you. I hope to see you soon. Meantime, here is our traditional newspaper closing:

-30-

Index

A

Adams, Eva, 38
Afflis, Bill "Dick, the Bruiser," 51-52
Ahearn, Major, 84-86
Aikin, Jim, 33,52
Akert, Ben, 196
Akert Family Market (Reno, Nevada), 49
Alcoholics Anonymous, 99
Allen, Jud, 113, 197
Allen, Terry, 88
Allison, Edward R., 141
Allison, Jimmy, 182, 190
Alpha Tau Omega, 45
American Newspaper Guild, 98, 100, 105-109, 112, 115-116
American Newspaper Publishers Association, 153, 159, 168-169, 189
Anderson, Verna, 115
Anderson, Victor, 114-115, 119-120, 144-145, 148
Andreini, Gloria, 57
Andrew, Marjorie, 57
Arentz, Sam, 54
Armanko's Department Store (Reno, Nevada), 49, 69
Army National Guard, 79
Armstrong, Bryn, 99, 107, 115, 118-119, 128
Armstrong, Charles J., 113
Armstrong, Henry, 103
Artemisia Hall (University of Nevada, Reno), 57
Associated Press, 71, 74, 179, 182, 185, 191, 202, 134
Ault, Chris, 199
Austin, Lloyd, 51

B

Babbitt, Nevada, 24
Baer, Max, 49
Bahan, Tom, 197
Baker, Sue Casey, 63
Banks, Idaho, 13
Barnes, B.L. "Bill," 182
Barnhart, Mrs. 22
Baxter, Mert, 71
Bean, Gerald C., 148
Bellinger, Harold, 40
Bend Bulletin, 22
Bend, Oregon, 22, 25
Benna, Bruno, 61, 196
Bennyhoff, Bob, 104
Berlin, Anne Gibbs (See Gibbs, Anne)
Berry, William, 105
Berscheid, Dewey, 138, 141
Bible, Alan, 38-39
Big Waldorf (Reno, Nevada), 49
Bigler, Clark, 105
Board of Regents, 64, 68-69, 99
Bohon, Robert, 119, 120
Boise, Idaho, 5-7, 10-11, 13, 15, 17, 19-21, 25
Bowers, Don, 98
Bowers, Emily, 98
Bowling, Robert, 197
Boyle, Hal, 88
Brackett, John, 158, 178, 211
Brady, Pat, 51
Brimmer, Andrew F., 202
Brokaw, Meredith A., 203
Brokaw, Tom, 203

Brown, Hattie, 28-29, 40
Buddy Baer's Bar (Reno, Nevada), 49
Buffet, Warren, 166
Bullis, Gary, 197
Bunker, Harry S., 116, 136, 146, 160, 183
Burdick, Al, 29
Burge, Florence, 140
Burksville, Kentucky, 6
Bush, George, 190-191
Byington, Douglas, 87-88
Byrd, Clarence, 45

C

Campo, Joseph L., 106-107, 114-116, 118, 141
Capital News (Boise, Idaho), 21
Cardoza, Norman, 141, 175
Carpenter, Jack, 38
Carter, Jimmy, 203
Carter, Rosalynn, 203
Caruso, Carmel "Crusher," 52
Cashell, Nancy, 199
Cashell, Robert, 199
Cease, George, 198
Chandler, Marilyn, 168
Chandler, Otis, 158, 168
Chapman, T.B., 19
Chicago Tribune, 168
Chico State University, 61
Chillicothe Gazette, 141-142, 173
Church, Foster, 175
Clark, Henry "Hank," 81
Clark, Peter B., 203
Clark, Walter Van Tilburg, 68
Class, Walter, 49
Cleveland Plain Dealer, 55, 71
Cobb, Ty, 37, 48, 54, 62, 73-75, 92, 100, 102-103, 105, 119
Cochran, Rosemary, 68
Coffee, Dana, 40
Colbrandt's (Reno, Nevada), 49
Combined Communications, 203
Conton, Betty Jean, 115
Copley, Helen, 168
Cousins, Norman, 199
Cox, Walter, 196
Crampton, Bert, 197, 200
Crest Movie Theater (Reno, Nevada), 50
Crocker, Len, 73, 92, 101-102, 119
Cronkite, Walter, 134

Crumley, Newton Sr., 54, 103-104, 121, 130
Curley, John, 202-204
Curtis, Mark Sr., 113

D

Daily Iowan, 114
Danville, Iowa, 4-5
Dempsey, Jack, 137, 197
Detroit News Corporation, 203
Diller, Phyllis, 199
Digino, Carl, 100, 116, 119
Digino, Levina, 115
Dixon, Mead, 138-139
Dondero, Don, 103, 115, 121, 127, 200
Donner Trail Guest Ranch, 127
Drackert, Harry, 127
Dunphy, Joan, 191
Dykus Family, 11-12

E

Earl, Clair, 72
Eaton, William W., 52, 65, 92-93, 99-100, 105-106, 108-109, 117, 213
Echeverria, Peter, 138-139
Editor and Publisher, 114
Edwards, Patricia, 57
Einstoss, Ronald H., 48, 183, 185-186
El Cortez Hotel (Reno, Nevada), 50
Elko Free Press, 115
Ely Daily Times, 38
Emmett, Idaho, 14, 15
Einstoss, Ron, 157-158, 165, 168, 174, 175, 177, 179
Erickson, Helgo, 108
Ericson, Fritsi, 203
Esplin, Willard "Red," 70, 85
Etchemendy, Leon, 83-85, 211
Etchemendy, Ruby, 84
Evans, Richard, 53

F

Fallon Eagle, 32, 34, 75, 98, 112
Fallon High School (Fallon, Nevada), 25, 28, 32-34, 38, 49, 51, 100
Fallon, Nevada, 23, 25, 27-28, 36, 42, 83, 92, 97-98

INDEX

Fallon Standard, 30-31, 33-41, 45-47, 54, 56, 58-59, 75, 92, 98, 101, 122, 168, 201, 211, 213
Fallon, Walter, 207
Farley, Cory, 197
Farrel, Arthur, 29, 39, 42
Federal Bureau of Investigation, 191, 203
Federal Reserve Board, 202
Federated Newspapers, 180
Feinberg, Abraham, 198
Ferguson, Don, 29, 161
Ferguson, Stanley, 42
Fife, Don, 37
Finch, Paul, 104
First Infantry Division "Big Red One," 82, 84, 86-88, 91
First National Bank of Nevada, 128, 130, 147
Fister, Don, 42
Fister, Larry, 42
Ford, Gerald, 169-170, 177
Forkner, Charles Robert, 17
Fort Benning, Georgia, 79-82
Fort Leavenworth, Kansas, 90
Fort Lewis, Washington, 70, 78
Fort Polk, Louisiana, 91
Fort Riley, Kansas, 81-83, 86, 88, 91
Fremont Tribune, 144
Fresno State University, 61, 71
Friel, William, 74-75, 100, 119
Fritschle, Jim, 18
Fulstone, Mary, 197

G

Gable, Clark, 121
Gagnon Apartments (Boise, Idaho), 12
Gallagher, Wes, 22, 202
Gannett, 168, 174, 179-180, 183-186, 189-195, 199-204, 207, 209
Garaventa, Gloria Cortesi, 197
Gardner, Paul, 38, 98
Gardnerville Record-Courier, 38, 63
Garfield School (Boise, Idaho), 11
Gasho, Larry, 163
Gazette Building, 99, 104-105, 108, 111-112, 114-115, 117
Gazette-Journal Building, 121
Gibbs, Anne, 29-30, 42, 46
Gibson, Ida, 31-32
Gilleland, LaRue, 165, 210

Glendon, Patricia, 140
Gold, William, 99, 105
Golden Hotel (Reno, Nevada), 23, 130, 198
Gonfiantini, Nello Jr., 177
Goodman, Julian, 203
Goodner, Helen, 37, 84
Goodner, Wes, 25, 28-30, 33, 37, 40, 84, 101
Goodwin, Rebecca, 197
Gorrell, Robert M., 47-48, 64
Graham, Kay, 168
Graham, Philip, 168
Granada Movie Theater (Reno, Nevada), 50
Grand Cafe (Carson City, Nevada), 102
Gray Reid's Store (Reno, Nevada), 50
Green Bay Packers, 51-52, 71
Green, Benjamin, 5
Green, Sylvan, 124-125
Greenwave Flash, 29, 42
Greenwood, Noel, 130
Gresham, Oregon, 22-23, 70
Griggs, Bill, 63
Grotto Bar (Reno, Nevada), 49

H

Haas, Laura, 81
Haas, William E., 81
Hageman, Adeline, 172
Hale's Drugs (Reno, Nevada), 50
Hamilton, George, 197
Hardy, Roy, 54
Harolds Club, 39-40, 48, 50-52, 54, 73, 91, 120, 197
Harper, Betty, 56
Harrah, William F., 176-177
Harrah's Club (Lake Tahoe), 135
Hartman Hall, 45
Hearst, William Randolph, 48, 183
Heath, Stan, 74-75
Hecht, Chic, 197
Hermiston, Oregon, 17, 20
Heselden, John, E., 202
Hettich, David, 126
Hickman, J.C., 174-175, 192
Higginbotham, Alfred Leslie, 38, 47, 55, 64, 67-72, 99, 135-136, 157, 211
Higginbotham, Marie, 67
Hirose, Toshi, 155
Ho, Chin, 180
Ho, T.K. Stuart, 202
Holiday Hotel (Reno, Nevada), 103

INDEX

Holy Cross University, 52
Honolulu Star-Bulletin, 180
Hope, Bob, 199
Howard, Clinton, 163, 193
Huckaby, Billie, 25
Hudson Lee's Restaurant (Reno, Nevada), 50
Hug, Jess, 10
Hug, Procter, 61
Hulse, James W., 73
Hume, Robert, 64
Hundred Eleventh Company, 79
Hushaw, Jim, 165

I

Idaho Daily Statesman, 14, 17, 19, 21
Idaho State College, 61, 71
Ingram, Carol, 39, 97
Ingram, James, 39
Ingram, Ken 30-42, 45, 58-59, 91, 97-98, 115, 148
Iowa City Press-Citizen, 144
Ireland, Bill, 69
Ireland, Jeanne, 69

J

Jackson, Joseph R., 74, 92-94, 97, 99-102, 107, 115-116, 118-120, 128, 131, 133-134, 140
Jackson, Sadie, 115
Janulis, Keiste, 46-48, 61, 55
Jeakins, William, 39
Jensen, Jackie, 104
John Ascuaga's Nugget (Sparks, Nevada), 170
John Ben Snow Foundation, 213
Johnson, Carl "Bucky," 36, 49
Johnson, Frank, 104, 144
Johnson, Lyndon B., 134, 202,
Jones, Clarence K., 115, 139, 144, 148
Jones, Lorna, 57
Junction City Union, 86
Junior Achievement, 128

K

Kansas City Star, 86-87
Karrasch, Karl, 136
Kelley, Pete, 98
Kellogg Charitable Foundation, 202

Kennedy, John F., 134, 195, 202
Kent, Mary Lou, 41
Kent, Muriel Smiley, 98
Kessinger, Paul, 201
King, Howard, 102
Klimasezwsk, Ted, 51
Knight-Ridder Group, 156, 168, 191
Koll, John, 163
Kottinger, William, 51
Kramer, James, 92

L

Laird, Charlton, 64
LaTossa, Louie, 24
Lawlor, Glenn "Jake," 53-54, 61, 71, 104, 198
Laxalt, Jackie, 197
Laxalt, Paul, 190, 198
Lazetich, Peter, 197
Leavitt, Myron, 53
Lee, Robert S., 144, 148, 212
Lemberes, Alex, 78
Lengel, John, 141
Lenz, Clair, 10, 13, 15, 24, 26, 208
Leon and Eddie's (Reno, Nevada), 49
Leonard, Gwen, 115
Leonard, Paul A., 73, 92, 115-116, 144, 148, 165
Leopard, William H., 163
Lerude, Les, 50
Lerude, Warren, 135, 140, 144, 149, 165, 168, 175, 177, 186
Lewis, Drew, 203
Licko, David, 163-164
Liechty, E.J. "Jack," 142-145, 149, 153, 155-163, 169, 173, 179, 182, 185, 202, 212
Life, 128
Lima, Marguerite, 31-32, 98
Lions Club (Reno, Nevada), 135
Little, Thomas, 64
Little Waldorf (Reno, Nevada), 49, 61
Lodge, Henry Cabot, 198
Lombardi, Louis, 54, 76
London Daily Telegraph, 105
London Mirror, 105
London Sunday Times, 173
Los Angeles Times, 158, 175
Louis, Josephine P., 202
Love, Malcolm, 51, 61
Lovelock Review-Miner, 38, 98

INDEX

Loyola University, 51
Lusk, Thomas, 31

M

McCabe, St. Clair, 172-174
McCarran, Patrick, 38
McCarthy, Joseph, 45
McClatchy Newspapers, 156
McCloskey, Jack, 38, 198
McClure, Robert, 39-40, 54
McClure, J. Warren, 202
McCorkindale, Douglas, 192, 203
McCulloch, Frank, 119
McCullough, David, 200
McDonald, Joseph Sr., 73, 92, 116
McDonough, Joanne, 112-113
McDonough, Robert "Lefty," 112-113
McGoff, John P., 167
MacKenzie, Walter, 99, 117, 119, 133-135, 140, 191
Mackay Stadium (UNR), 45, 51-52, 54, 198
Mail Tribune, 167-168
Majestic Movie Theater (Reno, Nevada), 50
Malcolm, Allen R., 213
Malone, George "Molly," 81
Manhattan, Kansas, 82
Manhattan Mercury, 86
Manitzas, Frank, 83-85
Manoukian, Don, 198
Manzanita Lake (UNR), 49
Mapes, Charles, 50
Mapes Hotel (Reno, Nevada), 50, 135
Margrave, Emma, 197
Marrs, Beulah Erma "Rusty" (nee Williamson), 3-5, 7-25, 27, 29, 35-37, 39-41, 97, 154, 157, 165, 210-211
Marrs, William, 14-15
Martin, Loretta, 156
Martin, Mabs, 198
Martinelli, Ernie, 196
Mason Valley News, 38, 98
Mathews, Willis, 86-87, 89
Matteucci, Al, 52
Mayhew, Catherine, 199
Melarkey, Alice, 115
Melton, Ann (nee Green), 5
Melton, Beulah (See Marrs, Beulah)
Melton, Bronna Lu "Brownie," 3-4, 7-17, 19-21, 23-25, 29, 36, 39, 54, 59-60, 97

Melton, Bufford, 6
Melton, Elijah, 5
Melton, Emelie, 154, 186, 192, 194, 214
Melton, Isabelle, 6-7, 9, 13, 15-18, 21-22
Melton, Jack, 6-7, 13-15, 17-18, 20
Melton, Jaime Gray, 122-124, 155
Melton, James, 6
Melton, John Allen, 6-7
Melton, John Jr. "Johnny," 6-7
Melton, Kevin Claude, 122, 154, 186, 192, 194
Melton, Margaret, 6, 13-15
Melton, Marilyn (nee Royle), 3-4, 57-63, 67-69, 72, 76-79, 81-82, 84-85, 87-89, 91-92, 94, 97, 101, 107-110, 112-113, 115, 117, 122-125, 129, 137-138, 144, 146-147, 154, 159, 164, 170, 176, 178, 179, 186, 191-196, 200-204, 207, 209-212
Melton, Martha, 60
Melton, Rollan Sr. "Bunk," 6-13, 15, 17, 19-23, 25-26, 41, 105
Melton, Royle William, 77-78, 87, 89, 97, 101, 108, 117, 122, 124, 154, 195, 213
Melton, Sarah, 6
Melton, Tiny, 6
Melton, Wayne, 87, 89, 97, 101, 108, 122, 124, 154, 213
Melton, William, 6
Menicucci, Bruno, 197
Mergen, Katharine, 105, 107-109
Meyer, Donald C., 161-167, 170-174, 177, 179, 181-184, 189, 192-193
Midmore, Joe, 141
Mill, John Stuart, 34
Miller, Dora, 21-23, 25
Miller, James E., 3, 6
Miller, Mary, 6
Miller, Paul, 179-180, 202
Miller, Robert, 202
Mineral County Independent-News, 38, 98
Mitchell, Joseph, 213
Model Dairy, 197
Mohr, Hans, 58
Monroe, Marilyn, 121
Montgomery, Edward, 119
Moore, Archie, 102-103
Morrison, John, 66
Morton, Lance, 61
Moscone, George, 189
Moser, Oscar, 29
Motley, Marion, 33

Murray, Charles G., 126, 128-145, 147, 149, 155, 158-159, 211
Murray, Nikki, 147
Mustang Ranch, 198

N

Nash, Ogden, 200
National Council of Juvenile and Family Court Judges, 213
National Judicial College, 53, 213
Neuharth, Allen, 168, 174, 179-180, 183-185, 189-194, 199-204
Nevada Appeal, 38, 72, 98
Nevada State Journal, 37, 48, 54, 62, 70, 72-76, 92, 100, 102, 104, 106, 108-109, 111, 113-115, 119, 123, 130-131, 136, 140-141, 144, 148, 153-154, 165, 170
Nevada Women's Fund, 203
New London, Iowa, 5
New York Daily News, 105
New York Post, 105
New York Times, 64, 173, 181
Newburg Evening News, 179
Newton, Marilyn O., 134, 197
Nielsen, Marie, 57
Nitsche, Robert, 116, 141, 170
Nixon, Richard, 164-165, 195, 202
Northside School (Reno, Nevada), 84

O

Oakland Tribune, 171
Olivas, Jimmie, 61, 90, 104
Olson, Edward, 104
One Sixteen Club (Reno, Nevada), 49
Owl Cafe-Casino (Fallon, Nevada), 24-25
Oyer, Boots, 142

P

"Pack Tracks," 64-68
Park School (Boise, Idaho), 12
Pedersen, Richard "Rap," 31
Petersen, Pete, 70
Petrini, Robert, 75
Petrinovich, John, 102
Phi Sigma Kappa, 45

Phillips, Phyllis Crudgington, 169-170
Piazzo, Chet, 50
Piazzo, Link, 50
Pintar, Ruth Fitz, 46, 77
Pittman, Vail, 38
Plummer, Marlene, 31, 56-57
Poughkeepsie Journal, 169, 179
Powell, Cecilia Schmitt, 46
Powell, Ralph, 29
Pratt, George, 119
Purcell, Jack, 184
Pyatt, James, 98

Q

Questa, Edward J., 130

R

Raggio, William, 100
Reagan, Ronald, 197
Redfield, LaVere, 138
Reese River Reveille, 38, 98
Remington, Lesley, 197
Renfro, Charles, 168
Reno Evening Gazette, 24, 62, 72-76, 92-94, 98-101, 104-106, 108-116, 118-121, 123, 130-136, 140-141, 144, 148, 149, 153, 154, 185, 211
Reno Gazette Journal, 4, 45, 136, 148, 155, 169, 174-175, 194, 200, 207, 213
Reno Little Theater, 126
Reno Silver Sox, 107, 110, 116, 119-120, 141
Reporter-Telegram, 182
Reynolds, Frank, 165
Reynolds Jr., Thomas A., 203
Rialto Theater (Boise, Idaho), 16-18
Rice, Grantland, 48, 183
Richardson, Frank, 64-69
Ridder, Dan, 183, 191
Ritter, Robert, 186
Riverside Hotel (Reno, Nevada), 50
Robbins, Kenneth, 112-113, 132
Rockefeller, Mary, 127
Rockne, Knute, 52
Rogers, Ginger, 170
Rogers, Lloyd "Punchy," 99, 108
Rogers, William, 195, 202
Rollan Melton Fellowship, 192

INDEX

Rooney, Mickey, 49
Rose, Patricia (nee Royle), 59, 97, 144
Rose, Ronald, 97
Roseman, Jean Brown, 155-156, 171-172, 191
Rosenberg, Ethel, 55
Rosenberg, Julius, 55
Ross, Harold, 119
Ross, Silas Sr., 54
Rowan, Carl T., 202-203
Royle, Dorothy Gray, 58, 62-63, 78-79, 212
Royle, William Jr., 59
Royle, William Sr., 58-59, 62, 70, 78-79, 212
Rueda, Dixie Fritz, 46
Russell, Charles, 38
Russo, Johnny, 102
Ryals, N. Walter, 48, 165, 177
Ryan, David, 61

S

Sagebrush, 48, 52-53, 57, 59, 62, 64-66, 68, 154
Saltzman, Estell, 140
Samuels, Frank, 76-78
San Francisco State University, 71
Sanford, Charlotte, 40
Sanford, John, 74-75, 92, 100-101, 105, 107, 115, 117-119, 126-128, 130-133, 137, 140, 149, 153
Sanford, Robert, 34, 98
Sanford, Myrtle, 115
Santa Cruz Sentinel, 165
Santini, Clark, 197
Savannah, Georgia, 5
Sawyer, Byrd, 33
Scales, William, 108
Schafer, Robert, 142
Schank, Stanley, 46
Schmidt, Donald, 161-162
Schon, Michael, 124, 126
Schurz, Nevada, 24
Schuster, Richard, 139, 144, 155, 174
Scripps, Edward "Ted," 55
Scripps Newspaper Group, 55, 183
Seale, Judy, 198
Seale, Robert, 198
Seaton, Fred, 86
Sei, Sandi, 196
Selkirk, Bert, 63
Semenza, Edwin, 124-125, 166
Sewell's Market (Reno, Nevada), 49

Sferrazza, Peter, 203
Shaw, Jack, 62
Sheeketski, Joe, 51-57
Sheffield, Johnny, 17
Shelly, Barbara, 75
Shelly, Bruce, 75
Shelly, Carl, 75-76
Sheppard, J. Craig, 61
Shields, Elaine Teel, 46
Shine, Albert, 76
Shoemaker, William, 7
Sinatra, Frank Jr., 135
Sinatra, Frank Sr., 135
Sioux Falls Argus-Leader, 144, 168, 186
Sky Room, Mapes Hotel (Reno, Nevada), 50, 77
Slingland, Ed, 99
Slipper, George, 56
Smee, James C., 52
Smernoff, Noah, 179, 197
Smith, Arthur M. Jr., 176
Smith, Claude H., 30-34, 37-39, 45, 56, 75, 92, 97-98, 211
Smith, Dean C., 48, 61, 141, 175, 183, 186
Smith, Ethel, 30-32, 75, 97, 98
Smith, Francis "Tank," 105
Smith, Harold Sr., 197
Smith, Pat, 40-41
Smith, Raymond I. "Pappy," 39-40, 50-51, 91, 197
Smith, Red, 48
Smith, William R. "Bob," 140
Smithwick, Hugh, 53
Snow, John Ben, 116, 146, 159-160, 170-172, 183
Snow, Jonathan, 213
Snow, Vernon, 213
Sparks Tribune, 72, 75-76, 79, 112
Speidel, Merritt, 159, 183
Speidel Newspapers, Incorporated, 48, 50, 72-73, 92, 116, 126, 131, 136-137, 142-149, 153-154, 180-186, 189-193, 201-203, 209, 212
Spina, Charles, 81
Spina, Nancy, 81
Stampfli's (Reno, Nevada), 50
Stanford University, 159-160, 168
Stephens, Edward C., 81
Steve, Del "Jugger," 29
Stewart, Jimmy, 18, 208
Stockton-Record, 4, 156-157, 167, 169
Stockwell, Daniel, 163
Stoddard, Robert, 50
Stout, Betty, 116

Stout, Charles H. "Chick," 92, 106, 114-116, 118,
　　126, 128-133, 136-137, 139, 141, 143-145,
　　147-149, 153, 155-163, 170-173, 179-183,
　　191, 211, 213
Stout, George, 116
Stout, Katherine, 116
Stout, Martha, 116
Stout, Minard, 61, 64-70, 176, 211
Stout, Richard, 116
Stout, Sue Steff, 163
Streeter, Jack, 88, 198
Strickland, Janie, 57
Strand, Bill, 29
Strong, Gordon, 171
Sullivan, Frank, 74
Sullivan, Pat Rogero, 140
Surber, Gordon, 62
Suverkrup, Arthur, 38
Swearingen, John, 86-91
Swenson, Edith, 39

T

Taylor, Jock, 38, 98
Terry, Alice, 65, 113
Theta Chi, 45, 58
Thomas, Lowell, 189
Thompson, Stanley I., 198
Thomson, Kenneth, 172
Thomson, Lord, 172
Thomson Newspapers, 171-174, 177, 179
Time, 46, 64
Tiny's Waffle Shop (Reno, Nevada), 50
Toomey, Jeanne, 140
Tory, John, 171, 172
Tower Movie Theater (Reno, Nevada), 50
Trachok, Richard, 115
Traynor, Buddy, 102
Trego, Peggy, 73
Trego, Robert, 73-74
Twenty-Ninth Infantry, 82
Tri-Delta, 57-58
Twin Falls, Idaho, 25-26

U

Uecker, Robert, 165
Ugalde, Wes, 122
Umbenhaur, George, 100

United Press International, 71, 74, 185
United States Marine Corps, 35-36
United States Military Academy, West Point, 80-81
University of Nevada, Reno, 46, 49, 51, 61-62, 64,
　　68, 71, 132, 154, 176, 212
University of Notre Dame, 52
Uribe, David, 108
USA Today, 22, 201-203

V

Vallee, Rudy, 16, 77
Van Sooy, Neal, 38
Vario's Restaurant (Reno, Nevada), 164
Vice, Floyd, 51
Vietti, Paul, 51
Visalia Times-Delta, 158, 174, 183, 211

W

Waldorf Hotel (New York City), 189
Wall Street Journal, 120, 168, 173
Ward, Thomas R., 91
Washoe County At-Risk Task Force, 213
Washington Post, 168
Wayne, Nebraska, 91-92
Weaver, Wayne, 29
Webb, Jim, 195, 202
Webert, Mary Jane, 164
Weil, Louis A. Jr., 202
Weissmuller, Johnny, 14, 17, 104
Wertheimer brothers, 50
Wessel, Mickey, 196, 199
West, Harold, 58
West, Sarah, 58
Whalen, Lloyd, 58
Wharton, Dolores, D., 202
Wheeler, Donn, 115, 119-120, 169
White, William Allen, 137
Whitehead, Edwin "Tip," 182
Whittington, Marie, 157
Whittington, Robert, 156-157, 161-182, 185-186,
　　189-192, 202
Wilkerson, Donald L., 81
Williams, Emelie (See Melton, Emelie)
Williamson, Daisy Edgington, 3-5, 7, 9-10, 13, 15,
　　24, 26, 28, 148, 154, 208, 210
Williamson, Hugh Osborn, 4-5
Williamson, Mary, 10

Williamson, Sherma, 10
Williamson, Wauneta "Aunt Neta," 3-5, 8, 208
Williamson, Wilbur, 3, 5, 10, 13, 17, 161
Wingard, Bob, 169, 192
Wiseman, Richard M., 81
Woodburn, William, 127

Y

Yasmer, Jenny Johns, 40